DSLR Cinema

DSLR Cinema:
A beginner's guide to filmmaking on a budget

3rd edition

Kurt Lancaster

Routledge
Taylor & Francis Group

NEW YORK AND LONDON

Third edition published 2018
by Routledge
711 Third Avenue, New York, NY 10017
and by Routledge

2 Park Square, Milton Park, Abingdon, Oxon OX14 4RN
Routledge is an imprint of the Taylor & Francis Group, an informa business

First edition published by Focal Press 2011
Second edition published by Focal Press 2013

Library of Congress Cataloging in Publication Data

Names: Lancaster, Kurt, 1967- author.
Title: DSLR cinema : a beginner's guide to filmmaking on a budget / Kurt Lancaster.
Description: Third edition.
New York : Routledge, Taylor & Francis Group, 2018.
Includes bibliographical references and index.
Identifiers: LCCN 2017050514 | ISBN 9780415793520 (hardback) | ISBN 9780415793544 (pbk.)
| ISBN 9781315210971 (e-book)
Subjects: LCSH: High definition video recording--Amateurs' manuals. | Single-lens reflex cameras—
Amateurs' manuals. | Composition (Photography)--Amateurs' manuals. | Digital cinematography—
Amateurs' manuals.
Classification: LCC TR862 .L36 2018 | DDC 777/.34--dc23LC record available at
https://lccn.loc.gov/2017050514

Printed and bound in the United States of America by Sheridan

CONTENTS

FOREWORD by Shane Hurlbut, ASC vii

ACKNOWLEDGMENTS ix

ABOUT THE WEBSITE xi

INTRODUCTION The Rise and Fall of the DSLR Cinema Revolution xiii

CHAPTER 1   Composition, Lenses, Blocking, and Camera Movement 1

CHAPTER 2   Lighting 19

CHAPTER 3   Exposure 35

CHAPTER 4   Recording Quality Audio 58

CHAPTER 5   Key Concepts in Postproduction Workflow 77

CHAPTER 6   Telling Better Stories 100

CHAPTER 7   Cinematic Gear on a Budget 123

CHAPTER 8   David Tembleque: Blackmagic's Pocket Cinema Camera
             in *Dear Tom* 153

CHAPTER 9   Joe Simon: Canon's C100 Mark II in *Fragments*
             by Dana Beasley 163

CHAPTER 10   Philip Bloom: Canon's 7D in *A Day at the Races* 177

CHAPTER 11   Kiril Kirkov: Documentary Intimacy with the Canon 5D
             Mark III in *Art of the People* 189

CHAPTER 12   Po Chan and Shane Hurlbut: Canon's 5D Mark II in
             The Last 3 Minutes 204

CHAPTER 13   J. Van Auken: Filming Action with Panasonic's GH5 in
             Unmasked 227

CHAPTER 14   Mari Cleven: Filming Documentaries on the Canon
             C100 Mark II 238

CHAPTER 15   Bibbi Abruzzini: Filming Documentaries on the
             Canon 5D Mark IV 255

CONCLUSION 269

INDEX 275

FOREWORD
(from the 2nd edition)

Shane Hurlbut, ASC

When Kurt Lancaster came to me with the idea of writing this book on DSLR film-making, I was honored to be a part of it. I have been neck deep in this technology since January 26, 2009. It has been a roller-coaster ride trying to figure out this new disruptive technology from a motion picture cinematographer's perspective. Forging ahead with normal operating procedure did not translate. I had to think out of the box and teach myself about menus and picture styles, and create a new checks-and-balances ritual for shooting. There is not much that this camera system cannot do because it can be small and compact or as big as you choose to make it. The platform is so liberating that I feel like a five-year-old again—full of possibility and endless creativity.

I refer to the Canon 5D Mark II as a game changer because the paradigm has shifted. This is the future, and as technology gets better so will the camera's data rates, processing power, and ability to do more uncompressed media capture. I shot with film for my entire career—that includes seventeen movies, hundreds of commercials, many music videos, and twenty-one short films—because the HD landscape never attracted me. It looked plastic and too sharp, with a depth of field that felt false. I have since found that if the story and characters are engaging and the film transports you, the capture medium doesn't matter.

Why the sudden shift in thinking about HD? The Canon cameras do not look like HD. It is what I call digital film because the quality is unlike any other HD camera available to date. The image looks unique. It is its own genre—one that I believe looks and feels the closest to film. In my opinion HD video capture has finally come from the right place: the still photography platform. Canon has been working on this sensor for years.

When directors Scott Waugh and Mike McCoy came to me to lens *Act of Valor* (2012), I told them that I didn't want to shoot another action picture unless we were going to reinvent the action genre. Seeing the potential in this small Canon 5D DSLR, we embarked on a mission: to capitalize on the compact nature of the camera, using it to our advantage by pacing and moving it in new and exciting ways that were a completely immersive experience for an audience. I wanted the audience to see the world through the eyes of the Navy SEALs. We wanted it to feel immediate, visceral, and immersive. As an audience member you became emotionally invested in the characters and their journey.

My creative journey with the camera involved a steep learning curve in 2009. The Elite Team and I made many mistakes in the beginning. Midway through the journey, everything just worked. I continued to hone my abilities with the 5D camera system and subsequent cameras by ingesting as much knowledge as I could and share it with the film community. That is how Hurlbut Visuals was born (see http://www.hurlbutvisuals.com).

Lydia, my wife of twenty-three years and soulmate, wanted to showcase my fearless, pioneering, trail-blazing spirit. She and our web developer, Ryan Fritz of Ryno Technologies, designed Hurlbut Visuals in the summer of 2009. Lydia convinced me that I had to change the way I think. The old rules of holding things close to your chest don't apply anymore. I began sharing everything as I was experiencing it while shooting *Act of Valor* and a variety of commercials.

Our shooting experiences became the HurlBlog (see http://www.hurlbutvisuals.com/blog/).

I answer every comment personally and give practical on-the-job learning. The unexpected benefit was the amazing dialog that occurs with our reader's input. I learn so much from the blog readers and feel excited about our forum. Lydia's vision of an intimate, personal, and heartfelt experience that was not just about an individual but about the synergy and team effort involved in creating beautiful images came alive and continues to expand.

Hurlbut Visuals has grown over the past three years. Our mission to create, innovate, and educate has also expanded. We are a creative collective comprised of writers, directors, producers, camera operators, first assistants, editors, and lighting technicians who have worked together for years. We are visual storytellers who use a variety of tools to achieve spontaneity and capture the best performance.

The Last 3 Minutes is where we figured out how to have Canon 5D imagery that held up on a 60-foot screen. The story is a result of the writing and direction of a very talented director, Po Chan. She has passion and a clear understanding of how to get the best performance from an actor by writing a backstory to make the characters come alive. Po embraces a visual style that is not ordinary. She is visionary, and I thank her for writing and directing a short that will continue to change the way people think about this technology. In March of 2012, Po and I collaborated again on *The Ticket,* which was Po's follow-up to *The Last 3 Minutes.* She wrote a beautiful and cinematic love story about getting one last chance. We used the latest in DSLR 4K capture: the Canon 1DC. This is the world that I have been trailblazing for quite some time. When the camera was delivered to Hurlbut Visuals, my Elite Team and I did various tests, using what we had learned from our collective experience with the Canon 5D Mark II. After the first night of testing, one word came to mind. WOW! Canon harnessed 4K in a small footprint with the processing power to record to CF cards without external recorders. This took our creativity and visuals to a whole new level.

Lastly, a huge thank you to Kurt Lancaster for giving a voice to DSLRs, specifically the Canon cameras, in this new book. I welcome him on the set any time after his assistance on *The Last 3 Minutes.* He jumped into action when our sound person was stuck in traffic and did excellent sound recording. Kurt was like a superhero sound guy in the night to save our project. Kudos, my man!

4 June 2012

ACKNOWLEDGMENTS

Many thanks to Emily McCloskey for pushing me to writer a third edition and setting up the contract approvals. Sheni Kruger transitioned into the project, followed by Katie Finn, who has worked with grace and patience. Her work is appreciated, along with members of the team who have helped me: Simon Jacobs and John Makowski.

Thanks to all of the manufacturers, artists, and photographers—too many to name individually—for permission to use their images in this book. Without the pics, it would have just been words, which would just not have been as exciting.

Furthermore, much appreciation for the critical eye and keen advice of Julian Grant and Dave Anselmi—my deep appreciation for their comments from an earlier edition. This book is better than it would have been without them.

Many thanks to the reviewers who gave comments at the beginning of the process: Dave A. Anselmi, Director/Producer/Instructor (PracticalMysticProductions. com), Michael Brennan, Director of Photography; Julian Grant, Producer/Director, Assistant Professor at Columbia College Chicago; Andrew Jones, Cinematographer; Eugenia Loli, Tech Reviewer, Software Developer, Videographer (http://vimeo.com/ eugenia/videos); Bruce Sheridan, Chair, Film and Video Department, Columbia College Chicago; Phil South, Tutor, Bristol Old Vic Theatre School. Additional thanks for those who provided blind peer review of the third edition proposal.

Hats off to Diana Copsey, Nathaniel Westenhaver, and Jessica Wolfson Cox for the transcriptions of many interviews from the first and second editions.

Thanks also to Peter Tvarkunas, Director of Education at Canon, who was open to the project and offered much support during the first edition.

I especially want to thank the international cast of filmmakers, cinematographers, journalists, and filmmakers who were generous with their time for interviews: First off, Philip Bloom, whose DSLR films and blog inspired me to delve into DSLR cinematography—he is a true British gentleman; American Jared Abrams at WideOpenCamera; planetMitch at planet5D.com—I look forward to his DSLR news updates every day; Rii Schroer, a German photojournalist working in England; Brazilian director Bernardo Uzeda and cinematographer Guga Millet; British ex-pat Neal Smith at Hdi RAWworks; American filmmaker and colorist Jeremy Ian Thomas (Hdi RAWworks); Kris Cabrera for insights into special effects with the Canon 7D; American writer and director Jamin Winans; and much appreciation for Hong Kong director Po Chan and ASC member Shane Hurlbut for letting me on the set of *The Last 3 Minutes*, so I could see the Canon 5D Mark II in action, as well as the Elite Team members who offered tips and allowed me to get underfoot as they shot, and of course Lydia Hurlbut, who not only offered invaluable assistance with the manuscript, but made sure I was in the right location for shoots over the greater LA area. Some of these people and their works did not make it into this new edition, but their original support and insight influenced it.

Thanks for the new filmmakers who agreed to be a part of the third edition. I'm grateful for their work. These include Lindsay Walker, who makes beautiful images on iPhones; David Tembleque, who dares to make personal cinema; Joe Simon, who makes the C100 Mark II a cinema camera; Brent Ramsey, from Canon, provided good feedback on the Joe Simon chapter; Kiril Kirkov, a visual anthropologist with a keen eye for cinematography; J. Van Auken, making action films out of a micro four-thirds camera; Bibbi Abruzzini captures the hearts of characters with her camera; and Mari Cleven, who creates documentaries with powerful characters and strong images. Some of these are my former students. I'm proud of them.

I also wish to thank my colleagues at the School of Communication at Northern Arizona University, who provided moral support during the writing of this manuscript as I held down a full teaching load: Bill Carter, Toni DeAztlan-Smith, Paul Helford, Janna Jones, Harun Mehmedinovic, Mark Neumann, and Jon Torn. Peter Schwepker, who retired a number of years ago, lent me his 5D over spring break before I decided to get mine—many thanks. I also want to thank my dean, Karen Pugliesi.

In addition, I thank my students, who inspire me to do even better work—both in teaching and shooting—some of whom were willing to experiment with DSLR cinematography when I encouraged them to use DSLRs for their projects before there were any books: Shannon Sassone, Shannon Thorp, Danielle Cullum, Taylor Mahoney, and Margo McClellan. Dana Beasley, one of our documentary graduate students at NAU, did a great job with proofreading the manuscript of this edition. Nikky Twyman was also indespensible with reading the final page proofs. And Kimberly Mitchell, a colleague in visual communication helped with advice on the layout of this edition.

I also want to thank my friend Beau L'Amour, who not only gave me a place to stay in LA, but offered detailed advice on audio and lenses, and got me contacts at Bandito Brothers.

Finally, special thanks to my wife, Stephanie, who has supported this project since day one (and helped proofread it), as well as to my stepson, Morgan Petrie. Both of them have been my family in Flagstaff. And of course to my mother, Judy Bennett, who opened up her home in Maine for my family on numerous occasions. It's good to get back home.

The website includes a number of additional resources, including videos of the films that are featured as case studies in the book.

Please be sure to visit!

http://booksite.focalpress.com/dslrcinema

Visit the author's DSLR Cinema blog:

www.kurtlancaster.com

Still from David Darg's and Bryn Mooser's *The Painter of Jalouzi*, shot on an iPhone 6s Plus (with a lens adapter) in Haiti. (©2015 RYOT Studio.)

The Rise and Fall of the DSLR Cinema Revolution

THE BEGINNING OF THE DSLR CINEMA REVOLUTION

Photographer Vincent Laforet redefined the game in late 2008, right at the birth of the DSLR cinema revolution with the release of the Canon 5D Mark II DSLR. Laforet's cinematic exploration of DSLRs liberated low budget filmmakers from the limits of prosumer video cameras, which were so full of compromises, including fixed lenses and tiny sensors, that it was nearly impossible to shape a film look. But not that many people noticed the potential of a DSLR as a filmmaking tool. Not at first.

It would take the eye of a photographer to turn a photography camera into a cinematic one.

Vincent Laforet, whose photographs have appeared in *National Geographic*, *Sports Illustrated*, *Time*, *Life*, and *Newsweek*, among others, remembers purchasing a Panasonic DVX100 (the miniDV 24p camera), but he quickly became "totally disinterested" in it, he tells me in an interview. "I was not impressed with the lens, depth of field, and the look and feel of it." He returned it within a week.

But in the fall of 2008, photographer Laforet redefined the video versus cinema game.

Laforet, one of Canon's "Explorers of Light" educators and a former Pulitzer Prize-winning photographer for *The New York Times* (2000–2006), had an appointment with David Sparer, Canon's senior manager of Pro-Products Technical Marketing.

It was a Friday and the team had just unpacked the prototype Canon 5D Mark II, a digital SLR camera, that was announced on September 17, 2008. Laforet took a peek, but they wouldn't let him touch the camera until he signed a nondisclosure agreement. Indeed, when he found out it was the world's first DSLR camera to shoot full-size HD video, he begged Sparer to let him borrow one for the weekend. But the cameras were to be shipped out to other photographers for testing on Monday, so the answer was no. Laforet made a pitch.

"This camera is basically going to sit for two days doing nothing," Laforet remembers saying. "Just let me borrow it for a few hours and I'll give it right back, so I can try shooting a sample movie." They eventually agreed, and told Laforet that Canon would not sponsor the movie. "You are just borrowing the camera entirely independently from Canon, and doing your own little thing. If the movie turns out good, we'll use it—if not, we won't," Laforet remembers them saying.[1]

> "I was literally stunned a number of times. I could not believe my eyes. ... [T]he way it captures light, it's absolutely stunning."
> -Vincent Laforet

He came up with a scenario and shot *Reverie* over a weekend (see Figure I.1).

When Laforet first saw the results of the 5D Mark II on-screen, he knew this was different from any type of video he had previously examined. "I was literally stunned a number of times," he mused. "I could not believe my eyes. It's one of the best still cameras out in the world. But between the size of the sensor and the lens choice and the way it captures light, it's absolutely stunning." In short, it looked like it was shot on film. After Laforet put *Reverie* online (Canon liked it), it received over 2 million views in a week, and Laforet's life changed overnight. The day after the upload, he received three different film project offers within a day. Independent filmmakers, video journalists, and students saw the results and many dumped their video cameras and started shooting their projects on DSLRs. Canon's 5D Mark II—when utilizing the proper settings and lighting conditions—started to be utilized as a cinema camera.

Although Nikon released the first DSLR that shot HD video (the D90 with 1280×720p resolution), it was Canon's 5D Mark II that captured the hearts of filmmakers. It not only utilized full HD 1920×1080p video, but it did so with a full frame sensor (36×24 mm)—essentially equivalent in size to a VistaVision cinema camera. But primarily, high-definition single lens reflex cameras, the hybrid DSLR (HDSLRs)—those that shoot stills and high-definition video—are designed for photographers. They're stills cameras. But thousands of DSLR shooters are using them as cinema cameras.

---

[1]Wallach, H. Interview: Vincent Laforet. <http://www.usa.canon.com/dlc/controller?act = GetArticleAct&articleID = 1286&fromTips = 1>.

FIGURE I.1
Still from Vincent Laforet's *Reverie*, the runaway Internet hit that changed Laforet's life overnight. (©2009 Vincent Laforet. Used with permission.)

SHANE HURLBUT, ASC, EMBRACED THE CANON 5D MARK II

Shane Hurlbut, ASC, who DP'ed *Terminator Salvation* (2009), among many other Hollywood film and television shows, also shot *Act of Valor* (2012) on the Canon 5D Mark II. He was originally trained on ENG cameras—a number of years ago as a student in mass communication at Emerson College in Boston. One eventful summer made him change his "religion." Over a summer break, one of his friends returned from USC film school and asked him to help shoot a movie in their hometown in upstate New York. He reminisces, "So I thought, 'All right I'll help Gabe out and learn.' It was all nights, so I started working on that project and fell in love with film. I just started looking at it and it was so different than TV video and I thought 'my God this is it.' So I went back that next semester and I changed everything I had from TV and mass communication to film and then I did a four-year film degree in one year."[2]

At the time, video just did not look like film. HD (at least at the prosumer level) may have been a game changer for news, sports, and event videographers—but not for many filmmakers.

---

[2] All interviews with Hurlbut were conducted by the author (in March 2010), unless otherwise noted.

The American Society of Cinematographers—that elite group who will give membership only by invitation—sponsored an event to show off the Canon 5D Mark II at Sammy's Camera in Los Angeles in February 2009. Hurlbut, among other ASC members, attended. "I went to Sammy's, and everyone was playing with it," but many weren't convinced at first, because of the stills camera form factor, and weren't sure on how to best harness its potential as a cinematic tool.

But Hurlbut saw the potential right away. "They had Vincent Laforet's film, *Reverie*, playing up there on a monitor. And I looked at that spot, and I thought, 'Whoa, that came from this camera?' And then I put the 5D in my hand and a light bulb went off. I knew that this was going to change everything. I was all in" (speech at Hdi RAWworks, 1 May 2010). He bought the Canon 5D Mark II that evening. "I realized that this is a game changer. I thought it was revolutionary. Then my mind just started thinking completely out of the box, 'What if we could do this, this, this, this, and this,' and it began to inspire me even more as a filmmaker." He worked his way through the various menu functions and taught himself how to use the camera. When McG, the director of *Terminator Salvation*, called Hurlbut and asked him to direct and shoot a series of webisodes to promote the movie—all based around a first-person perspective of a helmet cam—Hurlbut was all over it. It would allow him to take advantage of the Canon 5D Mark II. "The cameraman was the actor," Hurlbut says. "It was so exciting." Bandito Brothers Productions produced the webisodes for Warner Brothers. Bandito Brothers' directors were very impressed with the look of the *Terminator* webisodes, so they asked Hurlbut to DP their feature, *Act of Valor*, about the elite Navy SEALs where Hurlbut got to experiment more with the 5D—75% of the feature all of the action scenes was shot with Canon's DSLRs.

> Hurlbut saw the potential right away. "They had Vincent Laforet's film, *Reverie*, playing up there on a monitor. And I looked at that spot, and I thought, 'Whoa, that came from this camera?' And then I put the 5D in my hand and a light bulb went off. I knew that this was going to change everything. I was all in."

"Where did the idea of motion pictures come from?" Hurlbut asks. "It came from a brilliant individual, Louis Lumière. When he looked through his pin-hole camera, he asked himself the question, 'I wondered what it would look like if this image moved?' SHABANG!! Motion pictures were born. Why were the keys to the castle given to the ENG manufacturers to design our HD platform? Their specialty is capturing the news and sports. When I look at their images they don't look cinematic. I feel that the HD platform has now come from the right source, still photography." For example, Hurlbut explains, "I like to shoot a shallow depth of field, so the audience is drawn to what's in focus."

> Why were the keys to the castle given to the ENG manufacturers to design our HD platform? Their specialty is capturing the news and sports. When I look at their images they don't look cinematic. I feel that the HD platform has now come from the right source, still photography.

Up to this point, the HD video camera chip technology just doesn't quite do it for Hurlbut because the video looks overly sharp and has way too much depth of field. "New make-up is being designed, diffusion is being added, new LUTs [lookup tables] are being engineered all to try and make HD look good," Hurlbut says. "The Canon does all of this automatically without all the re-invention. You need to think much more out of the box, stop looking at all the numbers and drink the DSLR Kool-Aid, along with its limited color space and digital compression. This is what makes it look cinematic and organic. I call it digital film."

Because of this, Hurlbut embraces the DSLR over the high-end HD video cameras. "If I am shooting anything else, then I am shooting film," Hurlbut states. He often gets some strange looks when pulling out his 5D, especially when he hands it to the Technocrane technicians. "When I grab my 5D Moviemaker package, people who never worked with the still photography platform before view it like [a] UFO has just landed," he laughs.

But despite its alien look in the film world, Hurlbut tries to keep shooting simple. "What I like to do is try to keep it as close to the process of exposing film as possible." In the short produced for Canon, *The Last 3 Minutes* (see Figures I.2 and I.3), he notes how he used "my lighting monitor which becomes my viewfinder. It is intimate and my portal to view the light and composition." Not a big black tent with tons of wires running out of it, with waveform monitors, computers, and large HD monitors inside, nor did he utilize a digital image technician (DIT) seen on the set of *Battlestar Galactica*, for example. By embracing the simplicity of the Canon technology, he was able to keep the production simple, small, and intimate with the director and the actors, not a big circus. The camera becomes the DIT as well as the video playback technician. "Small footprint, big vision," he smiles.

FIGURE I.2
Shane Hurlbut, ASC, looks at his field monitor as he adjusts the focus ring on the Canon 5D Mark II for *The Last 3 Minutes*. "I light to the monitor," Hurlbut says. Note the red tape on the monitor setting the 1:85 aspect ratio; the 5D Mark II does not output HD when shooting in live mode, but standard definition. (Photo by Kurt Lancaster.)

FIGURE I.3
The shot from *The Last 3 Minutes* that Shane Hurlbut set up as seen in Figure I.2.
(©2010 Hurlbut Visuals. Used with permission.)

As Shane Hurlbut says, the camera "is exciting to me. And I think out of all this it's going to start a massive revolution."

Neil Smith, one of the pioneers of all-digital postproduction for the RED camera, was not so easily convinced as Hurlbut and Laforet about the potential DSLR cinema revolution.

NEIL SMITH'S TAKE ON THE DSLR CINEMA REVOLUTION

Neil Smith, a white-haired Englishman who retired from Microsoft, financed a grad school degree in neuroscience and became a documentary filmmaker. A few years ago, he started the former all-digital postproduction house, Hdi RAWworks, specifically for digital file-based workflows down in The Lot in Hollywood.

He attended the Collisions conference about the merging of filmmaking and DSLR cameras near the end of August 2009 at the Los Angeles Film School. Not only did Smith observe Shane Hurlbut, ASC, and Vincent Laforet speak, but Smith's Hdi RAWworks company put together their material that was to be projected at the conference. He looked at the work on a 60-foot screen and remembered thinking, "This is serious; this is cinematic-quality images."[3]

Rodney Charters, ASC, also convinced Smith to consider the potential of DSLRs as a cinema camera. As the DP on the TV series *24*, Charters purchased a Canon 5D Mark II and used it primarily for effects plate shots in the series. Neil Smith met him when he was shooting a CBS pilot, *Washington Field*, on a RED camera. He used Smith's posthouse for the postproduction work. Charters needed to get shots of the White House, Smith explains. "You try to film out in the streets of Washington, DC, anywhere near the White House with a RED camera and see what happens when an SUV with dark windows pulls up and six beefy chaps get

---

[3] All interviews with Smith in this chapter were conducted by the author in March 2010.

out and beat the crap out of you," Smith laughs. Charters, Smith continues, took the stealth approach. "He and his AC got his 5D Mark II, went outside, and took some background shots of the White House. He pretended to be a museum tourist. He got a shot where a cop car goes right in front of him, and nobody is stopping him," Smith adds.

Smith wondered how the HD video capabilities of the Canon 5D Mark II would compare to the 4 K resolution of a RED camera. Would it be cinematic or look as though it painfully stood out with a video aesthetic? Back in a screening room down at The Lot in Hollywood, they projected Charters' White House footage on a $100,000 2 K DLP projector. "We put it on the 20-foot screen downstairs," Smith remarks, "and I looked at it and I said, 'Ooh, that doesn't look as bad as I expected to look.'"

"We are a RED house," Smith continues, "we know image quality; we graded the first 4 K images off of the first RED. We understand all about color space and resolution." So even to consider using a hybrid DSLR that line-skips its images because the CMOS sensor processor is too slow to handle it was more than a leap of faith. It was, for the digital purist, like asking the ugly duckling to dance after turning down the prom queen. But in the right hands, the ugly duckling can shine. Smith asked Charters to do the ultimate test: shoot a series of demo shots at The Lot with the RED One, Canon 5D Mark II, and the Canon 7D and intermix the footage and see whether anyone could tell the difference.

They presented the work at the HD Expo in New York in the fall of 2009 in front of 200 filmmakers, Smith explains. "We asked everybody, 'If you can guess absolutely correctly which is RED, 5D, and 7D, we will buy you the best meal you ever had,'" Smith challenged. "We have not had to buy a meal." Despite the numbers and resolution charts, the 5D and 7D hold up against the RED—at least in the 2 K world. However, 4 K resolution is an entirely different story. Smith felt that Canon would beat out the other dedicated video cameras due to Moore's Law—faster, better, cheaper. The DSLR cameras can only get better, plus Canon has the sales distribution and mass market on its side.

> We asked everybody, 'If you can guess absolutely correctly which is RED, 5D, and 7D, we will buy you the best meal you ever had,' Smith challenged. 'We have not had to buy a meal.' Despite the numbers and resolution charts, the 5D and 7D hold up against the RED—at least in the 2K world.

In the end, Smith feels that the DSLR model for shooting movies "is a new form of filmmaking. This is cinéma vérité reborn." He adds: "There is something about the form factor about these cameras which allows you to work with actors in a totally different way."

Greg Yaitanes, a director of the TV series *House*, agrees with Smith. When they used the Canon 5D Mark II to shoot an episode of *House* in spring 2010, he said in an interview with Philip Bloom, "This was beyond a cinematic look. It gave a new level of being able to pull the actors out of the background and pull them right to your face, and give an intimacy that I haven't seen in digital or film."[4]

In addition to its size, Smith says the Canon sensor has a certain cinematic look to it. "To me, these HD digital SLRs have a 35 mm film aesthetic—there is something about the sensor and the color science," Smith muses. "You know, Canon had been making good 35 mm [still] film cameras for years; they've been making good 35 mm digital cameras for years. There is something in the sensor design, something in the spirit of the machine, the soul of the machine that is very organic. There is something that Canon engineers do with these sensors and their color science that produces a very film-like aesthetic."

Smith feels that due to "the form factor, the price, the image quality, and the new techniques of filmmaking" that it will "revolutionize anything with a micro budget. Anything under a million dollars where they used to consider a large HD camera they will now consider two or three DSLRs." Due to Moore's Law, Smith explains, "faster, better, cheaper" DSLRs will just get better. Because Canon has the R&D and the marketing, he feels it will remain king of the DSLR cinema world. Smith Spoke these words in 2010. The mirrorless cameras—smaller, cheaper, faster—delivered on Smith's prediction. But not before George Lucas experimented with DSLRs.

LUCASFILM TAKES ON DSLRs—WITH THE HELP OF PHILIP BLOOM

Independent filmmaker Philip Bloom, who, like Smith, initially dismissed the value of the Canon 5D Mark II, bought one and tossed it aside because he couldn't control some of the features manually. As a professional DP, he wanted that control. But late in the spring of 2009, he saw the potential. He started shooting some projects with it. He wrote about his experiences and put samples of his work on his blog (philipbloom.net). People noticed. Within several months, he became one of the key DSLR experts during filmmaking peak; he was invited to give workshops and asked by Canon and Panasonic to test out cameras for them. Rick McCallum, the producer of *Star Wars* (Episodes I–III) noticed as well and invited him out to Skywalker Ranch in Marin County, California, in October 2009. Mike Blanchard, the head of postproduction at Lucasfilm, called him up. They wanted to know how far the cameras could be pushed cinematically—can a DSLR be used as a cinema camera?

Bloom arrived with his equipment and shot around the countryside of Skywalker Ranch (see Figure I.4). He converted the files to Apple ProRes overnight and cut together a rough edit by morning. The big guys wanted to see it projected on a

---

[4] Bloom, P. "Exclusive: In-depth interview with Greg Yaitanes." philipbloom.net. 19 April 2010.

40-foot screen. That was the true test. Bloom knew the work looked good on his computer screen. And his stuff looked good on the web—but on a cinema screen? That was the true test.

For Lucas and his team, Bloom says, "If it looks great on the big screen then that is the most important thing. Not codecs, limitations, bit rates, et cetera. All those are very important, but the most important thing by far for them is how it actually looks and it passed with flying colors. That is what they really care about."[5]

Bloom blogged about his experience at Skywalker Ranch:

> I was nervous. Never having seen my work on a big screen as good as this, but also George Lucas came in to watch and also the legendary sound designer Ben Burtt. My heart was racing. I watched as the edit played and they loved it. My favorite moment was when the star timelapse came on and Ben Burtt said 'Hey, now, hang on!!' This was a very quick ungraded draft edit knocked together from a crappy grey day as a test, not supposed to be shown as an example of my work! Then Quentin Tarantino came in as he was due to talk at a screening

FIGURE I.4
Still from Bloom's Skywalker Ranch, a test video he shot for Lucasfilm to see how it would look blown up on a 40-foot screen. "My heart was racing," Bloom says. "I watched as the edit played and they loved it."
(©2009 Philip Bloom. Used with permission.)

---

[5]Bloom, P. "The tale of Lucasfilm, Skywalker Ranch, *Star Wars*, and Canon DSLRs on a 40 foot screen!" philipbloom.net. 12 Dec. 2009. http://philipbloom.net/2009/12/12/skywalker/.

of *Inglourious Basterds* and George said to Quentin, come see this. Quentin waxed lyrical, calling it Epic and William Wylersesque and was shocked it was shot on a DSLR. He had no idea you could shoot HD video on them or they were so good.

Bloom passed the test and Lucasfilm used Canon 5Ds on selected scenes in *Red Tails* (2012), a story about an African American fighter squadron in World War II. Mike Blanchard, Lucasfilm's head of postproduction, wasn't sure if the footage would hold up on-screen. "Certainly when we just look at the footage and put it on a big screen it holds up way better than it has a right to," he says. A lot of people get caught up in the numbers game, comparing one type of camera to another, he continues, such as the argument that "film is 4K, blah, blah, blah. You know, it's really not, because nobody ever sees a projected negative.[6] So by the time you do a release print and [put it] through its paces, it's no way near [what] a lot of people claim that it really is. So the great part about working at Lucasfilm, for people like Rick [McCallum] and George [Lucas]—working for them—is that you just show them things and that's where it ends. We don't do little charts about how it doesn't have that or it doesn't do that. We make it work. And that's just a beautiful way to do work, because it opens up everything" (interview with Jared Abrams, 15 April 2010; www.cinema5d.com/news/?p=3216). Now that most movies are released digitally, the degradation of the release print isn't a concern.

Yaitanes did note how there is a stark difference between those who are shooting stories and those who are shooting test charts: "Somebody could sit there and say to me, 'Well, you know, I looked at the specs and this doesn't line up and this and that.'" But Yaitanes said the proof comes from working "out there in the field." We "told a story and people have had an emotional reaction to that story, and, frankly, again, that trumps everything"—and they continued to use the 5D in the 2010/11 season.[7]

HOLLYWOOD NEVER REALLY EMBRACED DSLRs

Despite Lucasfilm's *Red Tails* and Yaitanes' work on *House*, Charters' work on *Washingtong Field*, and Hurlbut's cinematography on *Act of Valor*, there really was not widespread adoption of the Canon 5D Mark II in Hollywood. It never drove mainstream Hollywood cinematography. Certainly, low budget independent filmmakers, video production houses, and students embraced DSLRs as cinema cameras, propelling their work forward into cinematic aesthetics. DSLRs force shooters to think cinematically.

The biggest influence of DSLRs was their impact on sales. Because the sales were so high, the DSLR cinema movement forced video camera companies to change

---

[6] The raw negative can go up to 6,000 lines of resolution, whereas an analog projection print is typically around 2,000 lines (but digital intermediate scanned films can go higher).
[7] Bloom, P. "Exclusive: In depth interview with Greg Yaitanes." philipbloom.net. 19 April 2010. http://philipbloom.net/2010/04/19/in-depth-interview-with-executive-producer-and-director-of-house-season-finale-shot-on-canon-5dmkii/

how they approached their camera designs. In order to stay in the game—the demand for DSLR video was that big—they designed and released large sensor video cameras with interchangeable lenses, and what was once held by DSLRs (an inexpensive cinematic look), would morph into the creation of affordable cinema camera—from Blackmagic Design's Cinema Camera to the Canon C200. Initial cameras included Blackmagic's Cinema Camera, the Sony FS-100, Panasonic's AF-100, with some bloggers announcing them as "DSLR killers." But the early generation of cinema cameras didn't really deliver and the DSLR as a cinematic tool did not die as quickly as predicted. In fact, it was the DSLR that killed the prosumer video camera market, and they were forced to evolve in order to stay in the game. Even Canon entered the cinema camera market with the release of their C500 and C300, and Sony released the F3 and FS7. RED started evolving their cameras and releasing less expensive models. Although the DSLR still had game, others were gravitating to these newer cameras. Examining cameras used for films accepted into the Sundance Film Festival over the past few years, we can see a mix of cameras being used, from the iPhone to DSLRs, to Canon's new cameras and RED's new sensors (source: nofilmschool.com and indiewire.com):

2015

Tangerine: Apple iPhone 5s

Being Evel: Blackmagic Cinema Camera

The Royal Road: 16mm film

The Overnight: Canon C500

Advantageous: RED Mysterium X

Meru: Canon 5D Mark III

The Forbidden Room: Sony F3 and Canon 5D Mark III

The Strongest Man: Canon C300 (mostly); pickup shot with Canon C100

2016

Birth of a Nation: ARRI ALEXA

Nuts!: Blackmagic Cinema Camera

The Eyes of My Mother: RED Dragon

Miles Ahead: ARRI ALEXA and Super16mm

Operation Avalanche: Blackmagic Pocket Cinema Camera

Cameraperson: Compiled from 30 years of documentary footage from a variety of cameras

Hooligan Sparrow: Canon 60D

Equity: ARRI ALEXA

Love Song: Canon 7D

Belgica: RED Scarlet and Dragon

Christine: ARRI ALEXA and 16mm film

The Shining Star of Losers Everywhere: Canon C100 and Canon 5D

2017

Thoroughbred: ARRI ALEXA Mini

Landline: ARRI ALEXA
Patti Cake$: ARRI ALEXA Mini
Crown Heights: ARRI ALEXA
Berlin Syndrome: ARRI ALEXA
Pop Aye: ARRI ALEXA
Burning Sands: ARRI ALEXA Mini
To the Bone: ARRI ALEXA
Menashe: Canon C300
Golden Exits: Aaton XTR 16mm
Band Aid: ARRI AMIRA
Roxanne Roxanne: ARRI ALEXA
Ingrid Goes West: ARRI ALEXA Mini
Lemon: ARRI ALEXA
The Wound: ARRI ALEXA
The Nile Hilton Incident: ARRI ALEXA
The Yellow Birds: ARRI ALEXA and ALEXA Mini
Free and Easy: ARRI ALEXA
Don't Swallow My Heart, Alligator Girl!: RED
My Happy Family: ARRI ALEXA
It Happened in L.A.: ARRI ALEXA
Dayveon: RED Dragon
Rememory: ARRI ALEXA
The Hero: ARRI AMIRA and ALEXA
I Don't Feel at Home in this World Anymore: ARRI ALEXA Mini
Family Life: Sony FS7

The above list for 2017 does not include documentaries. It can be clearly seen that Arri cameras hold the forefront of higher budget independent feature films in 2017, while documentaries tend to lean towards a mix of DSLRs and low budget cinema cameras. In an interview with Shane Hurlbut, ASC, at the 2012 National Association of Broadcasters in Las Vegas, he still emphasized the fact that all of the new cameras—from DSLRs to 4K cameras—are tools to serve the story and the story will determine the right tools to use. He did admit that "we're at a crossroads, and 4K cameras is going to blow people's mind." 4K capture on Canon's 1D-C, and more recently the 5D Mark IV, would make Hurlbut exclaim with excitement that the footage "is the closest that I've ever seen video look like film, and it's looking like Kodak film." Indeed, after comparing RED and the Canon 1D-C 4K DSLR side by side, he felt that Canon had the edge: "It looked like I was watching 35 mm motion picture on the 1D-C, while the RED looked a bit more like video."

Hurlbut also feels that the Canon log file allowing for 12 1/2 stops of latitude adds to the cinematic potential. One of the detriments to high resolution cinema includes the recording of "imperfections" of a person's face, Hurlbut explains. But because Canon uses JPEG compression, he feels that it "rounds all of that incredible 4K sharpness off, just enough to make the skin look alive" without needing to use a diffusion filter to help hide blemishes.

This Sundance list also reveals the fact that many people are moving away from using DSLRs on their projects and moving towards high and low end cinema cameras. Athough still used by many students and some filmmakers, the success of DSLRs in filmmaking would become its defeat. Filmmakers with a good eye would shun the use of consumer camcorders, so they tried to rig them up with 35mm adapters, because high end cinema cameras were just too expensive for the projects they wanted to do. With the release of Canon's 5D Mark II, that all changed. The prosumer video camera was hit hard and they had to adapt in order to grow with this new demand.

Canon's photo division poached the sales of its video camera division. Canon designed and released the C500 (costing over $25,000), but they also came out with the C100 and C300, and more recently the C200. The C500 was phased out and replaced with the Canon C700. Sony and Panasonic have also released low end cinema cameras, but these companies have also created mirrorless cameras that put the power of filmmaking into cameras smaller than a DSLR. Some companies even make lenses for smartphones and a few filmmakers are experimenting with the form. Panasonic's GH5, sporting a micro four-thirds sensor, also shoots 6K anamorphic. For $2000, that's a lot of power in a small package. Blackmagic also released their Pocket Cinema Camera in 2013, which includes the ability to shoot CinemaDNG raw (in a compressed form), but it also shoots in 10-bit 422 MOV codec (a form used in professional broadcast standard cameras), while some of the more expensive DSLRs and low end cinema cameras (such as Canon's C100 and C200), shoot in an 8-bit format (the C200 can shoot in a compressed RAW codec at 12-bit, too). Blackmagic also released their URSA Mini, which includes RAW codecs and ProRes 444 XQ for around $6,000.

None of these newer lower priced cinema cameras and mirrorless cameras would have been desigend and released without the popularity of DSLRs as a tool for independent filmmakers. And a new form of cinema cameras are evolving to help take on the low end market: smartphone cinema.

SMARTPHONE CINEMA

Sean Baker's 2015 Sundance hit, *Tangerine*, was shot on an iPhone 5s. The cinematographers used Moondog Labs' anamorphic adapter ($175; http://moondoglabs.com) and the FiLMiC Pro app to help achieve cinematic quality (see Figure I.5). "If you don't have the money to shoot on, let's say 35mm [film], make the most of what you have," Baker said in an interview with *Variety*.[8] The smartphone is evolving into an alternative for low-budget cinema cameras. The Lensvid.com blog draws some conclusions about the market for photographers (and indirectly to filmmakers using DSLRs and mirrorless cameras):

> Smartphones killed the compact camera market—from over 100 million compact cameras sold in 2010 we will most likely see under 10 million sold in 2017. Just for reference, in 2016 the global sales of smart phones reached 1.5 billion units, an increase of 5 percent from 2015.
>
> Mirrorless are not fulfilling their promise—mirrorless are making lots of noise in the photo industry but looking at the numbers they have been more or less stagnant for the past 3 years at around 3 million cameras per year—far from impressive numbers.
>
> The DSLR market is shrinking—this was to be expected but it is not because of the rise of mirrorless. Why this is happening is probably a combination of reasons—at the entry level some people who might have considered buying a DSLR a few years back just settle for their smartphone camera which is better than ever and will soon improve even further with dual cameras, smart zoom technologies and more advanced features. At the mid to high end segments—there just isn't enough innovation to justify replacing gear as often as it used to be and on the more positive side—cameras are quite reliable and replacing a working camera for a new one which doesn't offer significantly more, just doesn't make sense to many users.
>
> Cameras are for older people—you can't see this in the numbers but we clearly see this all around us—aside from the professional segment—dedicated cameras do not interest the younger generation. The people who are still interested in photography are typically around the ages of 40-60 or more—the same people who maybe shot with analog cameras as youngsters and now have the time and money to invest in photography as a hobby—their children and grandchildren are far less interested in cameras and prefer to use their smartphones.[9]

Drawing two conclusions from this, serious low-budget filmmakers who want to be taken seriously tend to shoot their films on low budget cinema cameras rather than DSLRs and mirrorless cameras. There are others experimenting with smartphone cameras as cinema cameras, because they're cheaper, lighter, small, and available. There's even a Toronto Smartphone Film Festival (http://smartphonefilm.ca/), which included 217 submissions from thirty-four contries in 2016.

---

[8] "Sundance: Sean Baker on Filming 'Tangerine' and 'Making the Most' of an iPhone." *Variety*. http://variety.com/video/sundance-sean-baker-on-filming-tangerine-and-making-the-most-of-an-iphone/

FIGURE I.5
Sean Baker's *Tangerine* became a Sundance favorite in 2015. It would reveal the potential of a smartphone as a tool of cinematography.
(©2015 Magnolia Pictures. Used with permission.)

Lindsay Walker shot an experimental film, *The Courage Closet*, using her iPhone 6 and olloclip's 4-in-1 Lens Set (~$80; https://olloclip.com), allowing her the choice of shooting with a fisheye, wide, 10x macro, and 15x macro. (See Figure I.6.)

With potentially strong aesthetic results in the right hands, a smartphone, when tied to an inexpensive lens package, has become a viable option for many young filmmakers—especial those on a really tight budget. As the sales data show, many are avoiding DSLRs and using what they already own. A good eye, and with the right equipment, we can see such images found in *The Courage Closet* (www.youtube.com/watch?v=Gb8azalJOBA). (See Figures I.7 and I.8.) These images hold up cinematically and it reminds me of amateur 8mm experimental films. Walker says that her iPhone, along with the olloclip lens system, allows for filmmakers to experiment with "form" and "explore visual ideas" in order to "simplify" them. "It also forces you as filmmaker to really think about shots and what is actually achievable," she adds.

Walker has always been attracted to poetry writing and journals, providing a "good sense of my own identity and embracing that." She is a self-taught photographer, and would later get a master's in filmmaking,

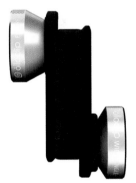

FIGURE I.6
The olloclip 4-in-1 Lens Set, provides a variety of lens angles for iPhones.
(Courtesy of olloclip.)

---

[9] "LensVid Exclusive: What Happened to the Photography Industry in 2016?" https://lensvid.com/gear/lensvid-exclusive-happened-photography-industry-2016/

allowing her to think about ways to combine her love of poetry writing with the moving image. "I wanted to know how my poetry would look in motion," she explains, "so I asked myself, 'How would the words I've written feel like and look like on screen?'" *The Courage Closet* was the result. It became a test case for her entrée into smartphone cinema, giving her visual ideas for her larger short film, *Bound,* a smart film about identity, connection, and memory (see https://www.youtube.com/watch?v=0zz0NB8nV9o). In addition, she continues, it's much cheaper to shoot on a smartphone, allowing her to test out her vision: "I wanted to use the iPhone because I had zero budget for *Bound.* I figured if I could pull off a short experimental by capturing feeling and tone with a smartphone then hopefully I'd be able to pull it off with a DSLR and a small crew of people."

It's not just experimental filmmakers using smartphones for filmmaking. Documentary filmmakers have also used the iPhone with lens adapters. David Darg and Bryn Mooser of RYOT Studio produced the short documentary *The Painter of Jalouzi* in Haiti (see https://vimeo.com/140249436). They shot on an iPhone 6s, using a lens adapter that allowed them to attach Canon and Nikon lenses, which helped them attain a cinematic look. (See Figures I.9 and I.10.)

FIGURE I.7
A wide angle image from Lindsay Walker's experimental short, *The Courage Closet,* shot on an iPhone 6s using an olloclip 4-in-1 Lens.
(©2016 Lindsay Walker. Used with permission.)

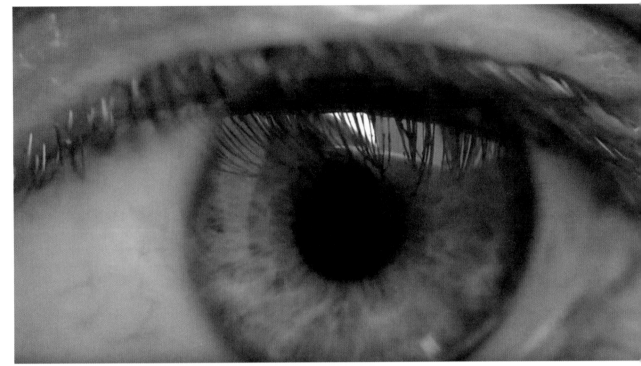

FIGURE I.8
A shot from Lindsay Walker's *The Courage Closet* using the olloclip 4-in-1 Lens Set for the iPhone 6 (macro setting).
(©2016 Lindsay Walker. Used with permission.)

Furthermore, those who take their smartphone filmmaking seriously should look closely at the $15 app, FiLMiC Pro (http://filmicpro.com), providing manual control of focus (shaping focal depth of field), exposure, white balance, zoom, focus peaking, zebra stripes, false color (for exposure control), audio meters, shutter speed, frame rates (1-240 fps for slow motion shots), a data rate of 100mbps at 4K and 50mbps at 1080p, and audio control. (See Chapter 4 for more details on recording audio.) In addition, in-app purchase for the iPhone 7/7+ provides flat log shooting modes. The app is also available to Android users. In short, it offers some features lacking in many DSLRs. This is the app used by filmmakers on the breakout iPhone hit, *Tangerine* (2015). (See Figure I.11.) Throw in a DJI Osmo Mobile gimbal stabilizer (for ~$300), a mini tripod, and external battery packs, and a filmmaker has nealy everything they need to produce low budget films. (See the end of Chapter 7 for an overview of some smartphone cinema gear.)

The DSLR revolution has evolved into the smartphone cinema reovluion, making filmmaking even more affordable than before. With the release of *Trangerine*, some might have considered smartphone cinema as an exception, a fad. But when Oscar winner Steven Soderbergh shoots his latest film on an iPhone, others are taking notice.[10] For additional resources on smartphone cinema, see http://nofilmschool.com/tags/smartphone.

WHAT THIS BOOK IS ABOUT

This book is designed for beginning filmmakers—or those trained in broadcast style of video production—who want to up their cinematic game, whether they're shooting a wedding, a student thesis film, a documentary, video journalism, an independent film for a festival, or a feature. It's designed to help shooters create cinema-quality HD video with the fewest possible people and with the least equipment—to maintain a small footprint of the one-person shooter, if needed, but with the ability to maintain a big vision.

Ultimately, video shooters can learn how to make their work look better by reading this book, but hooking that cinematic look to a good story is more than key. It's essential. It's what will impact an audience.

Philip Bloom, one of the original gurus of DSLR cinema, best sums up the purpose of this book, as he explained to me over breakfast at Venice Beach's Sidewalk Café:

FIGURE 1.9
David Darg sets up a shot using a Canon lens attached to an iPhone 6s Plus through a special adapter. (©2015. Courtesy of RYOT Studio.)

---

[10] Sharf, Zack. "Steven Soderbergh Shot a Secret Movie on His iPhone, Starring Claire Foy and Juno Temple." Indiewire.com. 18 July 2017. http://www.indiewire.com/2017/07/steven-soderbergh-secret-movie-iphone-claire-foy-unsane-1201856840/

FIGURE I.10
The result of a telephoto lens attached to an iPhone can be seen in this telephoto shallow depth-of-field shot.
(©2015. Courtesy of RHOT Studio.)

FIGURE I.11
FiLMiC Pro provides the smartphone filmmaker a lot of control over their image, including features found in cinema cameras.
(Courtesy of FiLMiC Pro.)

> Suddenly we are giving people an affordable tool to make high-quality imagery, and it's releasing potential in people they never realized they had. There are people out there who never thought that they would be able to shoot high-quality images like this, that they would have the opportunity to do it. And they will go out and do it and they may not do it as a full-time job—and most of them [won't]—but it's the passion brought out in people that is just incredible.

This book is about taking that passion, that desire to shoot cinematic images. Low budget cinema requries shooters to think like a cinematographer, rather than as a videographer.

The simplicity of pointing and shooting a DSLR camera as if you were shooting a video camera with everything automatically set is not the way to go. And shooting a low budget cinema camera in a point-and-shoot mode can be just as disastrous. Using cinema cameras requires shooters to understand lenses, focus, composition, depth of field, exposure, lighting, ISO (film exposure speed), color balance, camera movement, blocking, and separate recording of audio (when needed). This book was written to help guide those taking this next step into cinematic storytelling.

WHAT'S COVERED IN THE BOOK

This book assumes you already know how to shoot and edit. At the same time, the importance of basic cinematography will not be assumed, and even if you already hold this knowledge, the review may be beneficial because the examples draw not only from a DSLR perspective, but from the cameras that were influenced by the DSLR cinema movement, including such cameras as the Canon C100 Mark II, Panasonic GH5, Blackmagic Pocket Cinema Camera, among others. The first part of the book covers how to reach for a cinematic look, the "film look."

Chapters 1 through 4 include themes and a set of steps, so you can plan each element as you begin to master composition, blocking, camera movement, lighting, exposure, and audio. All the chapters include working examples from some of the best shooters in the field to illustrate the technical and artistic expression of low budget cinema cameras. It's not an exhaustive overview of of projects shot on these cameras, however. Only a few were selected for this book—based on the availability of subjects and the author's sensibilities. Chapter 5 covers postproduction workflow, but not as a software manual, but rather in ways that prompt you to think about what you can do with an image in postproduction based on the limitations of the source file, while Chapter 6 provides an overview and exercises on storytelling so you can quickly think about the number one reason to get a low budget cinema camera in the first place: to tell good stories. Chapter 7 covers what you should look for when purchasing gear, while the rest of the book goes into case studies of filmmakers in the field.

The goal isn't to master the entire art and craft of filmmaking in these chapters, but to expose you to some of the basic principles and potentials so you can begin shooting projects cinematically.

1. "Composition, Lenses, Blocking, and Camera Movement." This chapter provides the basics, the first tools needed to begin to master what it means to make cinema. It examines the golden mean in composition, the function of different types of lenses, the importance of working with actors to tell a story visually through body language, as well as why camera movement is one of the most powerful elements in cinematography. Some sections of this chapter have been revised to include examples from recent films.

2. "Lighting." Without an understanding of light and shadow, filmmakers will never break out of the flat video aesthetic. Lighting sets the mood of every scene, and just because many low budget cinema cameras are good in low light doesn't mean you should ignore one of the most important tools in cinematography. This chapter has been revised to include examples from recent films, including work by the Spanish filmmaker, David Tembleque (shooting on Blackmagic's Pocket Cinema Camera) and American filmmaker Joe Simon (shooting on Canon's C100 Mark II).

3. "Exposure." This chapter describes technical geek stuff, but cinematographers wouldn't consider themselves cinematographers without an understanding of how to utilize these tools to shape the look and feel of their digital films. A mastery of the tonal scale will teach you how much light to use on your subject and in the background. Exposure will help you determine not only how much light hits the sensor, but how much depth of field you'll have. This chapter has been revised to include more recent examples by David Tembleque and an explanation of shooting in flat log mode.

4. "Recording Quality Audio." Not enough can be said about the importance of getting clean audio. It's more important than capturing a good picture. Poorly recorded sound will prevent an audience from seeing your film. This chapter goes over some of the technical aspects of microphones and includes recommendations for equipment. It also includes the best way to get the cleanest sound for DSLR shooters: the external audio recorder. It includes workflow for using Magic Lantern, a firmware hack that allows Canon DSLR shooters to get audio meters, headphone jacks, and focus assist in-camera—a really important tool for run-and-gun video journalists.

5. "Key Concepts in Postproduction Workflow." Rather than attempting to teach software interface operation—something this book does not have the space to achieve—this chapter has been rewritten from scratch and digs into some of the key elements of what to look for and be aware of in the postproduction pipeline, including the steps needed to take in preparing footage, some of the

purposes behind editing for storytelling, rhythm and pacing, an overview of the tools used in editing, how to take a flat log look and make it look compelling, using LUTs to change the look and feel of a film, the function of sound mixing, mastering, and the power of sound design in post.

6. "Telling Better Stories with Your DSLR." This chapter is for those who want to make good on their traditional storytelling skills. It's one thing to buy a low budget cinema camera and start shooting, but to enter the world of professional cinema, a mastery of storytelling is essential. The chapter provides the basics of the three-act structure, covers the importance of visual storytelling through the actions characters take, and provides tips on writing good dialog. It uses Vincent Laforet's *Reverie* and Jamin Winans' *Uncle Jack* as case studies. In addition, it includes exercises on how to get good story ideas.

7. "Cinematic Gear on a Budget." This chapter has been fully revised, so rather than recommending one piece of gear over another, I describe what features you need to look for in a computer, editing software, camera, and audio gear that professionals need. Even though I do list some specific gear for those who want to get a sense of what's out there on a budget (including equipment for smartphone cinema), the most important elements in this chapter involve an overview of the features described.

8. "Blackmagic's Pocket Cinema Camera in *Dear Tom*." Some filmmakers fictionalize their lives. Others engage in essay films and talk about their experiences as we look at footage. David Tembleque relies on visuals with strong composition and use of natural light. He then adds a woman performing a break-up on a phone message. Is it fiction? Is it real? It's real. This new case study chapter examines Temblueque's approach to using the Blackmagic Pocket Cinema Camera on his award-winning short.

9. "Canon's C100 Mark II in *Fragments*." In this new case study, written by Dana Beasley, we see Joe Simon's approach to shooting a short fiction piece involving flashbacks. The end result is a 3-minute fictional short that utilizes a variety of technical applications and artistic approaches to visually and emotionally convey a couple's romance. "It's this whole time-shifting story of this person's life," said Simon, who served as director and director of photography for the film. "Basically, at the very end, you see that they're an old couple now, and you see that they're looking at the photo from their wedding as they reminisce through all those times when they first met and their courtship."

10. "Canon's 7D in *A Day at the Races*." One of the original case studies from the first edition of this book, it's still a classic in showing the results of a documentary by Philip Bloom, who shot it on a Canon 7D fitted with a special PL mounting plate that can take cinema lenses. He used high-end Cooke cinema lenses, revealing his signature style with close-ups of faces in and around horse stables and a racetrack in Los Angeles.

11. "Documentary Intimacy with the Canon 5D Mark III in *Art of the People*." In this new case study, Kiril Kirkov, a visual anthropologist, shot this film about Navajo artists in some of the most stunning locations in the southwest United States. He utilized observational cinema techniques to capture the details of painters' expressions and brush strokes, revealing an intimacy through the lens of the 5D Mark III, with audio recorded separatley on a Tascam DR-70D.

12. "Canon's 5D Mark II in *The Last 3 Minutes*." From the original first edition, this chapter tells the story of a short film was shot by Shane Hurlbut, a member of the American Society of Cinematographers, showing what can be done with a DSLR when pushed to its narrative limits. I was on set during the shooting of this ambitious film shot over a period of five days in eighteen different locations. The chapter includes interviews with the writer-director, Po Chan, as well as with Shane Hurlbut, ASC. The film holds up as one of the strongest shorts shot at the birth of the DSLR cinema movement.

13. "Filming Action with Panasonic's GH5 in *Unmasked*." This film was shot in Los Angeles and was written to include fight scenes designed to push the limits of the camera. Cinematographer J. Van Auken wanted to capture the ability of the GH5 by shooting in high-contrast situations, such as outdoors in high-contrast sun to stress the dynamic range of the camera. He also recorded fast lateral moves to push the rolling shutter of the sensor. Using a limited color palette, he isolated areas of high saturation as a means of showing off the camera's color separation capability, as well as its ability to shoot extra wide with its anamorphic lens feature. This new case study explores a camera that holds a lot of cinematic potential.

14. "Filming Documentaries on the Canon C100 Mark II." Another new case study shows off the capabilities of the Canon C100 Mark II as a news and documentary camera, featuring Mari Cleven's cinematic eye on three different short projects, one of which featured the return of a $160 million painting after it was stolen over thirty years ago from the University of Arizona. With documentary work, Cleven says that "instead of only pondering how to make a pretty shot, I now feel a sense of obligation that comes from being gifted the opportunity to tell someone else's story." She feels the C100 Mark II, for the price, allows her to shoot cinematically while at the same time utilizing integrated audio recording, 60 fps recording capability, and its all-around ease of use for solo shooters in the field.

15. "Bibbi Abruzzini: Filmming Documentaries on the Canon 5D Mark IV." The Canon camera is well represented as a solid documentary tool for Abruzzini, who takes it to Nepal and Lebanon, as well as the United States. She looks at girls and young women skaters in Nepal, examines a homeless person's life in Phoenix, Arizona, and finds that a small camera like the Mark IV allows her to enter other people's intimate lives.

This is one of the most exciting times to be a filmmaker. Over fifteen years ago, potential filmmakers and students got excited with miniDV and the later prosumer

HD cameras, but these didn't really break through to the cinema world, other than with a few exceptions. When it comes to the DSLR cinema revolution, there's been nothing like how it helped shaped this movement and forced manufactures to design and build new low budget cinema cameras. Not in the history of cinema. The closest we got was the breakthrough by Richard Leacock and Robert Drew, who developed a portable 16 mm sync-sound film camera that changed how documentaries were made (see, for example, *Primary*, 1960).

What kinds of projects and what styles of filmmaking will develop from the new cinema cameras of the future, including smartphone cinema? You, as a visual storyteller, will pave the way for a new kind of cinema, a kind of cinema never previously attained on such a small equipment budget.

Show us what you can do.

CHAPTER 1

Composition, Lenses, Blocking, and Camera Movement

Composition, blocking, and camera movement are the building blocks of your story. They're intertwined like DNA and you cannot have one without the others. This first chapter begins by defining these three elements and showing examples of how shooters compose their image along the golden mean, as well as how they tell a story through the blocking of performers, and how they utilize camera movement poetically.

COMPOSITION

Three-dimensional subjects and the scene they're in are composed through a lens. This composition relies on many factors, including lenses and shot sizes, as well as camera angles. But one underlying principle can't be understated: the golden mean appearing in nature, a ratio studied by mathematician and philosopher Pythagoras. Many cameras are equipped with rule of thirds grid lines which provide a decent way to compose your images—keeping eye lines on the top third of the image and your subject in either the right or left third, for example. But photographer Jake Garn argues that the rule of thirds isn't as naturally dynamic as the use of the golden mean, which we can see in one of his photos in Figure 1.1—the girl in the foreground composed along the golden mean.

Garn explains how Mario Livio explores this topic in his book, *The Golden Ratio: The Story of PHI, the World's Most Astonishing Number* (Broadway Books, 2003). The ratio provides a spiral and rectangular pattern that reflects a pattern found in nature and, when used by photographers and cinematographers, can create powerful compositions.

If you want to learn how to do this and train your eye to compose your images around the golden mean, the Shutterfreaks team—a group of photographers who have created a website with tips and tricks (shutterfreaks.com)—offer a Photoshop application that allows you to take stills of your compositions and see how well they fit within the golden mean. You may download Shutterfreaks' application for

FIGURE 1.1
Jake Garn's photo with the golden mean symbol laid out on top of it by the photographer.
(Photo ©Jake Garn. Used with permission.)

Photoshop, so you can analyze a still within a golden mean grid; see http://www.shutterfreaks.com/Actions/RuleOfThirds.php.

Let's look at a few random stills from Joe Simon's short, *Fragments*, and apply Shutterfreaks' golden mean app in Photoshop, just to see how it holds up compositionally along the golden mean (see Figures 1.2 and 1.3).

Another aspect of composition includes creating the illusion of three dimensions by providing depth to a scene. The woman in Figures 1.2 and 1.4 appears to stand out from the background since the light is behind her—this gives the scene depth. In Figure 1.4, we also see a fence receding diagonally to the background, which also provides depth to the scene. You may stage background and foreground objects or characters and move them along different planes of action to signify the sense of depth as well.

Practicing with depth, light, and placement of your subjects is the best way to train yourself for good composition. Ultimately, there are no rules, only what looks and feels right for the story. But an understanding of where and why these rules work—and a mastery of them in your shooting—is important if you want to create powerful shots. Don't break the rules until you know how to use each of them well.

FIGURE 1.2
In Joe Simon's *Fragments*, he utilizes strong compositional lines to pull us into the story. The light comes across her bed diagonally, causing us to go to Jessica Perrin's face. The flowers curve around her body, in silhouette, to provide balance. The horizontal line across the back wall rienforces the horizontal line of her body across the bed. Shot on a Canon C100 Mark II.
(Still from *Fragments*. ©2015 Canon USA, Inc. Used with permission.)

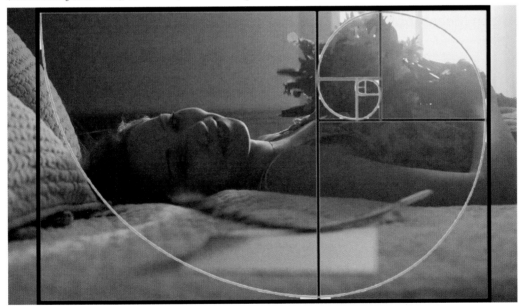

FIGURE 1.3
Overlaying a golden mean graphic on the above shot, we can see how Jessica Perrin is compositionally balanced.
(Still from *Fragments*. ©2015 Canon USA, Inc. Used with permission.)

FIGURE 1.4
Jessica Perrin and Dietrich Schmidt run outside, the composition balanced as they move along the golden mean, providing depth and energy along the diagonal line. Canon C100 Mark II.
(Still from *Fragments* by Joe Simon. ©2015 The Delivery Men. Used with permission.)

Golden Mean Application

To use the Golden Mean application from the Shutterfreaks team in Photoshop, first download the app from: http://www.shutterfreaks.com/Actions/RuleOfThirds.php.

How to Install the Actions
1. Open Photoshop.
2. If you haven't already done so, extract all the files from the ZIP file into a folder on your hard disk.
3. Click and drag the .atn file from that folder to your Photoshop window. If you look in the Actions window in Photoshop, you will see the action set appear there.

Using the Actions
Open the action set by clicking the little arrow just to the left of the name RuleOfThirds. You may need to scroll down in the Actions window to see the actions.

Open a photo you want to analyze.

Highlight one of the actions by clicking it, and then run the action by clicking the Play Selection arrow at the bottom of the Actions window.

The actions will make changes to a duplicate of your file so that you can protect your original.

Notes
1. If the Action window isn't visible, you can show it by going to the Photoshop menu and selecting Window/ Actions.
2. If you'd like an action that will help you crop your images to conform to the rule of thirds and the golden mean, check out our Rule of Thirds Pro Action (http://www.shutterfreaks.com/Actions/RuleOfThirdsPro.html).
3. If you are new to using Photoshop actions, http://www.shutterfreaks.com/Tips/GettingStartedPS.html offers an introduction to the basics.
4. If you see an error similar to "The Command Make is not currently available," you may be running the action on a 16-bit image in an older version of Photoshop that doesn't support layers in 16 bits. To correct the problem, convert your image to 8 bits before running the action.

Your Shutterfreaks Team (Used with Permission)

Checklist for Composition

1. Who owns the story and/or who owns the scene? Your compositional choice may revolve around your central character or characters. Know who they are so your composition can reflect the central power, point of view, and/or ownership of the scene.
2. What is in the frame? What you see is what you get. If you don't want something in the frame, get it out of the way or move your subject(s) until everything you see is meant to be there.
3. Place your main characters along the golden mean for strong composition. Follow the general principles of framing a character screen left if they're looking right, and screen right if they're looking left. Keep eyelines around one-third from the top as a general rule. Break these rules only when your story demands it.

LENSES

Lenses form the composition. Lenses do not reveal what the natural unaided eyes see. Rather, the cinematographer uses lenses as a way to shape the emotional equivalency of what the human eye perceives and feels. If you stand within typical talking distance from someone, this is what may translate on film as a medium shot. If the person is in a wide or long shot, this may be equivalent to someone standing on the other side of a room—shouting distance. A close-up would be equivalent to an intimate conversation, a kiss, or a fight—where you are inches from someone.

Different lenses render how we perceive the subject and setting descriptively and emotionally. Practically, a variety of lenses allow us to change the angle of what can be seen; they're measured by the focal length (a wide angle lens on a S35 mm camera would be a 20 mm focal length), and a long lens might contain a 100 mm focal length; a "normal" lens would be 35 mm or 50 mm focal length. The focal length on cameras is simply the distance of the lens to the imaging sensor when the focus is set to infinity.

A short focal length lens (a wider convex lens) bends the light sharply, bringing the image in focus only a short distance from the lens, but the image is smaller and therefore can capture more of the scene (and place much of the foreground and background in sharp focus). A long focal length lens is less convex, bending the light at a smaller angle, placing the focal distance farther away, making the image larger (with less of the foreground and background of the scene in focus).

As a comparison, the angle of view can be broken down to a 25 mm lens containing a field of view of 80 degrees, 50 mm at 46 degrees, 100 mm at 24 degrees, and 180 mm with 13 degrees.[1] In effect, the sharper the angle, the closer the view you can capture with the lens, if the camera is placed at the same distance (see Figures 1.5–1.8).

---

[1] The human eye can see about 240 degrees with peripheral vision. Most lenses do not provide a peripheral view. The field of view ultimately depends on the lens size and the size of the sensor chip of the camera. A 35 mm on a 7D has a 1.6 times difference in the field of view than a 35 mm on a 5D, for example. The 35 mm on the 7D will be similar to a 56 mm on the 5D (see "Canon 5D and 7D Lens Comparison Test." http://vimeo.com/14832168).

FIGURE 1.5
Zeiss 25 mm. About six
feet from the subject.
(Photo by Kurt Lancaster.)

FIGURE 1.6
Zeiss 50 mm.
Same distance
(Photo by Kurt
Lancaster.)

FIGURE 1.7
Zeiss 100 mm.
Same distance.
(Photo by Kurt
Lancaster.)

FIGURE 1.8
Leica 180 mm.
Same distance.
(Photo by Kurt
Lancaster.)

In addition, the ability to play with depth of field opens up the possibilities of utilizing more of the cinematographer's film tools to craft better and stronger visual stories. In Laforet's *Reverie*, for example, the opening shot and a shot later in the film are from the same setup using the same lighting conditions and position (see Figures 1.9 and 1.10). However, the angle of the lens is different. Laforet uses a tilt-shift lens (45 mm shot at f/2.8), which allows for selective focus. The first one looks as though it utilizes the shallow depth of field of a longer lens but was used with the tilt-shift lens, allowing Laforet to change the depth of field in the shot, placing the background out of focus, while his main subjects (the man and woman kissing) are in focus. If you look closely, you can see that in this moment of the shot (which changes focus over time), the arms of the man and woman are sharply focused while the heads are in soft focus. The second shot reveals the woman waiting, and the Brooklyn Bridge and skyline are in sharp focus.

In addition to the focal length and depth of field of lenses, another important factor is the speed of the lens. A "fast" lens has a wider maximum open aperture (iris). Less light is needed to expose the sensor—better for low light and night setups (and allowing for shallow depth of field). A "slow" lens means that it contains a narrower maximum aperture opening; more light is needed for proper exposure (with increased depth of field). A fast lens could be f/1.4 or f/2, for example, whereas a slow lens would be f/5.6. The difference in the two is significant: an f/1.4 lens lets in sixteen times more light than an f/5.6 lens! The terms "fast" and "slow" refer to the shutter speed when taking still shots. Typically, a slow lens would need to keep the shutter open longer to let in the same amount of light, whereas the fast lens allows for less time to let in light, thus a faster shutter speed.

The type of lens determines not only what you will see, but how much light will be exposed, as well as the potential depth of field. In the past, prosumer HD video camera filmmakers were stuck with a fixed zoom lens. Expensive adapters allowed for the addition of a 35 mm lens, but with the DSLR revolution, new cinema cameras, allows low budget filmmakers to change lenses as a standard option. Low budget cinema cameras have followed suit.

A zoom lens may be good for shooting documentaries, but many of the inexpensive lenses adjust the aperture speed when you change focal lengths. Zooming all the way in requires more light to expose, whereas zooming back out to the widest angle requires less light. Many lenses have fixed angles, so when you place a 50 mm lens on your camera, the only way to change the size of the composition would be to move the camera closer or farther away from the subject. The type of lens determines not only what you will see, but how much light will be exposed, as well as the potential depth of field.

FIGURE 1.9
Laforet uses a tilt-shift lens (45 mm, f/2.8) to attain selective focus.
(Still from *Reverie*. ©2009 Vincent Laforet. Used with permission.)

FIGURE 1.10
Laforet uses the same tilt-shift lens as in Figure 1.9, but alters the selective focus to bring the entire shot in focus, similar to the effect with a wide angle lens.
(Still from *Reverie*. © 2009 Vincent Laforet. Used with permission.)

Checklist for Lenses

1. Zoom or primes? Cheaper zoom lenses change the aperture speed rating. For example, an f/4-5.6 means that the lens pulled wide open will provide the greatest exposure of f/4; zoomed all the way in it will provide a stepped down exposure of f/5.6. Effectively, this means that you need to expose everything for f/5.6 or higher because you should not change the f-stop when shooting a scene (or the shots will look different). If you have the budget, more expensive zoom lenses will maintain their aperture rating all the way through the zoom—such as Canon's L series lenses.

2. Prime lenses have a fixed focal length and aperture rating. These are the best lenses but can be limiting in documentary and video journalism work because you may want to change lens angles quickly without having to change lenses.

3. What is the manufacturer's brand? Different lenses require different mounts to fit different brands and different lens sizes. PL mounts are standard cinema lenses. The Panasonic GH5 uses a micro 4/3 mount, whereas the Canon 5D uses Canon's proprietary EF mount, and so forth. It's recommended that you do not buy a camera with the kit lens, but invest in high-quality zooms and a couple of primes. What to look for: does the focus ring stop or is it mushy—free spinning past the point where it should stop? If you're using DSLRs in cinema projects with focus pullers or shooters needing precision, getting a lens type that stops is essential, especially when using different manufacturers' focus assists. Zeiss primes, for example, are designed for manual focusing with a lower turn ratio (a half turn usually covers the full focal range). Also, image stabilization is important because a slight shake or vibration can cause ruined shaky shots, especially on longer lenses. (The Panasonic GH5 has built-in stabilization.) Furthermore, when swapping out lenses, be aware of dust. You should get into a car or go inside if the wind is blowing or cover your camera with a jacket.

4. How much of the scene do you want the audience to see? Wide angle lenses present a wider field of view, whereas long lenses narrow what can be seen.

5. How much of the scene do you want in focus? Wide angle lenses put more of the scene in focus, whereas longer lenses decrease depth of field and narrow what's in focus. Both of these questions are answered by the length of the lens and the placement of the camera. If you want the audience to see more of the scene, then use a wide angle lens. If you want them to see less, use a long lens. If you want more of the scene in focus, then use a wide to normal length lens; if you want a shallow depth of field, then use a long lens.

6. Decide the speed of the lens. A fast lens (such as f/1.4) will allow you to shoot in low and natural light, better than a slow lens (such as f/4). Faster lenses will also allow you to lower the ISO setting, giving you more room to choose a richer look. Fast lenses allow you to open wide and get shallow depth of field, while slower lenses limit your depth of field choices.

BLOCKING

Blocking is where, when, and how subjects are placed and move in the composition, whether working with actors or characters in a documentary. How they are placed, when they move, where they move from, and where they go to are dependent on the story. There should be nothing random, because these movements (the blocking of the performers) need to be motivated; otherwise, random movements not grounded in the story will appear weak on-screen. One of the jobs of the director is to shape or choreograph the blocking (see Figure 1.11), while the cinematographer needs to capture these movements with the camera. (The cinematographer may offer visual concepts for blocking as an assist to the director in relationship to shot composition.)

Po Chan's approach to blocking in *The Last 3 Minutes* (featured in Chapter 12) is as precise as her direction on all aspects of the short: "All elements in this short film, from casting and the music to the wardrobe; from makeup (the choice of lipstick color) to the hairstyle and hair color; from the patterns and textures of the set dressing pieces to the looks of the crystal itself, are all carefully chosen so that they all work in harmony to tell the story," she explains to me in an interview on set.

FIGURE 1.11
Po Chan directs the blocking of William (performed by Harwood Gordon) in the opening sequence from her short, *The Last 3 Minutes*.
(Photo ©2010 by Kurt Lancaster.)

In the scene, Po takes time to set up the physical actions for actor Harwood Gordon, as his character William Turner has a heart attack and collapses to the floor. Po knows what she's looking for. She understands very well (and is glad) that Gordon has had no such experience before. She goes into extreme detail and wants Gordon to convey the pain in this moment. She explains to him the different layers of emotions that should be inside him in this scene. By doing so, she keeps the actor fresh in his imagination, and the physical action conveys that naturalness she's looking for. Some actors may be hands-off with the director, but Po says she looks for actors she can communicate with, heart to heart, look into their eyes, and know their feelings: "I trust them and I want them to know that they can trust me."

Every gesture Gordon does, every expression he makes, is carefully observed by Po. In this scene there is no dialog, so the physical actions are the main vehicle to convey the story. "I trust my instinct within—it's always correct," she says. She puts herself emotionally into the scene as she directs: "If my actor cries, I cry. I apply myself to them. Even though I can only live one life, I can experience many more different lives through the art of cinema." Figure 1.12 shows how the blocking in this scene is tied to the shots.

Each of the combinations described above changes the dynamics of the scene. There is no "right" choice since it depends on an understanding of the story and what you want to convey to the audience. Each scene contains an emotional shift, a change that alters the emotion of the scene, and an understanding of when this change occurs will help you make the better choice.

For example, in this particular scene (refer to Figure 1.12), the camera remains fairly static (with slight handheld motion, but no dolly or crane shots), and the character moves. In the second image, we see a low camera angle looking up before it cuts to the third image, when Gordon drops into a tight close-up frame of the camera. These two shots contain the shift in the scene—conveying to the audience the suddenness of his heart attack in the first, while the close-up expresses his surprise and pain. This is the first time the tight close-up is used in this scene. It's the crux, the point where the scene shifts into a new direction. In the beginning of the scene, William is mopping the floor, alone with his thoughts. But in the close-up, we see his pain and struggle, and the scene shifts as he struggles to reach for a meaningful heirloom in his pocket and his life flashes before his eyes. The filmmakers could have added camera movement at this point to emphasize this point, but it may have come across as melodramatic or overly manipulative, whereas the low angle followed by the tight close-up does the job well in this particular instance.

There are several possible combinations of blocking with a camera:

- A performer can stand still and the camera remains locked down.
- A performer can stand still and the camera moves.
- A performer can move and the camera is locked down.
- A performer can move and the camera can move.

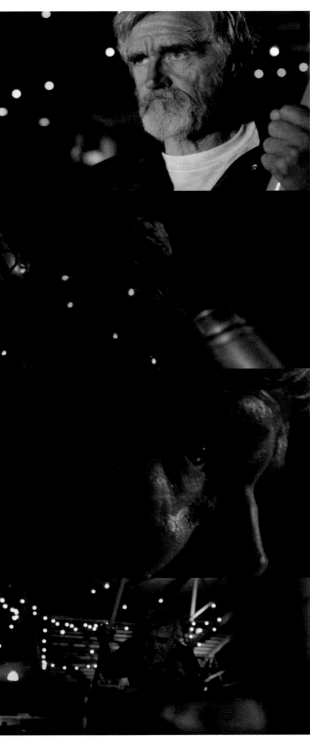

FIGURE 1.12
A series of shots from
the opening sequence
of *The Last 3 Minutes*
(Po Chan, dir.) reveal
how her blocking
visually reveals the
story. The movements
and position of
Harwood Gordon's
character, William,
on-screen provides
the information
for an audience to
understand what
is going on; Shane
Hurlbut's shots
support the blocking
by conveying these
emotions through shot
sizes, composition, and
lighting.
(Stills from *The Last 3
Minutes* ©2010 Hurlbut
Visuals. Used with
permission.)

In summary, blocking is the visual depiction of the story by actors' bodies—their body language, gestures, and movement through space—and this blocking must be tied to the shot, whether the camera is locked down or moving. In the opening sequence to *The Last 3 Minutes*, we can see how the story is fully told by not only how the character of William is composed in space, but how he moves and how the camera captures his movements. Whatever decision you make as a cinematographer, when shooting be aware that blocking and camera movement are intrinsically tied together.

Checklist for Blocking

1. Who owns the scene? This becomes the point-of-view character, the character who, perhaps, has the most to lose in the scene or the character impacted most by the events in the scene. When you know who owns the scene, then, as the director, you can determine what the emotional state of this character is at the beginning of the scene and at the end of the scene: where does this change occur? You need to know this in order to effectively block the scene (and determine how you'll emphasize this moment—through changes of shot size, angle changes, and/or camera and/or actor movement).

2. Set up your camera so that you capture not only the action of this character, but more importantly, the reaction of the character to the events occurring in the scene—especially where the scene change occurs. The character's actions and reactions will motivate where and what you capture on camera—and help immensely in editing. The choices for blocking and the use of the camera include these four combinations:

   • A performer can stand still and the camera remains locked down.
   • A performer can stand still and the camera moves.
   • A performer can move and the camera is locked down.
   • A performer can move and the camera can move.

   The choice you make should be dependent on the needs of the story; this takes analysis (see Chapter 6 on stories for more details).

3. Make a list of the shots you need to tell the story—and for editing, especially as it relates to the scene's emotional shift. Think about the actions of the characters and what they're doing from shot to shot. What shots do you need to tell the full story when you edit? Where do the performers' eyelines take us? This is one good clue in choosing shots to edit, and a good shooter needs to capture these eyelines. What will the shots look like as you edit? Do you have enough shots? Can you condense several shots into one shot with camera movement? The Renaud brothers, documentary filmmakers, mention in an interview with me how important it is for shooters to be editors: "We started out as editors as I believe all young filmmakers should do. If you can become a good editor first, it is easy to become a good shooter."

CAMERA MOVEMENT AND STABILIZATION

If blocking expresses the movement in the composition of a scene, the camera movement moves the composition and will result in strong visual dynamics. Just as a character needs to be motivated before moving on-screen, the camera needs to be motivated in its movement. The camera's movement needs to be tied to character motivations and movements because the camera captures emotions and actions through its lens.

To quickly attain an amateur look in your projects, just handhold the camera and move around a lot. Controlling the movement of a camera takes discipline and proper tools. When engaging in handheld movement, some smaller, ligher cameras can be awkward and difficult to keep stable for longer, sustained shots. One of the problems with handheld work is that it's hard; it's easy to make the movements unprofessionally shaky! Move in slow motion and make the camera feel heavy. In many of the shots of *The Last 3 Minutes*, Shane Hurlbut, ASC, handheld the camera, but his body was rock steady and the movements of the camera were slight and never jerky.

Several companies have designed a variety of stabilization devices for helping with handheld shots, but they can still provide poor results if you're moving around and bouncing too much. Holding still, moving in slow motion, and moving as if you're carrying weights will help your handheld work. Proper stabilization, whether using a tripod or a shoulder rig, when properly practiced, will help provide a professional cinema look. It's easy to whip light cameras around and make it jiggle too much as the body of the shooter fails to remain still. You must Zen your body and focus your attention on the shot. In addition, gimbals provide a strong amount of stabilization for camera movement.

When handholding shots, you may tilt up and down along the vertical axis (yaw) or move side to side, left to right (pitch). A roll occurs when you move front to back like a ship riding waves at sea (rarely used).

> It's easy to whip light cameras around and make it jiggle too much as the body of the shooter fails to remain still. You must Zen your body and focus your attention on the shot.

One of the safest ways to get a clean shot is to use a tripod or, my favorite, a monopod with feet and a ball joint, as well as a video head. It's one of the best ways to get stable and acceptable shots for light cameras. These monopods allow for small push-in and pull-out shots, as well as pan and tilt. Again, let your story determine the best way to convey the emotion you want in a scene. You may pan or tilt on a tripod (whether on a tripod or handheld), but be sure to move in slow motion to minimize shakiness and the "Jell-O effect" of the camera's CMOS sensor—when vertical lines shift diagonally while panning too quickly, because the sensor speed is too slow to keep up with the movement. Also, remember that the longer the lens, the faster the apparent motion and the more unstable the shot will be when handholding. It may be best to use a tripod when using a long lens.

Camera movement includes (see Figures 1.13a-e):

- Pan: left to right on the tripod axis
- Tilt: up and down on the tripod axis
- Push-in through space
- Pull-out through space
- Tracking (or dolly): lateral movement through space
- Crane: up and down movement through space

Despite the suggestion of using a tripod, one of the most powerful tools to create the film look revolves around camera movement—that poetic push-in or tracking shot that moves the viewer smoothly through the space of the cinematic world. However, there's an affordable way to get that high end filmic look: Cinerails has released a budget dolly for camera movement using PVC pipes as tracks that snap into place (see http://cinerails.com).

Panning a DSLR and the Jell-O Effect

A lot of online video tests reveal how a fast pan can cause verticals to shift. Critics point to these shifts as a weakness to the camera. At the same time, however, this issue doesn't seem to impact many professional filmmakers. Shane Hurlbut, ASC, says he's rarely encountered the problem. Vincent Laforet (dir. *Reverie*) said this about it:

> While the "Jell-O effect" exists with any CMOS sensor given their design, I didn't find it to be a factor in this project—or, for that matter, on any of my other productions. It's important to keep in mind that any camera out there, film or digital, has limitations on how fast you can pan it—especially when projected onto a large screen. (In general,

a DP will always plan for this on any camera moves they are directing the speed of the camera's move.) It's important to remember that a pan may look just fine on a 17-inch monitor—but the same pan may be a bit painful for the audience's eyes on a 50 foot silver screen. Unless you are doing dynamic and fast moving action sequences, where you are purposefully moving the camera at extremely high rates (whip pans, running sequences, etc.), I would say it's unlikely you will encounter issues with the "Jell-O effect."[2]

In the end, it's the DP's responsibility to know the strengths and weaknesses of his/her tools and to know how to shoot around those limitations.

---

[2] Laforet, Vincent. "VW Spec Ad posted with behind scenes video." Vincent Laforet Blog. 1 June 2010. http://blog.vincentlaforet.com/2010/06/01/vw-spec-ad-and-canon-digital-learning-center/

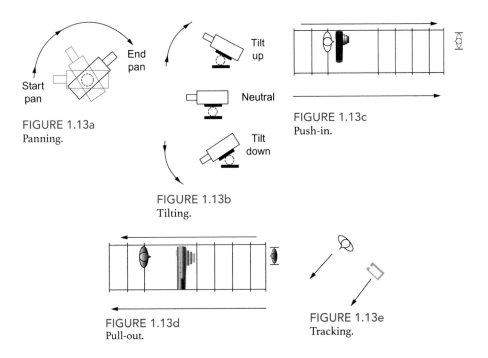

FIGURE 1.13a
Panning.

FIGURE 1.13b
Tilting.

FIGURE 1.13c
Push-in.

FIGURE 1.13d
Pull-out.

FIGURE 1.13e
Tracking.

Checklist for Camera Movement

1. What does your story demand? Your story—the emotional intention you're trying to express in your shot—should indicate whether the shot should be locked down on a tripod or contain smooth movement or a little bit more rough. Also, take note at what point in a scene the camera should move or stay still. This should convey the emotional shift in the story.

2. What angle of lens are you using? Long lenses = tripod in most cases. Normal and wide lenses = handheld and handheld stabilizers.

3. What kind of shot do you need? If you want the handheld look, providing a sense of immediacy or presence to the scene, then utilize a handheld stabilizer—such as the Steadicam Merlin or a gimbal—or even a monopod with a wide to normal lens. If you need a stable shot, no matter the lens size, then lock down the camera on a tripod.

4. Are you short on time? Do you need to "run and gun"? For video journalists and documentary filmmakers on the move use a handheld stabilizer or monopod (with feet, ball joint, and video head).

CHAPTER 2

Lighting

If the composition, blocking, and camera movement shapes the visual look of your film, lighting determines what that look feels like. No matter your lens choice, proper exposure, and ISO setting, a lack of understanding how to utilize light will destroy your cinematic look. A cinema camera will not provide a film look alone. Lighting is your most powerful ally in helping you sculpt a film look. Vilmos Zsigmond, ASC (*The Deer Hunter*), says that the "type of lighting we use actually creates the mood for the scene."[1]

This mood is what you, as the filmmaker, must try to shape and capture with your camera. It helps provide visual depth to your picture. If you shoot an off-white subject against a white wall, there's not much contrast—not much light and shadow—and the picture appears flat. If you shoot somebody white against a dark background, the person stands out, and if you add background lighting to the scene, the depth increases. Because of the large sensor of cinema cameras, along with high ISO settings, they maintain a strong advantage over small sensor cameras because of the capability to shoot in natural and practical low-light situations. Fewer lights are needed on set or on location.

The quality of light refers to what it looks like and what it feels like. What it looks like is what you see on the surface. The feel, on the other hand, conveys the emotion shaped by lighting. You can craft the look and feel of a film by paying attention to:

1. Light quality
2. Light direction
3. Light and shadow placement
4. Color temperature

[1] Fauer, J. *Cinematographer Style: The Complete Interviews*, Vol. 1. American Society of Cinematographers, 2008: 232.

FIGURE 2.1
Jessica Perrin runs from Dietrich Schmidt in Joe Simon's short, *Fragments*. A high three-quarter key from the sun sculpts their heads, arms, and shoulders as a crew member bounces soft reflected sunlight into Perrin's face. Shot on a Canon C100 Mark II.
(©2015 Canon USA, Inc. Used with permission.)

LIGHT QUALITY 1: SHOULD IT BE HARD OR SOFT?

Hard light is direct, producing harsh shadows, and results in a high level of contrast. This can come from a sunny day or an unshaded light pointed directly at a subject. Hard lights are especially effective as backlight and rimlight sources, such as the example in Joe Simon's short, *Fragments* (see Figure 2.1.) Jessica Perrin runs from Dietrich Schmidt as a high three-quarter key from the sun sculpts their heads, arms, and shoulders. (A crew member bounces soft, reflected fill light from the sun onto Perrin's face.) As an additional note, the saturation of color is more prominent when the source comes from the front, while colors become desaturated when the lights are placed in the rear, as we see in these two images (Figures 2.1 and 2.2). See https://vimeo.com/120850943.

Soft light is indirect, created by reflecting or diffusing the light (an overcast day, a scrim, or sheet dropped between the light source and the subject, or simply bouncing light off a white art board, or even reflecting light off a wall or ceiling). This type of light provides a soft quality to the image. Perrin's face is lit from the side using a light bouncing off a silk screen outside the window to mimic daylight. Because the light is bounced, the quality feels soft. (See Figure 2.2.)

One of the counterintuitive properties of light is the fact that as the lighting instrument is brought closer to the subject, the softer the lighting gets, while farther away, the harder it is because it becomes more of a point source, causing the hard light quality to stand out. A diffused light source from farther away may convey a harder light quality than a low-watt Fresnel lamp up close, for example.

FIGURE 2.2
Joe Simon utilizes a soft side key light (motivated by a window) on Jessica Perrin in *Fragments*, shot on the Canon C100 Mark II. He utilizes shallow depth of field to bring out the beauty of the face. In addition, a hard light source from the rear window reflects off the table behind her to provide a sense of depth to the shot. (©2015 Canon USA, Inc. Used with permission.)

LIGHT QUALITY 2: DIRECTION

The direction of the light will determine the placement of shadows and, consequently, the physical texture of objects and people. There are fewer shadows when the lighting is on-axis of the camera (the front). Shadows increase as the light shifts off-axis of the camera and to the rear of your subject. Light from the side will increase the texture of the scene. When lighting is "motivated," it refers to a light from a particular source, such as a fireplace, window, lamp, or the sun. The motivated light source in Figure 2.2 is a window out of frame, screen left. Notice how the side lighting, here, brings out the texture of Perrin's face.

Light Placement Terminology

- Key: The main light source of the scene (a window, a table lamp, overhead lighting, a fireplace, and so forth). Know where your motivated light source is and add lights, if needed, to reinforce it accordingly. Can be hard or soft quality.

- Fill: Lights used to fill in shadows caused by the key light. Usually a soft quality, less intensity than the key in order to provide a sense of depth (if both sides were equal, the image would become flat).

- Back and Rim: Lights placed behind characters to separate them from the background. A rim light specifically is placed high with the light falling on a character's head, her hair (and often the cheekbone), lit in such a way as to differentiate her from the background.

- Background: Lighting occurring in the background of a scene, designed to separate it from the foreground, giving the scene visual depth. These could be street lights, lights in a store, a hallway light inside, and so forth.

Below (Figures 2.3-2.7) are a series of stills from a the music video *Bandit* shot on the Canon 5D Mark IV in 4K mode. Each shot illustrates a different light source direction using natural and practical light sources. See video at: https://youtu.be/puybMhAWwWM.

Light Source Direction: Side

FIGURE 2.3
A still from the music video, *Bandit* by Hunnymoon, shot on a Canon 5D Mark IV, 4K mode. The side lighting brings out the texture of the concrete columns and the performers' faces.
(©2016 Canon Europe. Used with permission.)

Light Source Direction: Back

FIGURE 2.4
A still from the music video, *Bandit* by Hunnymoon, shot on a Canon 5D Mark IV, 4K mode. The backlighting, using natural light, silhouettes a romantic moment in a car.
(©2016 Canon Europe. Used with permission.)

Light Source Direction: ¾ Rear

FIGURE 2.5
The sun is placed as a three-quarter rear key, offering a hard quality light source on the face along the cheekbone of the performer in *Bandit* by Hunnymoon, shot on a Canon 5D Mark IV, 4K mode. This natural rear key light helps separate him from the background. Note the fill on the screen right-side of his face. (©2016 Canon Europe. Used with permission.)

Light Source Direction: Front

FIGURE 2.6
Soft front light fills the faces of the performers in *Bandit* by Hunnymoon, shot on a Canon 5D Mark IV, 4K mode. Note the sunlight used as a hard rim light, causing an edge of light around the woman's face, separating her from the background.
(©2016 Canon Europe. Used with permission.)

Light Source Direction: ¾ Frontal Key

FIGURE 2.7

A soft three-quarter rear key light brings out the beauty of the performers in *Bandit* by Hunnymoon, shot on a Canon 5D Mark IV, 4K mode. Note the background lighting, a soft focus background, but no fill on the woman's upside face, which is in shadow.

(©2016 Canon Europe. Used with permission.)

LIGHT QUALITY 3: LIGHT AND SHADOW

Related to light direction is the placement of shadows. Shadows bring out drama and are essential when creating a night or dark scene (see Figure 2.8 and 2.9). The direction and height of the light determine how shadows fall in the composition. Lights from the front will minimize shadows, whereas lights from the rear will increase shadows seen on camera. The higher the light source, the shorter the shadow. If you want long shadows, shoot at sunrise or sunset, or place your lights low, instead of high, in the background. Side lighting will increase texture.

FIGURE 2.8
Red lights and dark shadows offer a sense of danger and romance in *Bandit* by Hunnymoon, shot on a Canon 5D Mark IV, 4K mode.
(©2016 Canon Europe. Used with permission.)

FIGURE 2.9
Light and shadow provide texture and a sense of edgy romance in *Bandit* by Hunnymoon, shot on a Canon 5D Mark IV, 4K mode.
(©2016 Canon Europe. Used with permission.)

LIGHT QUALITY 4: COLOR TEMPERATURE

Digital sensors see lights differently than people do. Computer chips are not as smart as human perception and have a hard time adjusting precise and subtle differences in color caused by different kinds of light sources. Different chemicals burn at different wavelengths, producing different color qualities depending on whether the source is halogen, tungsten, fluorescent, sunlight, and so on. Also, sunlight changes its color temperature depending on the time of day and whether or not it's cloudy (see Figure 2.10). Color temperature is measured in Kelvins (K).

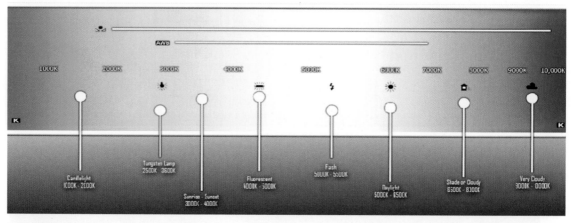

FIGURE 2.10

An overview of the color quality during different times of day. Sunset can also refer to sunrise. The warmer and cooler label refers to the quality of the tones, not to actual temperature. Blue looks cooler (and feels cooler emotionallys), but it's actually hotter than warm tones on the temperature scale (which are actually cooler in temperature, but feel warm). (Based on image from http://www.sunper.net/Bloglightingeducation_How-The-Color- Temperature-Relates-With-LED-Lighting/).

Our eyes adjust to these varying color temperatures automatically. Indoor settings for cameras are usually set at 3200 K, whereas outdoor settings are usually at 5600 K; both of these numbers are averages for indoor tungsten lighting and outdoor daylight. Even though cameras have automatic white balance systems, the white balance setting of your camera allows you to adjust the setting manually. You may set your camera to manual mode and adjust it with a white or gray card. Many cinema cameras allow you to control the color temperature by dialing it in. Balancing correctly is important in controlling the image. Sometimes you may want to experiment with color temperature as a way to change the look of the scene, but you should always control this important element of lighting. (See Figure 2.11.)

Cinematographer Tip

Color Temperature
Shane Hurlbut, ASC

When shooting in an 8-bit color space (4:2:0), you have to get the in-camera look as close as possible to the final vision for the project. It is compressed and that color space can be limiting. I find it is the compression that makes it look the closest to film, so embrace it. As a cinematographer, you really need to micromanage the color temperature. If you want a day exterior to feel consistent throughout a day from morning till sunset, you need to start with your color temperature so that it is consistent with that of the sun. In the morning it could be around 3400 degrees Kelvin. To keep the light looking white and not orange, you will need to set your color temp at 3400 Kelvin. By midday it should be around 5200 to 5500 Kelvin. You repeat the same approach at sunset. We had a sequence in *Act of Valor* on a dry lake bed that posed for a landing strip in the Horn of Africa. We started before the sun came up and were there until it went behind the Sierra Nevadas at around 7:45pm.

I used this micromanaging approach and the image is so consistent. In the final color correction we hardly had to do any manipulation other than dialing in contrast. (Hurlbut, Shane. Collision Conference. Video. 9 Nov. 2009, http://shanehurlbut.smugmug.com/Professional/CollisionConference/10137672_ia4ZS#697099091_Bqx5z-A-LB)

In addition, many of these cameras allow you to create presets for the picture look. Several shooters have mimicked the look of a variety of film stocks to create different looks as well. In addition, postproduction color grading allows you to further shape the look of your project.

There is no one way to determine color balance. Do you balance for tungsten if you're indoors near a window, do you just go with the camera's preset (daylight, indoor, outdoor shade, and so forth), or do you dial it in? You need to look at the image and think about how it relates to the story to best determine what you need. Shane Hurlbut, ASC, dials in his color temperature by eyeballing the monitor or the camera's LCD screen and getting the look as close as he can get it before turning it over to postproduction. Others suggest using the presets for consistency depending on the lighting type you're in, and setting manual white balance only when in a mixed lighting setup (halogens, fluorescents, incandescents in one room, for example). A good rule is to set it based on your key, the brightest source.

FIGURE 2.11
Three shots of the same model using three different color temperatures. The middle one is "correct." The first one is too blue, and the third is too warm for the standard look. However, the color temperature is a guide; you may decide the warm image is the color temperature you're looking for to capture the feeling of your story. (Photos by Kurt Lancaster.)

White Balance Tip
Do not manually white balance during a sunrise or sunset because you would be adjusting the nice golden flow into white, and you don't want to lose the golden glow! During the sunset scene in *The Last 3 Minutes*, Shane Hurlbut, ASC, dialed in his color temperature at 4700 degrees K (see Figure 2.12).

FIGURE 2.12
Shane Hurlbut, ASC, dialed in the color temperature to 4700 degrees K for the beach scene from *The Last 3 Minutes* (featured in Chapter 12). Shot on a Canon 5D Mark II. (See Chan, Po. and Hurlbut, Shane. *The Last 3 Minutes*. Vimeo.com. 2010. http://vimeo.com/10570139) (©2010 Hurlbut Visuals. Used with permission.)

SAMPLE LIGHTING SETUPS

The following stills with brief explanations show basic setups for shooting outdoor day, outdoor night, indoor day, and indoor night as tied to the idea of composition and light quality. Below, I examine David Tembleque's award-winning short, *Dear Tom*, as an exemplary work of natural lighting shot on a Blackmagic's Pocket Cinema Camera. An example from his *Wonderful People* was shot on the Sony FS700.

Outdoor Day

When shooting outdoor locations, time of day and weather are the two most important factors to consider; they determine your light source and shadows. Big-budget films may use generators with daylight lamps, but when shooting a documentary or an outdoor wedding, for example, you need to be aware of the sun's location because it will be the primary light source. Mornings and afternoons tend to provide better shooting because the color temperature will provide warmer skin tones; it will also provide long shadows, so you can shape the look around this light and shadow placement. (See Figures 2.13 and 2.14.) However, when shooting during the "golden hour," you'll have less time to shoot and a bit more challenge in post to match the color temps from shot to shot (and sometimes within the shot), because the lighting is changing quickly (and thus the color temperature). In addition, to soften the quality of the light you may want to use a scrim to remove the harshness of the light on a subject's face, or you may want to bounce light off a reflector to provide fill light.

FIGURES 2.13 AND 2.14

David Tembleque utilizes outdoor light (daylight and magic hour) in these two shots from his award-winning film, *Dear Tom*, shot on the Blackmagic Pocket Cinema Camera. Take note of the color temperature change.

(©2015 David Tembleque. Used with permission.)

Indoor Day

In shaping the interior during the day, many cinematographers will use windows (see Figures 2.15-2.17). They may add a daylight lamp from the direction of the window on longer shoots, so as not to lose light direction when the direction of the sun changes over the course of a day. Otherwise, use a scrim and bounce light off of the scrim.

FIGURES 2.15 AND 2.16
David Tembleque utilizes windows and practical lights at a restaurant in these two shots from his award-winning film, *Dear Tom*, shot on the Blackmagic Pocket Cinema Camera. Take note of the changes in lighting using windows and television sets. The time of day could be day or night in Figure 2.16.
(©2015 David Tembleque. Used with permission.)

FIGURE 2.17
David Tembleque uses outdoor light with midday light from a window in his new short, *Wonderful People*, shot on the Sony FS700. Notice how the light reflects off the walls, providing a soft fill light on her face, while the window is a hard light, causing rim light along her hair, nose, lips, and chin.
(©2017 David Tembleque. Used with permission.)

Outdoor night

At night, rather than setting up lights, Temleque uses existing practical lights to his advantage. (See Figure 2.18.)

FIGURE 2.18
The couple kiss in a phone booth as David Tembleque takes advantage of practical lights on a street to capture this shot for his film, *Dear Tom*. Shot on the Blackmagic Pocket Cinema Camera.
(©2015 David Tembleque. Used with permission.)

Checklist for Lighting

1. What is the mood of the story, the scene?

2. Decide the quality of the light: hard or soft; direct lighting or bounced (or scrimmed) lighting for each light you're going to use.

3. Choose the kinds of light you're using: key, fill, back, background. (Yes, there are many different types of lights—from sunlight with a reflector to hardware store halogen work lights, but you need to determine how they're going to be utilized.) Many scenes will have all four of them, but there's no rule. Sunlight with a reflector may be all that's required. With cinema cameras, you can use as much natural and practical light as possible before bringing in other lights.

4. Decide light placement of each light. A frontal ¾ key will make the scene look different than a rear ¾ key with a frontal fill light. Lighting placement will determine shadow placement, all of which will convey different moods.

5. Lighting zones or contrast range:

   A. Will everything be lit evenly?

   B. Will there be some contrast between bright and darker areas?

   C. Will there be great contrast between the light and shadows?

   D. Will you need to scrim the lights to dim them, use a dimmer, move lights closer or farther away from the subject?

   E. Do you have barn doors on the lights to control where the light falls?

   F. Do you have blackout scrims (flags) to control where the light and shadows are placed?

6. If you're shooting outdoors, what time of day will provide the best mood for the scene? Because sunlight is your key light source, it will determine to a large extent the mood of your scene. A high-contrast scene with harsh light might be best during late morning through early afternoon, while early morning or early evening will provide the golden hour look with long shadows and rich sunlight hues. Reflectors and scrims will help you control outdoor lighting. Night shots may require additional lighting setups if there aren't enough practical lights (from storefronts and street lamps, for example).

7. Control your color temperature. Indoor lighting is different than outdoor lighting. A fluorescent light will look different than an incandescent bulb. Know your primary light source and adjust your white balance accordingly.

Still from David Temblegue's *What If* ©2017. Used with permission.

CHAPTER 3

Exposure

THE ZONE SYSTEM, HISTOGRAMS, AND ISOs

One of the tools to shape the ratio of light and shadow revolves around the zone scale—an arbitrary scale indicating the tonal values from dark to light in an 11-step black-gray-white gradation, numbered 0–10 (0 = black; 10 = white; see Figure 3.1). Zones 0-3 represent black and deep shadow values (details and texture in an image can begin to be seen in zone 2, while 3 shows dark details and some texture, and 4 reveals landscape shadows and dark foliage). In addition, zones 4–6 represent face tones (from dark-skinned to Caucasian facial tones).

The mid-gray of 5 represents brown skin tones and sky; this is also the value of an 18% gray card used for white balance. Zones 7–9 hit lighter grays and highlights (an 8 would reveal texture in snow, whereas 9 would represent blown-out highlights, and 10, pure white). Each zone number indicates a doubling in brightness from the previous zone; the gray in 6 is twice as bright as the gray in 5; the gray in 7 is four times brighter than 5 (each step is a multiple of two). The black in 1 is half as bright as in 2. The doubling and halving of the gray scale is similar to the doubling and halving of the exposure range in f-stops.

Shane Hurlbut, ASC, explains, "Film has about 13.5 stops of latitude. Eight of these fall in the over-exposure (highlights) while 5.5 falls in the underexposed areas (the shadows)." The Canon 5D "goes in the other range," Hurlbut tells me. "It's got 7 in the under and 4-5 in the over." He adds: "So you're not able to handle highlights as well" as in film, with the 5D containing about seven stops in the shadows and

FIGURE 3.1
Zone scale from 0-10, referring to a quantification of a black-to-white gradation. One zone is twice as bright as the next when moving toward the white, while it's half as bright when moving toward the black. This matches the changing values of f-stop settings.
(Based on Zone System. Wikipedia.com. https://en.wikipedia.org/wiki/Zone_System)

four to five in the highlights. This refers to the dynamic range of a camera, the ratio of brightest to darkest areas of the shot. Generally, old school video expressed a contrast latitude ratio of 25:1, whereas film contains a 256:1 ratio (each zone is a doubling of brightness, so 4 zones is 16 times difference, 8 zones is 256 times difference). Digital cinema cameras reach this level and some of them exceed this, hitting 13 to 14 zones of dynamic range.

In general, standard video has about a 4½-zone scale range, whereas DSLRs and cinema cameras can double or triple that. Knowing this, you can make choices as to proper exposure for a person's face; for example, lighting the set accordingly so that your ratio of darks to bright stays within four to five zones and letting the rest fall off. And if you want the audience to see details throughout the shot, you can set up your lights so that everything stays within four zones, for example.

> The ISO setting of cinema cameras allows you to change the "speed" of the film: the lower the number, the more light you need.

In other words, each of the camera's exposure settings (the f-stop or T-stop), matches the change in the zone scale; a stop down will halve the value of the exposure, whereas opening one stop will double the brightness. So the filmmaker can take advantage of the zone system by either setting up lights and adjusting exposure or using natural lighting and adjusting exposure. The f-stop (or T-stop) doesn't measure tonal values; it's simply a representation of how much light is reflected on the surface of what's being shot—the light coming through the lens. Looking at an image doesn't reveal the f-stop setting, but when you use the zone system, you can get a fairly accurate read of the tonal values to the point that you could re-create the look of the shot. In addition, the ISO setting of cinema cameras allows you to change the "speed" of the film: the lower the number, the more light you need. Each standard increase in ISO (200 to 400, for ecample) will be as if you're opening the aperture one stop, or if you're going down one standard ISO setting (from 400 to 200), it would be similar to closing the aperture one stop.

The typical place to start with exposure is to measure your primary subject in the setup with an 18% gray card. Set your ISO and take the measurement. This will set your proper exposure (you'll get the correct f-stop setting), placing it in the middle (zone 5). If you control the lights, you could also go the other way. Open the aperture all the way and then adjust the lights until you have the 18% gray card at the proper exposure. So if you want the audience to see details throughout the shot, you can set up your lights so that everything stays within four or five zones or stops of exposure, for example.

Let's look at an indoor night shot from Vincent Laforet's *Reverie* to see how we can use the zone system practically. In Figure 3.2, we see tonal values of 0–6—black to light skin tones. By keeping the dynamic range within six stops and exposing the brightest part of the face at 6, Laforet is able to shape the rest of the scene around the blacks, letting the exposure of the man's body fall down to 0; blacks dominate

FIGURE 3.2

We could re-create Vincent Laforet's interior night shot from *Reverie* (see https://vimeo.com/7151244), using the zone system by quantifying the tonal range of black-gray-white. To accent the darkness, Laforet lets the blacks fall off, revealing little to no detail in much of the setup (0–1). We can begin to see details in the 2–3 range, while 4 and 5 allow us to clearly see the patterns on the pillow, the texture of the T-shirt, the man's arm and hand, as well as the table. Zone 6 is typically the value of Caucasian skin tones, and, save for the soft focus on his feet, we would clearly see the detail. The screen-right side of his face is shadowed, and we lose detail here, whereas the screen-left side of his face reveals details in the skin tone, edging on being a bit bright (7). The blue's brightness (tint and shade) changes depending on the tonal values; it's really dark in the background (where the 3 is), a bit brighter in the zone 5 areas, and really light in zone 6.

(Still from *Reverie*. ©2009 Vincent Laforet. Used with permission.)

the scene (stressing the nighttime feel of the shot). He allows the Caucasian skin tone to shine the brightest with the face and feet, while part of the arm and hand to hit zone 5, and leaving the shadows falling off into the blacks.

FILMMAKING TIP FOR ADVANCED SHOOTERS

For those who really want to master this material and get the most out of postproduction imaging—especially if you want to get the best dynamic range in a shot—shoot flat in order to go deep. Most cinema cameras contain a cinema log mode (C-log, S-log, flat mode, etc.). It spreads the data across the exposure spectrum, making the image look like it's flat. In reality, it's recording extra data in the highlights and shadows that you can dig out in post. See the section, "Shooting Flat for the Curve," later in this chapter.

Tip: Zone Scale in Practice

A typical Caucasian face has a reflectivity of 36%; a brown face, about 16%; a black face, 10%. Green leaves have a 14% reflectance, while black velvet is at 2%. Light grays reflect 70% of light, while off-whites reflect 80% (see Viera, D., & Viera, M. *Lighting for Film and Digital Cinematography.* Wadsworth, 2005: 54).

If you want to expose for zone 5 (the "correct" exposure for an 18% mid-range gray card), set your lights and place your subject, angle the 18% gray card so that it reflects the same light as your subject, and take your reading. The 18% gray card refers to the reflection and absorption of light (18% of the light is reflected, while 82% is absorbed). If you get an exposure reading of f/5.6 on your light meter for your particular ISO setting, then that's your f-stop setting, and the rest of the tonal range will fall off or increase depending on the amount of light in other areas of the applied shot. If you're trying to control the amount of detail in the shadows and/or highlights, you can adjust your lights accordingly. You really need a light meter to attain this level of work.

Most independent filmmakers and video journalists will usually just eyeball the exposure so that the image on the LCD screen looks right. But if you're really trying to control the image and know that you want the audience to see details in the background, you could plan for it to be two stops dimmer than your main subject in the foreground (which you've exposed at f/5.6 on zone 6), for example. You would light the background for zone 4 (two stops down), and you would know you're in zone 4 when you get a metered reading of f/11 (two stops down from f/5.6: f/8, then f/11) at the same speed (ISO setting). Do not change ISO in a scene so your shots will remain constant shot-to-to shot in a scene. Let's say you want the background half as bright as a character—control your lights in the background (dimmers, scrims, and/or flags) so that you meter it at f/8 (one stop closed down from an f/5.6 is half as bright). If you want it four times dimmer, conrol the lights so the meter stays around f/11.

When shooting outdoor daylight, the black to white on the zone scale doesn't mean that you can shoot in bright sun and dark shadows. The eye's contrast ratio is as high as 1,000,000:1. A camera's sensor on an 11-stop dynamic range is 1024:1, while 12 stops would give you 2048:1, 13 stops would be 4096:1. So you need to control the lighting in order to block or dim light that's too bright and add light to places that are too dark.

Tip: Lighting and the Zone Scale

A fast way to set your lights so as to brighten or dim your subject is to remember the inverse square law as a main property of light. Doubling the distance of the light from your subject (by either moving the light or your subject) drops off the brightness four times. If you halve the distance, the brightness increases by four. So if your subject is being lit inside by a window, and she's too bright for your exposure range, you can move the subject farther away (or scrim or place a gel filter on the window). If you're using lights, then you can simply move the lights farther away or closer to the subject to change the intensity (or you could use a dimmer on the light—although this will tend to change the color temperature of the light, thus impacting your white balance). In either case, moving the light or moving the subject toward or away from the light source will change your zone scale.

So choosing which zone to expose provides an idea of where your highlights and shadows will fall out of the exposure range. Choosing to properly expose at zone 5, for example, allows you to capture a fair amount of detail when exposing in zones 4–8 or 3–7.

Tip: The Histogram

FIGURE 3.3
If you don't have a light meter, you could use the histogram graph found on most cameras to "read" the range of tonal values in the shot, and adjust the camera's exposure or ISO setting accordingly. Here we see a histogram of a still from David Tembleque's *Dear Tom* (from a Photoshop tool). The readout on cameras show the same thing. The histogram represents the amount of your scene that's bright or dark (the tonal values). If the meter shows a high amount on the left side of the screen, the image is overall dark, showing the image to be "crushed" (a lot of detail lost in the blacks); high values on the right side of the meter reveal the image to be mostly bright and could be blown out. The gray values fall in the middle, so the 18% gray card reference representing the midrange point will be equivalent to a histogram reading in the middle of the graph. When applied to the zone scale, the readings on the left 40% of the graph would represent 0–3 (the dark grays and blacks), 4–6 (the middle gray tones) would fall into the middle of the graph (20–30%); while brighter gray tones, highlights, and white would fall along the right 30–40% of the graph.

(Shot from *Dear Tom*. ©2015 David Tembleque. Used with permission.)

Photographer Michael Reichmann tells his students that when he shoots, "I'm barely even aware of the image on the LCD; it's the histogram that commands my attention." Perhaps this is an exaggeration because getting good composition is key, but once the composition has been chosen, getting proper exposure is just as important, and the histogram is one of the tools to show what your image looks like across the tonal range. Reichmann believes that there is no "bad" histogram because it's simply giving you what the reading is. Histograms are valuable for showing you how much of an image is blown out or crushed. But you can adjust your light and shadows accordingly if you're trying to place your subject in the middle of the histogram exposure zone. (See Reichmann, M. "Understanding Histograms." http://www.luminous-landscape.com/tutorials/understanding-series/understanding-histograms.shtml)

EXPOSURE AND DEPTH OF FIELD

Exposure represents the amount of light allowed to fall on a camera's sensor—and it also determines the depth of field of the focal plane—what's in focus. Cinema lenses have T-stops placed on the barrel of the lens, and you adjust the stop manually rather than through the in-camera setting (see Figure 3.4). An iris—like the pupil of your eye—controls this. When it is opened all the way (low f-stop or T-stop number), more light falls in. When it is nearly closed (high f-stop or T-stop number), less light enters.

For photo lenses, the range of the aperture opening is measured with f-stops:[1] 1, 1.4, 2, 2.8, 4, 5.6, 8, 11, 16, 22, 32), while cinema lenses use T-stops. F/1 (or the lowest number available on the lens) represents the iris opened all the way, whereas 32 (or the highest available on the lens) is nearly closed. Each number in the sequence represents a doubling of light when opening up (f/1.4 lets in twice as much light as f/2), while a stopping down of the exposure halves the amount of light (f/2 receives half as much light as f/1.4; see Figure 3.5 for the iris range of a Zeiss Contax 50 mm f/1.4 lens). These are really fractions, since each step down of the iris is one half o f the previous stop.

Furthermore, the lower the f-stop, the more shallow the depth of field becomes. Higher f-stops increase the depth of field. You can download a depth of field calculator or go to: http://www.dofmaster.com/dofjs.html. You input the type of camera, the distance to the subject in inches, feet, centimeters, or meters, and it'll calculate

FIGURE 3.4
This Zeiss Contax 50 mm/1.4 photo prime lens places the f-stop settings on the lens itself. This lens has an f-stop range from f/1.4 to f/16.
(Photo by Kurt Lancaster.)

---

[1]T-stops are also used in this terminology; f-stops are determined mathematically (focal length divided by the diameter of the aperture), whereas T-stops are similar but include the light absorption quality of lenses. For practical purposes, they're nearly the same.

the proper distance. (See the changes in Figure 3.5.) Note how the depth of field (DoF) increases with the corresponding higher f-stop values. Also note, as the distance to the subject decreases, the depth of field decreases, and with a subject farther away, you'll also get increased depth of field. For example, a subject 20 feet away with a 50 mm lens at f/1.4 has a depth of field of 4.15 feet, while a subject at 2 feet has a depth of field of less than half an inch!

f/1.4

Distance ~4' f/1.4: DoF = 1.92" (from 3.92'-4.08')

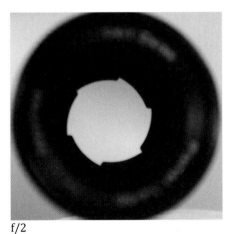

f/2

Distance ~4' f/2: DoF = 2.64" (from 3.89'-4.12')

FIGURE 3.5
The f-stop setting determines the depth of field, as can be seen with the focal plane changing in the corresponding images with Preston. At f/1.4, 2, 2.8, and 4, the background chairs are out of focus, while they begin to get sharper at f/5.6 and above. Depth of field calculation based on 5D Mark II, Zeiss Contax 50 mm/1.4 at a distance of approximately 4 feet (using the depth of field calculator at: http://www.dofmaster.com/dofjs.html).
(Photos by Kurt Lancaster; model: Preston.)

f/2.8

Distance ~4' f/2.8: DoF = 3.85" (from 3.85'-4.17')

f/4

Distance ~4' f/4: DoF = 5.4" (from 3.79'-4.24')

f/5.6

Distance ~4' f/5.6: DoF = 7.68" (from 3.71'-4.34')

FIGURE 3.5 (Continued)

f/8

Distance ~4' f/8: DoF = 10.92" (from 3.6'-4.51')

f/11

Distance ~4' f/11: DoF = 15.6" (from 3.45'-4.75')

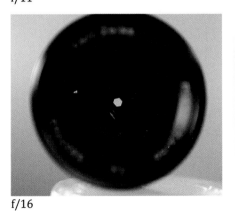

f/16

Distance ~4' f/16: DoF = 22.68" (from 3.27'-5.16')

FIGURE 3.5 (Continued)

Most people eyeball the exposure by using the LCD or an external monitor, but this approach will not provide an accurate reading. Philip Bloom doesn't recommend it. "Don't use the LCD screen to expose," he says. By using the camera's metering system, Bloom feels you can get a more accurate read—important for professional use. You can meter an average exposure with DSLR cameras, but using a light meter is better.

Use a light meter to determine the precise value of the exposure, moving it if you want to get a reading on another part of the scene. By using the zone system you can find the accurate exposure range for your project.

FIGURE 3.6
The same shot with three different f-stop settings. The top image is at f/8, the middle is f/11, and the bottom is f/16, each one letting in half the light as the one previous. F/8 is the proper exposure where you can still see some details in the shadows without the subject's face being blown out. Notice that the depth of field of the subject is sharp throughout, because of the high f-stop settings providing a depth of field between 2.11' to 4.64'. Zeiss 25 mm, f/2.8.
(Photos by Kurt Lancaster.)

CINEMATOGRAPHER TIP

Film Look with Exposure, Shutter Speed, and Filters

Shane Hurlbut, ASC, says, "Making HD video look like film has a cocktail and one of the essential ingredients to this flavorful recipe is neutral density (ND). You have to keep your exposure on a [Canon 5D Mark II] around a 5.6 to get that beautiful shallow depth of field. The 7D should be around a 2.8, and the 1D around a 4.0. This gives the focus puller a chance and still retains a beautiful fall off of focus."

The 7D has close to a 35 mm sensor so you would shoot around a 2.0/2.8 split to give a decent focus range, but keep the background out of focus enough to battle aliasing and moiré issues. Use a shutter speed of 1/50 or 1/40 all the time. I do not like to go above it. When you go at a 1/60 or higher it starts to look like video, and it's too sharp for me. I use the motion blur at a 1/50 and 1/40 to help with the crispness of HD and make it look more like film.

In addition, Hurlbut, who shot *Terminator Salvation* (2009) and *Act of Valor* (2012), recommends using neutral density filters to change the exposure value without altering the f-stop setting). "Tiffen's Water White NDs and Water White IR NDs looked the cleanest of all the available filters. This filter was specifically designed for the HD world. It is very pure glass to give you the best image for your post color correction. The filters that were originally made for film had brown and green in the glass that was no problem to dial out in film because of the uncompressed 4:4:4 color space. But now with HD 8-bit compressed color space [of DSLRS and many low budget cinema cameras], you do not have that range of manipulation in color correction. In addition, by using neutral density at higher levels to achieve a shallow depth of field, you must deal with the problem of infrared (IR) pollution. The Water White IR NDs counteract this issue and give an image that does not have so much pink/magenta. As a cinematographer, I want to limit this contamination because it ends up showing in the blacks as well as skies in day exteriors."

(Shane Hurlbut, personal notes. See Hurlbut, Shane. "Filtration: Beware of the Reaper of Cheap Glass. Hurlblog." 10 February 2010. http://hurlbutvisuals.com/blog/2010/02/10/filtration-beware-of-the-reaper-of-cheap-glass/)

TIP

If you need the exposure wide open for best shallow depth of field work, then you will need to add neutral density filters so you can lock your iris open. If you don't have an ND filter, then you can increase shutter speed—it'll make the image sharper, but you'll maintain a shallow depth of field. (See p. 48.)

FALSE COLORS

False colors are another tool to measure exposure. You set the values of the colors in-camera, such as red for clipping at 95%, green for midtone exposure, blue for under-exposure at 15%, and so on. By switching to false color, the cinematographer will see a variety of colors on screen, letting her know where the exposure values are located in the shot. In Figure 3.7, red shows over-exposure, reading above 99%, while yellow shows over-exposure at above 95%. Green, proper exosure, reveals 42%. Blue is used for under-exposure below 12%, while purple indicates deep underexposure below 5%. These values are adjustable. If a camera does not contain a false color option, you can find it on many external LCD monitors.

FIGURE 3.7

A screen grab of false color tools to read exposure. Different colors and vaules can be set to show under-, proper, and over-exposure. Here, green is at around 42% value, blue is under 12% value, purple falls way under (below 5%), while red reveals clipped highlights at 99% and above.

(Image courtesy of Kurt Lancaster.)

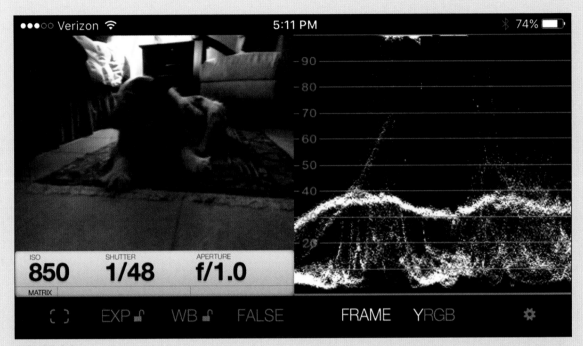

FIGURE 3.8
The waveform monitor on the Cine Meter II app by David Wilt. It also show colors, exposure levels, false colors, among other featrues.
(Image courtesy of Kurt Lancaster.)

Cine Meter II App

To help with making the proper exposure on your camera (especially if you do not have a light meter or a waveform monitor in your camera), and you could use Adam Wilt's Cine Meter II app lcoated here: https://itunes.apple.com/us/app/cine-meter-ii-an-exposure-color-meter/id846918884.

It is a light meter for a smartphone that contains a waveform monitor, which reads the amount of luminosity for pixels related to the image you're exposing, going from left to right. See Figure 3.8. The bottom represents shadows, while the top represents highlights. As can be seen in this

shot, it is dark. The few clipped highlights represent the light at the top of the image, while the graph falling down toward zero reveals the shadow areas. Midtones would typically be between 55–75 on this scale.

In addition to the waveform monitor, the app also contains false color readings (showing in color over- and under-exposed areas of the shot), as well as providing light meter readings, among other tools. The app is ~$25.

CINEMATOGRAPHER TIP

Jim Mathers, president (and co-founder) of the Digital Cinema Society, discusses how he approaches exposure:

> With exposure tests, what I'm basically looking for is the sweet spot somewhere between two competing extremes of underexposure on one side, where the image would start to become unacceptably noisy; and on the other, the point where I would start to clip, or lose detail in the highlights. It would seem logical to flatly expose a chip chart, then simply count out the number of steps between the two limits to find the median value. However, I find that this is not always the exact center between these poles; it can be more of a creative choice, and it can vary depending on the subject. And while it would be nice to assign a corresponding ASA/ISO number to a given sensor, this also depends on the shooting situation. For example, in a high contrast daylight exterior, I might tend to rate the sensor a little higher, looking to protect the highlights, which would lead me to allow less exposure to reach the sensor. However, in a low key setup I might be looking to capture shadow detail, treating the sensor as if it is less sensitive, allowing more light to pass through to help insure my shadow areas stay free of too much noise. Now, I'm way too pragmatic to have a different meter setting for every scene, but I have found two or three different ratings varying with the broad category of the shot to be appropriate, just as I might shoot a movie on two or three different stocks.
>
> (Digital Cinema Society Newsletter. 26 March 2010: #6.2)

USING ND FILTERS

The most important filters are designed not only to protect your lenses from scratches, but filter the amount of light hitting the lens; they are called neutral density (ND) filters. This type of filter allows you to keep the aperture open under bright light confitions; the filter essentially stops down the f-stop aperture setting—without closing the iris—the amount depending on the type of filter used, allowing the filmmaker to keep the shallow depth of field of an open iris in high-exposure situations. Filters can be screwed onto the lens or dropped in front of the lens when using a matte box, or they can be conveyed electronically if the camera has a built-in neutral density function; some cameras, such as the Canon C100, contain analog ND filters that can be adjusted with a dial.

Filters are assigned different numbers depending on their density, their ability to block out light. ND2 will be labeled 0.3, providing for a one f-stop equivalent reduction (see Table 3.1). Companies also make variable ND filters (called ND faders) so you can adjust the filter without having to switch them out.

In addition, when you're choosing an ND filter, consider getting one that includes infrared filtration. The IR is especially useful for DSLR cameras because they're sensitive to infrared, causing oversaturation of red, as well as focusing and interference issues.

Table 3.1	Filter Name, Density, and f-Stop Reduction	
ND Filter Type	Density	f-Stop Reduction
ND2	0.3	1
ND4	0.6	2
ND8	0.9	3
ND16	1.2	4
ND32	1.5	5
ND64	1.8	6

Questions to Consider When Using Filters

1. What is your exposure latitude? Are you shooting in bright sunlight, for example? Set your ISO level where you want it and then set the exposure. If you're blowing out the highlights, then it's too bright. Adding a neutral density filter will change your exposure latitude and allow you to get the shot you need.

2. Do you need shallow depth of field in bright light? Use an ND filter when you want to open up your iris and maintain shallow depth of field without overexposing your shots.

3. How much light do you want to come through? The density determines the strength of the filter. The higher the number, the less light will come through. Be aware of the changing exposure latitude with ND filters. A 0.9 filter, for example, provides three stops of exposure across your entire range. So if you're using an ND filter only to prevent a blowout of the highlight, be aware that your shadows will deepen, and you may lose detail, although before the ND placement, it was fine. You'll need to brighten the shadow if you don't want to lose the detail.

CONSIDERING SHUTTER SPEED

The shutter in a film camera would normally be half a circle (180 degrees), so if the film speed is 1/24 of a second (24 fps), you would double that to get the shutter speed (1/48). NTSC video shoots at 30 fps, while PAL (European standard) is 25 fps, so with NTSC you would typically shoot at 1/60 of a second shutter speed. Shane Hurlbut, ASC, however, considers this "a recipe for delivering images that look like video, not film":

> I use a 1/40th or a 1/50th of a shutter. You never go above that. Anytime you go above, it starts looking like video. By just going up to 1/60th of a second it instantly takes a beautiful 5D that gives filmic images and turns it into a video camera. The more you sharpen the image, the more it looks plastic. I use the motion blur to soften the crispness of HD video. Shooting at a 1/50th is like shooting with a 200 degree shutter. I shot the whole *Rat Pack* (1998) on a 200 degree shutter—I loved that look.[2]

Setting the proper shutter speed becomes an important tool in helping to attain the film look with cinema cameras.

CONSIDERING FRAME RATES

Before addressing in-camera settings, I want to address frame rate. Currently, film has a 24 frames-per-second (fps) rate, and provides one of the benchmarks for getting the film look (video shooting at 24p), which engages a judder effect when shooting (and that's part of the film look).

However, such filmmakers as James Cameron offer a different opinion. He feels that unless you're transferring your project to film or have it projected on a 24 fps player, then you don't need to shoot 24p. In an interview with David Cohen of *Variety*, Cameron actually argues for a faster frame rate in order to create a smoother quality of the image:

> I've run tests on 48 frame per second stereo and it is stunning. The cameras can do it, the projectors can (with a small modification) do it. So why aren't we doing it, as an industry?
>
> Because people have been asking the wrong question for years. They have been so focused on resolution, and counting pixels and lines, that they have forgotten about frame rate. Perceived resolution + pixels = replacement rate. A 2 K image at 48 frames per second looks as sharp as a 4 K image at 24 frames per second with one fundamental difference: the 4 K/24 image will judder miserably during a panning shot, and the 2 K/48 won't. Higher pixel counts

---

[2] Seymour, Mike. "Red Centre Podcast: Red Day & Shane Hurlbut." Fxguide.com. #56. 15 February 2010. https://fxguide.com/quicktakes/red-centre-podcast-out-red-day-shane-hurlbut/

only preserve motion artifacts like strobing with greater fidelity. They don't solve them at all.[3]

Cameron argues for 48 frames per second because the quality doesn't vastly increase at a higher number and it's compatible with film projection (doubling the standard 24 frame rate). For shooting, 24p will best represent the film look because that's the current aesthetic of film and best engages the film look when shooting with video. But getting the film look isn't just about shooting 24p. You need to sculpt light and shadow and work within a specified dynamic range, engage smooth and stable camera work, choose lenses and filters, and get proper exposure at the proper shutter speed when telling your story as powerfully as possible.

SHOOTING FLAT FOR THE CURVE

What does it mean to shoot flat? Why would we want to shoot flat? We're dealing with digital data when shooting on contemporary computer-chip cinema cameras. The human eye distinguishes changes in brighteness much better than detecting changes in darkness or nuances of subtle shadows. If the collected light and shadows—translated as digital data—are treated evenly (the same amount of data spread across from shadows to brightness), then the data collected and stored on the shadow side becomes wasted. We can see this in the zone scale (Figure 3.1), where the brights are easier to distinguish than the changes in shadow detail. We don't perceive light in a linear way.

A camera's sensor does respond to light in a linear way and if you record linearly, what you see is what you get—an accurate low dynamic range image (assuming an 8-bit recording) with proper exposure, focus, and color balance. It places the same amount of data throughout the image spectrum evenly. Kind of.

When we talk about how data gets recorded, all bets are off. In low budget cinema cameras most of them record 8-bits of data—256 pieces of information (shades of color and light intensity) recorded per pixel. When shadows are being recorded, less digital information is being used (black represents zero, while a blown-out highlight, would hit the high range of 255.

Place that on a linear scale that represents a doubling of information represented by each stop of a lens—and you'll soon discover that the brighter an image gets recorded the more data it uses, the highlights hogging the high end values of brightness. For example, let's assume a 10-stop dynamic range with a linear recording: each stop is an exponential increase of data being recorded. Divide 256 pieces of information along a linear eight-stop range and it's not 32 (256/8), which is what we would assume, due to the exponential increase

[3]Cohen, D. S. "James Cameron supercharges 3-D." *Variety*. 10 April 2008. http://www.variety.com/article/VR1117983864.html?categoryid51009&cs51

of light. Remember that f/1.4 does not let in eight times more light than f/22, even though that's an eight-stop range—but it delivers in 256 times more light.

In a similar way the light intensity hitting the sensor at the brightest value falls on the high end of the scale, while the low end shadows uses less data. Therefore, the value of the highest intensity utilizes half of the 256 points of data (128 to 256), while the lowest end is using 2 points of data (0 to 2), while the middle levels use 16 to 64 (0, 2, 4, 8, 16, 32, 64, 128, 256). Therefore, half of the 8-bits of data are being utilized by the highlights and if there are only 8 to 16 pieces of information in the shadows, there's not going to be much data or detail there to pull out in post (and if you adjust the shadows in post, it'll fall apart fast).

But this is not how our eyes perceived the world. Indeed, as Phil Rhodes says:

> [The] human visual system is very much better at discerning the differences between comparatively bright objects than it is at discerning the differences between comparatively dim objects. See [http://hyperphysics.phy-astr.gsu.edu/hbase/vision/bright.html] for a graph of perceived against actual brightness—at the dim end, the curve is almost vertical, indicating that we don't see the difference between "really dim" and "not quite so really dim" very well; whereas, we see the difference between "bright" and "really bright" much better.[4]

Film stock reacts similarly to the world as our eyes. Data is spread evenly in a non-linear way in what is known as a logarithmic (log) gamma curve (see Figure 3.9).

Digital data can be treated in a similar way, too. With log data conversion, equal amounts of data are reserved for the low end (pushing those values up and removing contrast) and making the image appear flat or washed out. Less data is used in the highlights (where it's not needed) and more in the shadows (where we do need it).[5]

That flatness needs to be treated in post by placing a curve or a LUT (look-up table) in order remove the washed out look by boosting the contrast of the image. Since there's more data in the lower half, the dynamic range of the image increases and the change in contrast makes it appear that it has more data than it does (there's still only 256 in an 8-bit image). (See Figure 3.10.) This is why recording in 10-bit, with 1,024 pieces of information is better and is standard on high end cameras. 12-bit raw is even better with 4,096 pieces of information and allows for a lot more headroom for color and tonal changes in post. Raw shooting does not require log curve settings, since the raw data can be manipulated in nearly every way in post (unless the highlights have been clipped, then there's no recovering of that data).

Because the data is recorded in log, the film-like curve, applied to digital data, helps emulate an aspect of the film look through the roll-off of highlights and shadows,

---

[4] Rhodes, Phil. "Logarithmic vs Linear" discussion thread. Cinematography.com. 2 December 2008. http://cinematography.com/index.php?showtopic=33270

[5] See "Understanding Log-Format Recording" by David Adler for more information. (https://bhphotovideo.com/explora/video/tips-and-solutions/understanding-log-format-recording).

the dropoff of the "toe" and "shoulder." So if the camera is placed in a "cinema" mode, it will record the light (and color) data in a non-linear log curvy way.

Each camera manufacturer tweaks this log curve in different ways and, as Rhode notes, they

> include proprietary deviations of the manufacturer's own divising which are intended to enhance the performance of the device. Add to this the fact that no imaging device is perfectly linear in response to light in any case, and the processing you choose to apply to log (or indeed linear) images tends to be based partially on mathematics and partially on what makes a subjectively nice picture.[6]

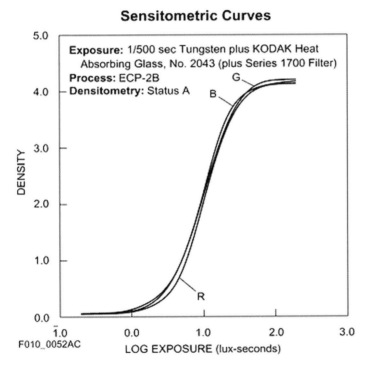

FIGURE 3.9
Film curves are logarithmic. The film stock increases or decreases in density based on exposure. The highlights and shadows "roll off" along the "toe" and "shoulder," creating a unique property of film similar to how the human eye perceives light and shadow. Digital data clips, cutting the data off, rather than rolling off.
(Image courtesay of Kodak.)

[6] Rhodes, Phil. "Logarithmic vs Linear" discussion thread. Cinematography.com. 2 Dec. 2008
http://cinematography.com/index.php?showtopic=33270

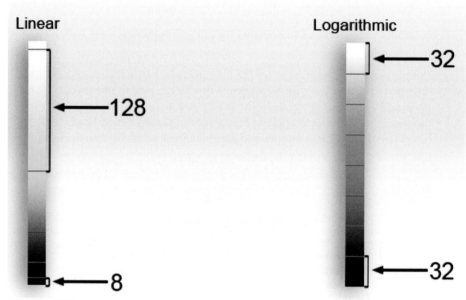

FIGURE 3.10

Linear vs log scale. In linear, half the data within an 8-bit recording is reserved for the highlights (where we don't need it), while only a little bit of data remains for the shadows (where we do need it). The log curve fixes this, spreading the data over the entire image range in more even fashion, allowing for details to be preserved and recovered in post and in effect, increasing the dynamic range.

For more information, see "How to Understand 'Log' or CineStyle Recordings" by Phil Rhodes. http://www.redsharknews.com/technology/item/1975-how-to-understand-log-or-cine-style-recordings (Images ©2016 Phil Rhodes. Used with permission.)

Setting cameras to shoot flat is almost mandatory when attempting to shape a cinematic image. However, if the original image is already low contrast, you may not need to apply the log curve. Test the image through postproduction to discover what works best. See Figure 3.11 for a before and after image of shooting flat and then applying a grade to the image.

FIGURE 3.11
When recording in Canon Log, the image comes out "flat" or washed out. When grading, it shines, bringing out more information in the highlights and shadows.
(Image courtesy of Canon.)

A tight close-up in the music video *Bandit* by Hunnymoon, shot on a Canon 5D Mark IV, 4K mode. (©2016 Canon Europe.)

Checklist for Exposure

1. Set your camera to manual (for DSLRs).

2. Determine your exposure latitude. Knowing your latitude range from shadows to highlight will help determine how much light you need for your subject, foreground, and background. If you know the dynamic range of the camera, you can determine how much light and negative fill you need to control the amount of light throughout your entire exposure range. A light meter is helpful for this process, but you can also use the histogram or waveform monitor to see the dynamic range from dark to bright. As you practice with image, light, and shadow, you'll be able to eyeball the exposure range for your particular camera.

3. How rich do you want the image? The ISO level—the "speed" of the exposure—determines the richness of the image. The higher the number, the more light sensitive it will be but will result in more video noise; the lower the number, the richer the image will look but will require more lighting. Outdoor daylight will allow for ISO 100, whereas outdoor night shots will require a high ISO setting. The lower the setting, the lower the noise. Increasing the ISO will add more noise to the image. Recommended indoor ISO = 400, 640, 800, 1250. Recommended outdoor day ISO: 100 or 200.

4. How much light do you want? Set your aperture's f-stop (the lower the number, the more open the iris, letting in more light; higher numbers close up the iris, cutting off the amount of light falling on the sensor). Neutral density filters are used to cut out light without changing your f-stop.

5. How much depth of field do you want? Choose your lens and open up the aperture for more shallow depth of field; when the iris is more closed, the focal depth of field will increase. Adjust light intensity and/or ND filters accordingly.

6. Set your shutter speed. It should remain at 1/40 or 1/50 of a second to maintain a nonvideo look and get you closer to the film look.

CHAPTER 4

Recording Quality Audio

RECORD SOUND LIKE A PRO

The cinema law of sound: No one can watch a film if the audio sounds bad. No matter how good the image, poor audio quality will block your viewers from ever appreciating the image. Do not ever skimp on sound. It is the most important element in scenes with dialog. In fact, you can present a fairly poor image and if the audio is spot on, people will enjoy the movie—more so than good images accompanied by bad sound. Bad sound is a dead giveaway that the film was made by an amateur.

With DSLR cameras and some of the early model Blackmagic cinema cameras (Production, Pocket, etc.), it's pretty easy to get bad sound, but most of the new low budget cinema camera include XLR inputs that help in recording professional audio recordings. With some basic audio recording knowledge and the proper tools, we can overcome the limitations of cameras without XLR inputs, and this foundational knowledge must also be used by shooters using cameras with XLR inputs. Most cameras with built-in microphones deliver poor audio. Dialog should never be recorded with the built-in camera mics—ever. Jared Abrams (WideOpenCamera.com), says he likes the fact that cameras lacking XLR inputs make you go "back to basics" of filmmaking:

> The way they started motion picture was one frame at a time. And eventually they just strung 'em together until it looked like some-thing they were used to and liked, and off we went. The DSLR cameras are doing just the same thing. It's a great sync-sound camera. If you treat it like that, then you'll get the most out of it. If you run separate sound, you will get better sound. And the fact that they didn't jam all this audio into it just makes it a more potent camera. That's one of the bad things about standard little video cameras is that they're trying to jam all this audio technology into it.

Still from Kurt Lancaster's *Occupy Wall Street*. ©2011.

Whether you're shooting with a DSLR or a cinema camera with XLR inputs the best sound will always come from an external recorder with a field mixer. This is what professional filmmakers use. And if you treat your cinema camera as if it needed external audio recording, then you're well on your way in getting clean audio recordings. Ideally, recording sound separately, or at the very least, disabling the automatic gain control (AGC) in the camera, getting the proper microphones, and for cameras lacking XLRs connecting the mic to a professional audio adapter (containing a preamp with limiters) are essential in getting the best possible sound.

Despite this, I have some students now who will record with external audio recorders with XLR inputs, and they still get bad recordings! The most important factor in getting good audio involves proper mic placement and setting correct levels. It doesn't matter if the camera contains XLR inputs or not—a bad mic placement will result in poor audio and improper levels every time.

This chapter defines sound quality, provides terminology for different microphone types, the different audio gear you can get, how to use Magic Lantern to get in-camera monitoring of audio on some Canon DSLRs, and a case study on capturing "run-and-gun" audio with a Canon 5D. The most important factor in getting good audio involves proper mic placement and setting correct levels. These principles of audio are requisite in order to get clean audio recordings, whether you're using a Canon C200 or a Blackmagic Pocket Cinema Camera.

The following are some basics filmmakers should consider when recording audio for projects:

1. What is the sound quality of the space you're recording, whether indoors or outdoors?

2. What type of microphone will you use, such as a shotgun mic or a lavaliere? Or are you stuck with just an onboard mic? The choice will determine your pickup pattern (what area of sound the mic will favor when recording).

3. Will you use a condenser or dynamic mic? Will it be powered through its own battery or from the camera's power, providing "phantom" power? (Most cinema cameras provide phantom power.)

4. Is the audio input high impedance or low impedance—minijack input or XLR input? A high impedance mic can pick up interference, placing noise in the recording.

5. Can you disable automatic gain control of your audio and manually control the sound?

6. What is the compression of your audio recording? 24-bit will provide more headroom in post, than 16-bit audio.

7. Where will you place the microphone? Will it be a camera-mounted mic, or will you use a boom pole or pistol grip? Microphones mounted on a camera must be close to the subject in order to get a clean signal.

8. Will you use an external audio recorder or just record it to the camera (or both)?

The answers to these questions will determine your audio quality. This chapter covers these topics so you can be more informed in your choices as you shoot and know the impact of compromises. You should test through postproduction and into a final export of your project to understand what your final field audio recording will sound like.

SOUND QUALITY

Just as the cinematographer must be aware of the quality and source of light in a scene, filmmakers need to be aware of the ambient room quality. Is it hard or soft? Hard walls and hard floors will reverb your audio, providing micro-echoes of sound in the space. Test the sound quality by yelling in the space. If you hear an echo, reverb will be abundant and the audio may sound a bit tinny. A room with carpeting, furniture, and so forth will absorb the sound and break up the soundwaves, so the reverb will be minimized. Outdoors (other than an alley, for example) will likely provide a soft sound quality. A windy day will cause audio impacts, pretty much ruining the recording. Using a windscreen will minimize this damage—not the foam windscreen that usually comes with the mic, but a large, thick, furry screen covering a sound blimp for wind production.

In addition, the filmmaker must decide if the subjects should sound close or far away. In most cases, their voices should sound as though they're close, so the microphone must be brought in close (less than 2 feet or closer). If distance needs to be conveyed, then pull the microphone back so it sounds as though someone is talking across the room, for example.

In addition, some cameras and audio recorders provide an option to utilize automatic gain control (AGC), which means it will adjust the levels of the audio coming into the recording, depending on how much sound is hitting the mic. A lot of sound will lower the input, whereas soft sounds will force the camera to increase the levels, typically causing unwanted hiss. In either case, the AGC will result in recording uneven audio levels and adding extra noise when the levels are low. In most cases, you want to turn off the AGC. Some cinema cameras and DSLRs do not allow you to change this setting, so BeachTek and juicedLink are two companies that provide devices to disable the AGC of cameras and allow you to input XLR microphones. These devices trick the camera so that it thinks all the audio is even, allowing manual control of the audio.

Furthermore, audio is recorded at different qualities. A 44.1 kHz, 16-bit recording provides less headroom than a 48 kHz, 24-bit recording. The first number refers to the sampling rate—the number of times per second the audio is sampled (44,100/second), and the second number refers to the amount of information recorded per sample (16-bit or 24-bit). If you're using an external recorder, you have the option of setting different compression schemes. Just make sure you set the same compression as the camera so you can sync them up in post. Do not use compressed MP3 recording—no matter how high the bit rate. Keep your audio data as raw as possible!

Also, when recording audio, such as dialog, be sure to record room tone in every space you record. Have everyone on set be quiet and record blank audio for at least a minute. This will capture the ambient sound you will need in editing in order to fill in gaps between takes or to even out the sound quality from different takes.

The following sections provide an overview of some of the equipment you may think about using on your shoots. They include a justification of what works well and why. Some of this information may be a review for experienced filmmakers, so feel free to skip over it. If you're relatively new to filmmaking, the information may be useful, especially if you're trying to get better sound for your projects. The final section of the chapter includes several checklists for different types of audio setups.

MICROPHONE TYPES

Microphone types sound differently; they will convey distinctive audio qualities depending on the space you're in. The major mic types include lavaliers (lavs), omni-directionals (omnis), cardioids, and shotguns. They will never sound the same.

- Lavs are needed for wide shots with dialog (we'll see the boom pole with a shot-gun mic in a wide shot).
- Cardioids are for use indoors.
- Shotguns are for outdoor medium and close-up shots.

Cardioids provide the best sound recording but pick up too much noise outside. Because shotgun mics have the rear lobe pickup pattern, they'll pick up reflections of sound off the ceiling and wall, resulting in interference when shooting indoors. Lavs, although useful for picking up dialog in a wide shot, don't sound as good and need to be postprocessed to bring back the warmth of a person's voice. For run-and-gun jour-nalists and documentary filmmakers, the shotgun is the best choice if you can choose only one mic.

Many of these mics include space for a battery, but you will want to use phantom power if available because it will increase the quality during recording, although it will reduce the battery life of your recorder. The voltage allows the signal to be picked up when sound waves hit the front plate, changing the value of the air quality against a capacitor and turning it into an electric signal. On the other hand, dynamic micro-phones—the ones you see reporters use on television news—are more rugged and do not require any external power. But the sound quality is not as good as condenser microphones.

Shotgun microphones are unidirectional, oftentimes with a cardioid or supercardioid pickup pattern. A cardioid pattern allows you to record sounds from the direction the microphone is pointed (see Figure 4.1), whereas a supercardioid—found in shotgun mics—does the same thing but also picks up some sound from the rear (see Figure 4.2).

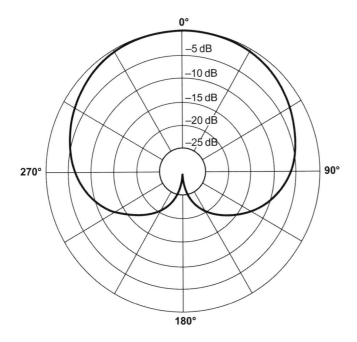

FIGURE 4.1
Cardioid pickup pattern. "The Microphone, Your Voice's Gateway to the World." Voiceover4us.com.
(http://www.voiceover4us.com/blog/2008/07/15/14/).

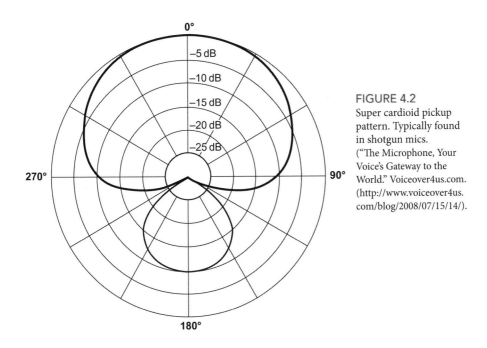

FIGURE 4.2
Super cardioid pickup pattern. Typically found in shotgun mics. ("The Microphone, Your Voice's Gateway to the World." Voiceover4us.com. (http://www.voiceover4us.com/blog/2008/07/15/14/).

One of the popular mics that can be attached to a DSLR or cinena camera's accessory shoe is the Rode VideoMic Pro (see Figure 4.3), a light shotgun mic that attaches on top of the camera (see Figure 4.4 for a polar pickup pattern chart for this mic). If you're traveling light and shooting a news piece, documentary, or a wedding solo (without anyone helping out with sound), then this is probably one of the most useful mics you can get for your DSLR. It will not be as good as a shotgun mic with an XLR adapter, but it will provide usable sound for your production.

FIGURE 4.3
Rode VideoMic Pro with foam cover. This mic includes a built-in shock mount to reduce noise from movement. The foam windscreen is not useful against wind; you'll need a wind muff that's designed for this mic. The frequency response of this mic ranges from 40 Hz to 20 kHz. This mic uses a minijack connector; it's a high impredance mic but can connect directly to a microphone jack without any kind of adapter. This minijack mic could be plugged directly into an external audio recorder.
(Image courtesy of Rode.)

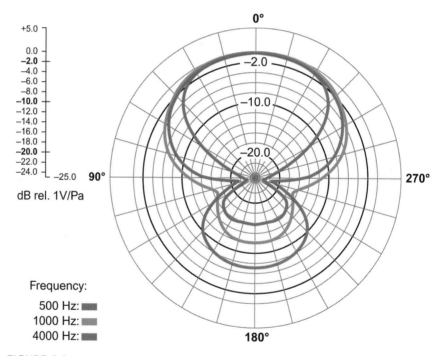

FIGURE 4.4
Rode VideoMic Pro's polar pickup pattern measured in frequency response. The Hertz refers to the wavelength. The lower number is low-frequency sounds such as rubles and bass. The higher frequency expresses higher tones. A human voice can range from 80 Hz to 1100 Hz.
(Image courtesy of Rode.)

The Rode VideoMic Pro will provide usable sound for run-and-gun style documentary and journalism work, but it's recommended that it be used to record decent reference audio and as a backup source in case your audio recorder fails. It is better to use a higher-end XLR mic, especially if you're submitting for broadcast or to a film festival, where audio really matters.

If you're shooting solo and going for speed, attaching an on-camera mic, such as the Rode VideoMic Pro, is a decent choice. When you're talking to someone, be sure that person is close, no more than three feet away, if you want to capture as clean a sound as possible. This may work great for news and documentary. However, when shooting short fiction pieces and commercials, you will want wider shots and still pick up clean audio.

But because the performers are more than a few feet away (even five feet is too far), you'll need to run longer cable. Be aware that microphones with minijack plugs (the standard tip-ring-sleeve, or TRS, connectors) are high impedance using unbalanced cables and the signal will weaken over distance, and these mics are prone to picking up noise and interference (such as a radio station). It's best to use a balanced cable (XLR).

The Rode NTG-2 shotgun mic is a good dialog microphone, most useful for outdoor shots or indoors if sound reflection is minimal (see Figure 4.5), and if you're shooting solo, attach this mic to the XLR input and use phantom power, and you'll get really good sound. If you have a sound person, this type of mic is a great choice when attaching it to an external recorder (such as a Tascam or Zoom).

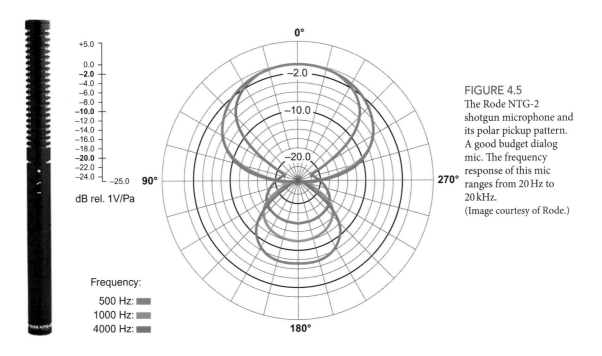

FIGURE 4.5
The Rode NTG-2 shotgun microphone and its polar pickup pattern. A good budget dialog mic. The frequency response of this mic ranges from 20 Hz to 20 kHz.
(Image courtesy of Rode.)

Whatever shotgun mic you end up using, knowing its strengths and weaknesses is important. Note, for example, the frequency response of the Rode VideoMic Pro compared to the Rode NTG-2. The NTG-2 can go as low as 20 Hz, whereas the VideoMic Pro is limited to 40 Hz. Fewer low frequencies will be picked up by the VideoMic Pro. However, often a boom pole sound operator will engage the low-cut filter to minimize boom pole handling or wind, removing the lower frequencies from the shotgun mic.

Shotgun mics provide the best sound in your recording work, but using a shotgun inside a room with a lot of reverb will cause extra audio muddiness.

If, instead, you use a mic with an XLR connector (with balanced cable, which will resist the noise that high-impedance lines will pick up), you will have the advantage of running long cable, and it'll pick up very little to no noise, and the audio quality will stay high. Interference will be minimized. But you will need to hook it up to an XLR adapter if shooting with a camera without XLR inputs or use an external audio recorder with XLR inputs.

It must be noted that the interference tube in shotgun mics doesn't work well indoors—unless there's a lot of sound absorption material, such as furniture. Sound reflecting off the wall skews the frequency and draws attention to the echo sounds. If all you have is a shotgun mic, typical of run-and-gun-style doc shooters, video journalists, and indies, be aware of the space you're in and adjust the direction of the mic, as needed. Holding the mic from below, for example, may minimize sounds bouncing off the walls.

When pointing a shotgun mic at someone, remember that it will pick up sound behind the person, so if she is standing on a sidewalk and you're facing the street with the camera-mic setup, you'll get loud traffic noise. If you have the person turn around so you're facing a storefront, you'll get much cleaner sound. When shooting a documentary in Hood River, Oregon, I interviewed many people on the street asking them about their Sasquatch sightings. The shotgun mic was held close to them, and traffic noise was minimal, despite the number of cars and trucks rumbling by. In addition, holding your mic up in the air (with a boom pole or pistol grip) and pointing down toward your

Getting the Right Mic and Using a Boom Operator

Filmmaker David Anselmi says that "even a crappy mic sounds better on a boom! A mic with a boom pole and a good boom operator can give you great sound—much, much better than a $1,000 Sennheiser 416 mounted on the camera!"

In addition, Anselmi recommends going for microphones in the $600–$1,000 range. "You may want to do an A/B comparison of a lower end mic with a high end mic with excellent audio monitors, so you can hear the difference— you'll never be satisfied with a $250 mic again. Also, for outdoors—especially in heavy wind—a blimp is essential." Words of wisdom as you shop for the right microphone. Testing is always the best rule of thumb. If you're in New York City, B&H Photo has an audio room where you can test microphones (other professional video/audio gear stores will also allow you to test microphones).

performer's voice will also minimize external sounds, because extra noise reflection is minimal when pointing toward the ground.

Most lavaliere mics are omnidirectional, picking up sound from all directions. If you want someone to sound close up and personal, the lav mic, when wired properly, provides good, clean sound. Lavs require a transmitter that typically hooks to the subject's belt, and a wire attached to the mic is strung up beneath the subject's shirt and hooks onto the shirt collar (see Figure 4.6). An XLR wire connects the transmitter box to the camera's XLR adapter. There are also wireless

FIGURE 4.6
Sennheiser's wireless lav G3 microphone system. It's expensive at about $600, but the wireless will give you a lot of flexibility on shoots. (Image courtesy of Sennheiser.)

models, which allow the transmitter to send the audio remotely to a receiver that connects to the XLR adapter.

Built-in camera mics, no matter the camera, are nearly useless and usually provide poor sound quality. They're useful only for reference audio if you're recording sound externally on a digital recording device. If you must use the onboard mic, make sure it's not windy and make sure your subject is standing less than 3 feet away. For DSLR cameras, phantom power is provided only with onboard external XLR adapters or external digital recorders.

WINDSCREENS

Windscreens are absolutely essential when shooting outdoors, even if there's only a light breeze. Wind impacts a microphone's diaphragm hard and can easily damage your audio. The foam covers that come with microphones are really designed to soften the speech of the performer; they're not windscreens and will not hold up to outdoor use even on a light windy day. Rather, using a wind muff or windscreen is the way to go when there is a breeze. They slip over the microphone, and their thick, furry cover breaks up the impact of light breezes. Some of these are "dead cat" wind muffs that slip over the hard shell of the windscreen to disperse the wind energy (see Figures 4.7 and 4.8).

FIGURE 4.7
The Rycote Softie offers some protection against wind but is not good for moderate levels of wind.

FIGURE 4.8
Rycote's Miniscreen is a great budget option (~$80) for taking out moderate wind noise on a shotgun microphone.

XLR ADAPTERS

If you want to get good sound out of a cinema camera lacking XLR inputs, utilizing a preamp with XLR connectors is one of the best options if you're not using an external recorder. You'll get a rich and clean signal. This option also allows you to use professional XLR microphones for cameras lacking them.

Furthermore, using an XLR cable is a must for recording over a distance of a few feet, and because DSLR cameras and some cinema cameras do not contain XLR inputs, you'll need to use an XLR adapter. JuicedLink and BeachTek are two popular companies that build XLR adapters. The two products I'll describe here also allow for audio monitoring (with headphone inputs), provide phantom power for microphones, and subvert the automatic gain control of the audio in-camera. As noted before, most, if not all, DSLR cameras use AGC.

Be sure the adapter has the proper transformer and circuits; otherwise, the noise resistance natural to the XLR cable will be lost. In addition, the XLR adapter box contains a mini-jack that plugs into the camera's mic input; this input can easily break. Some people hot-glue the right angle connector into the minijack and cable-tie the slack to the camera, connecting and disconnecting the cable from the adapter box.

FIGURE 4.9
BeachTek's DXA-SLR model.
(Image courtesy of BeachTek.)

BEACHTEK DXA-SLR XLR ADAPTER

BeachTek's DXA-SLR model includes a microphone preamp (15 dB) to help provide a clean signal for your microphone (see Figure 4.9). It's designed so you can access the battery of the Canon 5D. It also utlizes 48 volts of phantom power, which is an added bonus for powering your mics. It doesn't contain LED meters for monitoring audio input levels, but it uses a single LED to indicate red when audio clips.

JUICEDLINK'S PREAMP DT454

JuicedLink's preamp DT454 provides clean audio with the circuitry of its preamp—a product designed for cameras needing XLR adapters (see Figure 4.10). It overrides the automatic gain control of some DSLRs. It allows you to use up to two XLR mics, as well as two minijack unbalanced mics (useful for those who own Rode's VideoMic Pro but want a clean connection and clean sound). It also includes LED level meters, a headphone jack (a must-have!), as well as 48 V and 12 V of phantom power.

FIGURE 4.10
JuicedLink's preamp DT454.
(Image courtesy of JuicedLink.)

PISTOL GRIP AND BOOM POLE

Pistol grips and boom poles are basic tools if you're working with a crew. If you're running and gunning, then stick with your onboard external microphone, but if you have at least one other person helping out on the shoot, use a boom pole to bring your mic in close to your subject. A pistol grip provides a similar tool for medium and close-up shots (see Figure 4.11). I've sat in a chair during an interview and handheld the mic with a pistol grip, just out of frame, and received excellent quality sound because I can place the mic a foot or two closer to the subject than just placing it on-camera. In this kind of setup, I put the camera on a tripod, use an external audio recorder, and sit beside the camera so I can monitor the image during the interview.

EXTERNAL RECORDERS

If you want to get good clean audio, several products by Zoom and Tascam offer external recorders with professional XLR inputs. (See Figures 4.12 and 4.13.)

Essentially, these recorders allow you to hook up a professional microphone to their XLR inputs, so you'll get the clean audio. There are also a variety of settings that can be chosen, but be sure to pick a non-MP3 compressed format. Use 44.1 kHz, 16-bit or 48 kHz, 24-bit (or the one that matches the audio compression of the camera—if it's a different rate, you may get material out of sync). You will still record audio on the camera's microphone and use it as a reference, and replace it with the clean audio after you've synced it up. As a back-up (in case you have to do a manual sync), record a slapping of hands or use a slate at the beginning of the take, and make sure everything's recording; it's sometimes too easy to forget to turn on the external recorder!

Use the Rode VideoMic Pro connected to the camera's shoe as your reference and backup sound (or hook up a shotgun mic to your video camera; then bring in the XLR mic as close as possible). You could consider putting the device on a small tripod. If you're using a minijack microphone, you may want to consider getting the Marantz PMD620 audio recorder. It doesn't have XLR inputs, but it'll give you a clean recording—much better than the on-camera mic.

FIGURE 4.11
A Rycote pistol grip. Great for getting a mic in close when you have tighter shots. The device is designed to minimize handling noise when holding a shotgun microphone. (Image courtesy of Rycote.)

FIGURE 4.12
Zoom H6 audio recorder. (Image courtesy of Zoom.)

FIGURE 4.13
Tascam DR-40 audio recorder. (Image courtesy of Tascam.)

If you do not want to deal with an external recorder and you want the best possible sound out of any video camera or DSLR, you may want to consider a more expensive option (~$750): Sound Devices MixPre-D (see Figure 4.14). It's a portable field mixer and mic preamp that contains unclippable limiters, so, if set properly, it will not blow out any sound. It's made of metal, so the rugged device will hold up to some impact abuse. If you're utilizing this with a DSLR, the MixPre-D includes a locking connector to the DSLR, feeding the field mixer's clean audio to the camera. The chief advantage is the ability to use XLR microphones, but you can also monitor audio, engage phantom power for mics, adjust the levels, and view an LED level meter. Hooking this up to an audio recorder (such as the Zoom H6) will provide pristine sound.

Always record your audio between −24 dB to −6 dB in order to receive a strong signal and to minimize the risk of clipping audio if a subject or performer gets too loud.

FIGURE 4.14
Sound Devices MixPre- is a powerful preamp fo adding quality audio to your recordings. Clean and quiet preamps with unclippable limiters make this one of the most powerful tools in your audio arsenal. It includes a DSLR feature that allows you to input this device directly to th camera's unbalanced (hi impedance) microphon input.
(Image courtesy of SoundDevices.)

HEADPHONES

You need to monitor audio when shooting. The problem with most, if not all, DSLRs is their lack of a headphone jack—thus, the importance of getting an XLR adapter with a headphone input or using an external digital audio recorder. Cinema cameras do contain headphone jacks. Monitoring sound will allow you to know when something's not working right.

With that said, there are headphones designed to sound pretty, and then there are headphones designed to sound accurate: monitor headphones. You want the headphones that sound accurate. One of the best websites detailing unbiased ratings and sales of headphones is: http://headphone.com. For studio use—"Headphones for Studio Use" with a price range of $50–100, go to: https://www.headphone.com/collections/50-100/studio.

Getting the right headphones—within the parameter of making sure they're designed for monitoring sound accurately (studio and/or field production)—is essential. But once you have the choice paired down to headphones that are designed for accurate monitoring, the ones you purchase should be those that are comfortable for you to wear.

MAGIC LANTERN FOR CANON DSLRS

The Magic Lantern firmware hack (instructions and software located here: http://magiclantern.wikia.com/wiki/Unified) adds menu options by installing software on the camera's memory card, adding such professional features as audio meters, headphone monitoring, spot meter, histogram, among other functions on most Canon DSLRs. It is free, but it works only on a limited numbers of cameras. Installing Magic Lantern does void your warranty, and it is not supported by Canon, and this author only recommends it for experienced shooters (he and Focal Press make no warranties or guarantees for your camera). You proceed at your own risk.

Furthermore, Magic Lantern adds audio meter bars on the LCD screen so you can see what the audio is doing. Sescom makes a cable that plugs into the AV port of the camera and converts it to a headphone jack for some of the Canon DSLRs lacking this important feature.

In addition, this tool contains a focus assist that lights up the focal plane with blue pixels, so you don't have to wonder if you're close on the focus—you know you're there (the feature doesn't work well in low light, however).

Another feature includes the focal length of a zoom lens, as well as the focal plane distance, so focus can be pulled more precisely and helps with marking tape. (See Figure 4.15.)

The installation instructions are located here:

- http://magiclantern.wikia.com/wiki/Unified/Install

The user guide instructions are located here:

- http://magiclantern.wikia.com/wiki/Unified/UserGuide

My Magic Lantern menu settings (default unless otherwise noted; read the manual for an explanation of the all the settings):

Audio
- Audio Gain: This is where you adjust the levels. Mine is currently at 23 dB.
- Input Source: You can adjust to include external and internal at the same or choose "external stereo" (which is what I normally do).
- Output Volume: Sets headphone levels. I've set mine to the maximum of 6 dB.
- Audio Meters: ON.

Live (I keep everything off, except the following):
- Global Draw: ON
- Focus Peak: D1xy, 1.0, local (aside from the audio settings, this is the key reason I use Magic Lantern—the ability to know where you are in focus.)
- Spotmeter: Percent, AFF
- Waveform: Small (sometimes I'll use this instead of the histogram).

Movie
- Movie Restart: ON (when the camera hits the 4GB file size limit around 12 minutes, instead of the recording shutting off, it'll turn itself back on, so you'll only lose about a second).

I don't adjust any of the other menu settings.

FIGURE 4.15
Magic Lantern Unified on a Canon 60D. Along the top, we can see the audio meters that change color (green for within the zone, yellow getting hot, red for clipping). It shows the remaining space on the memory card (11.8 GB). The spot meter in the center places the exposure at 34%, while the histogram hovers above center to the right. Along the bottom can be seen the size of the lens and the f-stop setting (50 mm at f/1.8), the shutter speed 1/41, the ISO (400), and the color temperature preset (Sunny).
(Photo by Kurt Lancaster.)

Magic Lantern Case Study—*Occupy Wall Street* with the Canon 5D Mark II

When shooting on the run, it's important to travel light. I was in New York City on other business in October 2011, when I decided stop sta Zuccotti Park and observe *Occupy Wall Street*. I brought my Canon 5D Mark II with two Zeiss Contax 50 mm f/1.4 and 35 mm f/2.8 lenses with a Lightcraft ND fader, a Sennheiser ME62/K6 omnidirectional condenser microphone (it is a great dialog mic and short), a Lightwave windscreen, a special XLR to minijack connector (made by ETS), a Sescom AV headphone cable, and headphones. I had one spare battery and two 16 GB memory cards. (See video at: http://vimeo.com/30500114>.)

Pulling out my gear, I noticed many others using larger video cameras, but with my low-profile setup I had easy access to many different subjects. I handheld all of the shots (with no rig attached to the camera). I kept the camera close to the subjects (in most cases 3 feet or less) so as to get their audio clear on my mic as possible (see Figure 4.16). Although I wished I had brought along my shotgun mic, I couldn't find the right windscreen, so I kept with the low profile mic, because I had a windscreen, and I felt that was more important than getting the directional sound of a shotgun mic.

I attached the Sennheiser mic to the shoe mount using a shockmount, and plugged it directly into the mic input of the 5D using an XLR to minijack camera balun (the ETS PA910) series, providing a low to high impedance connection to the camera. (See Figure 4.17.) In other words, in a pinch, it'll provide decent audio when you don't have a separate digital audio recorder on hand (such as the Tascam DR-40). Magic Lantern allowed me to see audio meters while recording and monitoring the audio by plugging into the AV port of the 5D. Indeed, I adjusted the audio several times based on the levels I watched.

The omnidirectional aspect of the ME62 picked up a lot of side and background noise, but it ended up adding to the atmosphere of the piece. Furthermore, I stood close to the subject, so the microphone was less than 3 feet away. I shifted my head to the left, while hand holding the camera, so the subject being interviewed would look at me and not the camera. The project was edited by my friend, Stacey Sotosky.

This was my test whether the step-down cable with a high-quality mic could record usable audio. It did. At the same time, Magic Lantern's capabilities for audio monitoring

allowed me to treat the project as if I were using a cinema camera—but with the benefits of the cinematic quality of a Canon 5D Mark II.

FIGURE 4.16
By keeping the camera close to the subject (2.5'–3') at Occupy Wall Street in New York City.
(Lancaster, Kurt and Stacey Sotosky. *Occupy Wall Street*. 2011. http://vimeo.com/30500114.)
(©2011 Kurt Lancaster.)

FIGURE 4.17
Run and gun: Canon 5D Mark II, Zeiss Contax 50 mm f/1.4 lens, shockmount, Sennheiser, ETS step-down cable (XLR to minijack), headphone adapter by Sescom, and Magic Lantern is installed.

Checklist for Sound Quality

1. Are you indoors or outdoors?
2. What is the surface quality of the environment? Will the sound reverb, or is it absorbed in the environment? If you're getting a lot of reverb, get the microphone in really close.
3. Do you want your subject to sound close?
4. Do you want your subject to sound far away?
5. Can you turn off the automatic gain control? If not, then use an audio adapter (or Magic Lantern on some Canon DSLRs) that turns it off or use an external digital audio recorder.
6. What is your compression value, 16 or 24 bit?

Checklist for External Onboard Minijack Mic

1. Choose your microphone (such as the Rode VideoMic Pro or a shotgun mic with an XLR to minijack step-down cable if shooting with a DSLR), attach it to the accessory shoe plate, and plug the mic directly to the microphone jack of the camera.
2. Turn on the mic (be sure you put a fresh battery into the microphone).
3. If possible, turn off the AGC and set the audio input levels of the camera at 212 dBu to minimize clipped audio (keep the levels under −6 on the meter).
4. Keep your subject no more than a few feet away or so; this will provide the strongest audio signal.
5. Monitor with headphones and adjust levels as needed. If you're shooting with a DSLR with no audio monitoring capabilities, consider installing Magic Lantern.
6. Input your files normally. The audio is recorded simultaneously with the video.

Checklist for External XLR Mic with XLR Adapter

1. Choose your microphone (such as an XLR shotgun mic).
2. Attach the XLR adapter and connect the XLR's minijack plug into the camera's minijack microphone input. (Make sure you put fresh batteries into the adapter.)
3. Plug the mic's XLR cable into input 1 of the XLR adapter.
4. If the camera has automatic gain control (most DSLR cameras do, but read the manual to find out), turn on the XLR adapter's AGC disabler.
5. Use either a boom pole or pistol grip, or mount it to the camera with a shockmount with an accessory shoe adapter. Plug the mic to the microphone input of the XLR adapter.
6. Turn on the phantom power (it'll be either 48 V or 12 V). If you have a 12 V option, you may want to use this to save battery life, but be sure the mic you choose can utilize 12 V of phantom power.
7. Plug in your headphones.
8. Set the max levels of your audio to 212 dBu (−6 on the meter) to help prevent clipping if a performer or subject gets too loud. This will give you 12 decibels of headroom.
9. Keep your microphone less than 3 feet away from the performer.
10. The audio is recorded simultaneously with the video, so no additional steps are needed when you export your files from the camera to the computer.

Checklist for External Recorders (Tascam DR-40)

1. Do two recordings: one on-camera for reference and backup and the other externally. Choose your microphone type and follow the previous checklist for mini-jack on-camera recording. For DSLR shooters, don't worry about an external XLR adapter because that just complicates the workflow. You could just use the camera's mic, but if you hook up a Rode VideoMic Pro, for example, you'll get usable sound, so if something did go wrong in the external recording, you'll have a backup.

2. Most audio recorders contain a tripod screw hole, so you can mount the recorder onto its own tripod, if desired, or mount it to a DSLR rig.

3. Put fresh batteries into the recorder.

4. Choose your microphone for the digital audio recorder (XLR shotgun, XLR lav, or both—using the two different inputs) and hook it up to a boom pole, pistol grip, or tripod. Make sure it's no more than 3 feet away.

5. Attach the XLR cable to the mic and the input of the audio recorder (if you're using two mics, plug both into the recorder).

6. Set your audio recorder's audio compression scheme; be sure it matches the camera's recording capabilities (it'll most likely be 44.1 kHz, 16-bit or 48 kHz, 24-bit). Some recorders can do 96-bit, which will give you an even better recording to work with in post. Just be sure the kilohertz (44.1 kHz or 48 kHz) matches the camera setting.

7. Unless you're using a field mixer with limiters (such as the MixPre), set the max levels of your audio to 212 dBu (keep the levels below −6 on the meter) to help prevent clipping if a performer or subject gets too loud. This will give you 12 decibels of headroom.

8. Turn on the phantom power (it'll be either 48 V or 12 V). If you have a 12 V option, you may want to use this to save battery life, but be sure your mic can utilize 12 V of power. Otherwise, just stick with 48 V.

9. Plug in your headphones. There's a separate volume control for the headphones, but what you're hearing isn't exactly what you're actually recording!

10. Press Record on the digital audio recorder. The first time you press the Record button, it'll flash red and provide an audio level signal so you can test your levels before actually recording.

11. Set your levels by doing an audio test.

12. Press the Record button a second time to start recording. Double-check the timelapse clock to see if it's ticking; this will assure you that you're recording the audio!

13. Start recording on the camera.

14. Clap your hands or use a slate.

15. Begin the scene.

16. When the scene is completed, press the Stop button. (If you press the Pause button, you will keep one file if you press the Stop, then each time you record, a new file will be created—which is useful when recording multiple takes of video.)

17. Take note of the file number on the audio recorder, so you can match it to the right take on the camera.

18. Export the camera's video-audio footage into your computer.

19. Export the audio from the audio recorder.

20. Sync audio in post.

Still from Kurt Lancaster's *Tracking Alewives for the Passamaquoddy*. ©2016. Used with permission.

CHAPTER 5

KEY CONCEPTS IN POSTPRODUCTION WORKFLOW

It does not matter what software you use for editing. Most software engage in the same tools, but use different types of interfaces and capabilities. For example, DaVinci Resolve contains the most tools and control when color correcting, and they've added tools for picture and sound editing. Can the software do what you need it to do? And does the software give you a certain amount of pleasure—or cause the least amount of frustration—when editing via the interface? If both those answers are yes, then that's the one you should use.

SOFTWARE COMPARISON CHART

Software	Avid	Final Cut Pro	Premiere	DaVinci Resolve
Cost	Free (for limited version) $50/month ($600 per year)	$300 (additional cost for Motion and Compressor ($50 each)	$35/month $420/year	Free $300 pro version
Platform	Apple and PC	Apple	Apple and PC	Apple and PC
Cloud or stand-alone	Cloud and stand-alone	Stand-alone	Cloud	Stand-alone
Learning curve	High	Low	Medium	Medium to High
Penetration rate	Hollywood and some news outlets; some independent productions and production houses.	Independent films, production houses, and some news outlets.	Independent films and production houses.	Unknown for editing.

The steps in workflow are similar across all software—they're designed to allow you to put different clips together, trim them, slow down and speed up footage, move clips around in a different order. It's where sound gets mixed and mastered, where footage gets cleaned up. It's where flat log footage becomes beautiful. It's where the look and feel of a movie are created. And those are just a few of the steps comprising postproduction. The postproduction phase separates the amateur from the professional, where technical skills and artistry come together in what can be considered a painstaking, but creative, task of the filmmaker. It's for those who pay attention to details.

Rather than attempting to teach software interface operation—something this book does not have the space to achieve—this chapter will dig into some of the key elements of what to look for and be aware of in the postproduction pipeline, including the steps needed to take in preparing footage, some of the purposes behind editing for storytelling, including rhythm and pacing, an overview of the tools used in editing, the differences between color correction and color grading, how to take a flat log look and make it look compelling, using LUTs to change the look and feel of a film, the function of sound mixing, and the power of sound design in post.

I will zoom in on some visual examples using DaVinci Resolve when describing color correction and grading and when I need to show an example of an editing tool and/or a sample in Final Cut. Again, I'm not teaching how to use software step-by-step. There are plenty of books and online tutorials that will guide you far more adeptly than I can in the limited space of this chapter. I will provide visuals from the software I'm familiar with as a way to show processes that leads to results.

The most important thing for me is to guide you through the thinking process of why you may want to make certain choices as it relates to story. Workflow is about organization and planning.

HOW CAMERA CHOICES IMPACT THE EDIT

The following technical information provides you with information that will lead you to choose how different types of cameras impact your postproduction workflow. Knowing what these terms are and how they will impact what you want the final image to look like is a core concept behind this chapter.

RESOLUTION, CODECS, SAMPLING, AND BIT DEPTH

This can be the most confusing and most of this occurs in-camera. But it's also important in the postproduction workflow, since you need to make sure your timeline contains the proper settings—although most software contains options so the timeline can conform to the footage.

In either case, you must know how resolution, bit depth, and codec of your footage impacts your creative choices as a filmmaker. It is key in deciding the first steps of the workflow process, what you can really do with it. For example, shooting in 4K with a compressed 8-bit codec will not give you the richness of a 2K or HD shoot with a 10-bit or 12-bit codec. And most of the cameras used by shooters in this book shoot in an 8-bit codec, which is the worst state to be in when facing a need or desire to engage in color correction and grading. When you record in 12-bit raw or 444HQ, you'll have the most headroom in changing the look of your footage in post.

Resolution

The number of pixels recorded. The higher the number, the higher the resolution, but that does not necessarily mean that there is higher visual perception for the audience.

- SD Standard definition 640x480. Old format no longer used in new cameras.

- HD High definition 1280x720 and full HD 1920x1080. Current standard for Blu-ray DVDs and broadcast television. The 1280x720 is not used as much, but it still is an option on some contemporary low budget cinema cameras.

- 2K Cinema resolution 2040x1080 quality for projection.

- 4K UHD (ultra high definition) 3840x2160 and True 4K 4096x2160. 4K is the future, according to marketing forces trying to get you to buy new televisions.

- 8K UHD 7680x4320 and True 8K 8192x4320. Anything above 4K is not needed and it's arguable that 4K is really needed.

Cinematographer Steve Yedlin, ASC (whose latest film is *Star Wars: The Last Jedi* (2017), presents a compelling data-driven case about resolution in "A Clear Look at the Issue of Resolution," published on American Cinematographer's online site (24 July 2017) (see https://theasc.com/articles/a-clear-look-at-the-issue-of-resolution). In it he does a comparison of several high-end cinema cameras, including Arri (35mm film and digital), Red Weapon (6K), Sony F55, an Imax 65mm camera (scanned at 11K).

> There is no perceptual difference between a 6K source scaled down to 4K projection and the same source choked to 2K amount of data, then scaled up to 4K.
>
> -Steve Yedlin, ASC

He argues that cameras collect data and different brands of cameras do not necessarily contain different looks, as well as arguing that the visual perception of the audience hits a limit and when perceived in a cinema situation—and not a pixel-by-pixel analysis—there is no perceptual difference between a 6K source scaled down to 4K projection and the same source choked to 2K amount of data, then scaled up to 4K.

In about five and half minutes into the second video on the site, Yedlin shows his experiment based on controlled variables ("the variables are controlled in the absolute, ultimate way possible," he explains). He feels that people certainly can "compare 6K to 2K" with different cameras containing "different noise, different photosites—everything's different," but he was interested in using literally the same image for the comparison. Not only the same camera, but the same frame, so you don't even have frame-to-frame variables impacting the comparison. So the idea was, what if I only have 2K of this 6K image—what if I have to choke it all the way down to this[?] What does that image look like in comparison to the 6K original after it is scaled up to 4K? And then we see how very little the resolution actually matters; it's almost indistinguishable.

(See Figures 5.1 and 5.2.)

FIGURE 5.1
This image is cropped in, showing a close-up of a subject shot on a 6K Alexa and then scaled down to 4K UHD.
(Courtesy Steve Yedlin ©2017 Steve Yedlin.)

FIGURE 5.2
The same shot, now showing a 6K Alexa source choked down to 2K, then upscaled to 4K. Yedlin argues that there is no perceptual visual difference between this image and the 6K to 4K image shown in Figure 5.1.
(Courtesy Steve Yedlin ©2017 Steve Yedlin.)

What does make a difference, he says, is the type of scaling algorithms used to output the image to 4K resolution—not the pixel count. Indeed, Yedlin found that the 3K camera was more "resolute" in image perception than some of the 6K cameras. Ultimately, Yedlin feels that the function of a camera (whether film or digital) is to collect data, information that can be manipulated. Indeed, he contends, "how you display that information later [is] not enforced by the camera brand." But he feels marketing teams of camera brands have sold us a bill of goods that's not necessarily true, but we accept the manufacturer's take on a camera, because

> it's been so ingrained in us that the machine that takes that measurement decides what to do with the data. We're so conditioned to believe this that we don't even look at a lot of the stuff that's down the road in the image pipeline and can be far more instrumental in the final image quality. But because of the feedback loop, we've tended to believe that cameras do have different inherent looks. And we make decisions based on that false premise.

The best way to determine the quality of the resolution is to test several cameras in a controlled variable experiment, Yedlin says, in order to best determine what camera you should use for a production.

> We've tended to believe that cameras do have different inherent looks. And we make decisions based on that false premise.
> -Steve Yedlin, ASC

As for 4K versus 2K, most theaters uses 2K projection, so those who are shooting 4K now will not have a large audience see their work in 4K, since most of cinema projection is still 2K and most television sets are full HD—although more and more televisions are being released with 4K capability. However, there are increasingly more cameras being released that shoot 4K. There are several benefits to shooting in 4K now:

- Future proof. Store your film or project in 4K so it's ready when there's a market for it.

- Cropping a shot. The editor may want to crop an image and if you have a large area of resolution (such as 4K), then the image can be cropped or recomposed for an HD or 2K project without losing any data, such as the image going soft.

- Fixing unwanted motion in a shot. There might be a wobbly shot that allows software to fix that motion. If you're shooting in full HD or 2K, that software will share and grab data around the wobbly shots in order to fix it. If there's no space around the shot, then the image will lose some resolution, but if there's a lot of space around it (4K), then it can pull data above full HD and 2K without losing any resolution.

- If you're doing work for Netflix, HBO, among others, 4K production is required.

Codecs

Codecs are video and audio coding formats, essentially a software coder/decoder for compressing and decompressing footage. Consumer and even low-end cinema cameras (such as the Canon C100) compress footage to a great degree, increasing recording space while maintaing good image quality. The higher the bit rate, the higher the quality. DVDs and web videos utilize compressed formats.

Some of the video codecs include:

- MPEG-2: An older lossy video compression used for broadcast transmission and DVDs.

- H.264/MPEG-4: A compression standard used in most applications, from Blu-ray DVDs to web streaming, as well as digital cinema camera encoding.

- H.265: The next generation beyond H.264, offering double the compression while maintaining the same level of video quality. Important for 4K compression. This format supports up to 8K.

- Containers wrap particular formats around codecs, providing metadata.

- AIF/WAV: Uncompressed audio formats, the former developed by Apple, the latter by Microsoft and IBM.

- AVCHD: Popular container holding H.264/MP4 formats.

- AVI: Standard audio/video containers for Microsoft.

- MOV: Apple ProRes QuickTime container for MPEG-4 and it is really interchangeable with MP4—although some cameras, such as the C100 Mark II, record compressed audio (MP3) when using the MP4 format.

- MP4: Audio video container for MPEG-4 formats.

Sampling

The eye perceives the nuance of brightness more than color. To take advantage of this, chroma (or color) subsampling compresses color information to save space. In this type of compression, there's one piece of information for luminance (black and white or brightness) and two for color (chrominance). The numbers represent the one brightness sample rate (given as a 4) and two-color sample rates among a group of pixels (given as a 0—no sample; 2—half sample; or 4—full sample, no compression). All pixels get full brightness or luma values, thus these sequences always begin as 4. (When there's a fourth number 4, that represents the chroma channel for green screen work.)

4:4:4

No compression. All light and colors are sampled at the same rate. There is no subsampling, so this provides the strongest image for postproduction work. Each pixel contains luma (brightness) and chroma (color) data. Provides for the most headroom in post, especially when doing green screen work, which is called the alpha channel and it is represented by a fourth digit). Greatest ability to alter color and exposure values in post color correction and color grading work. This is the 12-bit RAW standard.

When you're shooting an 8-bit compression format, the look is baked in—not much can be done in post. When working with RAW or in 10-bit workflow, you can shape the look of the film in post. You can either design or apply existing look up tables (LUTs) to a project—which provides color grading to the work, giving it a specific style of film look. This is why RAW is so attractive to some filmmakers—you can shape nearly any look you want without destroying the original, so in many ways it's a throwback to shooting on original film stock, but with more freedom.

4:2:2

In a four pixel sample, all the luma values are used (4), but only half the color data (2:2) is used. The image is considered very good and nearly indistinguishable from 4:4:4—except when you need to do heavy post work, when the image will fall apart into blocky, noisy artifacts, and banding across colors. This is the standard ProRes codec, providing a clean image with some ability to change color and exposure values in post. Circumventing the 8-bit compression scheme of many cameras, Atomos and Video Devices make video recorders that allow such cameras as the 8-bit compression found in the C100 and DSLRs to record in 10-bit 4:2:2 with a feed from the HDMI out (some higher-end models do record 4:4:4). On the other hand, Black-magic Design created their cameras that allow for ProRes recording in-camera.

4:2:0

Same level of luminance, but now half the color data of 4:2:2. And this is the sampling rate found in nearly every DSLR and consumer video camera (and Canon's lower-end cinema cameras), recording in different versions of H.264 compression wrappers (such as MP4 and AVCHD). The image will fall apart quickly in post if you have to make changes to the image—so the importance of getting the image right in-camera.

See Chapter 7 for a chart summarizing the compression scheme of the most popular types of codecs found in cameras.

Below we see similar images with different codecs from the documentary I shot, *Tracking Alewives for the Passamaquoddy*, the original shot on a Digital Bolex D16, 12-bit (uncompressed CinemaDNG RAW), imported into DaVinci Resolve for color correction, and then exported as ProRes 444XQ (4:4:4), 422HQ (4:2:2), and in H.264 (4:2:0).

(See Figures 5.3–5.6.)

FIGURE 5.3

CinemaDNG, 12-bit CinemaDNG RAW image of Asha Ajmani from *Tracking Alewives for the Passamaquoddy*, shot on a Digital Bolex D16, uncorrected (image as shot in-camera).
(Courtesy Kurt Lancaster.)

FIGURES 5.4 AND 5.5

Above, a CinemaDNG, 12-bit image (a few beats later from the CinemaDNG file in Figure 5.3), after applying a basic color correction in Resolve, then exported as a ProRes 444XQ. Screengrab from QuickTime player.

Below, the same image exported as ProRes 422HQ. Screengrab from QuickTime player.
(Courtesy Kurt Lancaster.)

FIGURE 5.6
Now I've exported the color corrected image from Resolve as an H.264 file (subsampled at 420). Screengrab from Quick-Time player.
(Courtesy Kurt Lancaster.)

Outside the basic color correction applied in DaVinci Resolve from the original in Figure 5.3, there's not much of a difference among the images, but I also haven't attempted to change the image in the extremes. (The color correction is not the final look of the film, since additional correction was made in Final Cut with Koji Color film emulation appled. See the complete short documentary at: https://vimeo.com/135755739. There is really no perceptual loss of image quality among these codecs. On a close-up examination, we can begin to see differences in quality. (See Figures 5.7–5.9.)

FIGURE 5.7
I've zoomed all the way in on Ajmani's eye using the ProRes 444XQ, where we can see nuances of color among the pixels.
(Courtesy Kurt Lancaster.)

FIGURES 5.8 AND 5.9

Above, I've zoomed all the way in on her eye on a ProRes 422HQ file, where we can begin to see some color data loss among the pixels.

Below, I've zoomed all the way in on her eye, again on an H.264 file subsampled at 420. Here we see a lot of color data loss among the pixels, revealing an increase in blocky artifacts.

(Courtesy Kurt Lancaster.)

Bit depth

The color bit depth of a camera is far more important than resolution. It is the amount of data provided for color information per pixel on the sensor. Chroma subsampling refers to how this data is handled from the sensor to the recording of the data—compressed (4:2:2, 4:2:0, or uncompressed 4:4:4). You can do more with a 10- or 12-bit camera in 2K than a 4K camera shooting 8-bit. Bit depth provides more data, especially when it comes to the thickness of images. When it comes to post-production work, the more bit depth there is, the more that can be done with the images in post.

8-bit

Most of the cinema cameras profiled in this book shoot 8-bit, which means the cameras do put out images that look good—it just requires accurate processing of color and exposure during production. It represents 16.7 million shades of color (8 bits = 256 reds x 256 greens x 256 blues). That's certainly enough for viewing accurate color! However, when you start altering colors and brightness in post, it's not quite enough. Any correction or changes made in post must be minimal, or the image will likely fall apart if pushed too hard, resulting in resolution issues and artifacting/pixel blocking, as well as increase in noise. Shooting in 8-bit is similar to shooting a JPEG image in a stills camera and putting it into Photoshop and realizing that there's not much that can be done with the image without losing image quality.

10-bit

Delivers 1024 bits of information per color channel. We're now up to over a billion colors or 1074 million colors, which provides some decent headroom in post. A professional codec found in professional broadcast cameras and higher-end cinema cameras. A 10-bit codec allows for some changes in postproduction. Blackmagic Design's cameras can shoot with 10-bit codecs.

12-bit

Offers 4096 bits of information per color channel. Now we're up to nearly 68.7 billion colors! It offers the densest capabilities for altering footage, where an image's color and exposure can be completely changed with little to no image quality loss. The Digital Bolex D16 shoots in 12-bit RAW, while the Canon C200 shoots in a compressed 12-bit RAW, allowing for a lot of leeway in shaping the look of the film in post.

KEY ELEMENTS IN THE WORKFLOW PIPELINE

ORGANIZATION AND BACKING UP FILES

Whether you're using a cloud server or physical hard drives next to your computer, be sure you have multiple backups of your footage and edits. Hard drives fail. If you only have one, then all of your hard work on shooting and editing will vanish in seconds. Back up your files daily.

Furthermore, control where your files are—name folders, name files, and keep different types of material in different folders. For example, audio should have its own folder, photos and images go in another, while footage from your camera can go into its own folder or subfolders (interviews, dialogue, action shots, etc.). In the end, there are no rules on how you organize your footage, but you should have everything clearly labeled, so if someone needs to take over your project they could find all the elements with logical names.

PREPPING FOOTAGE

Most 8-bit cameras shoot in what's called long groups of pictures, where data in one frame is shared (interpolated) with other frames—this is done to save data space, but it's not so good for editing, since if you slice between key frames in the middle of the shared data, the image may not display correctly. If your software can't play back and edit certain types of footage, then you need to process the footage into a form that it can handle. This usually occurs during the import stage and you can determine how the files are decompressed (or decoded).

And even if an 8-bit camera shoots in a format that allows for the recording of every frame, the image may still be in a form that's still compressed (such as recording in an 8-bit 4:2:0 chroma subsample). For example, with Canon's C200, it can shoot in a mode called Cinema RAW Light in a 12-bit, 4096x2160 resolution at 24p on a CFast card. But if you were to use an SD card, then the camera would record an MP4 file at a range from full HD to UHD resolution in an 8-bit chroma subsample of 4:2:0. This is fine as a reference, but not nearly as good as RAW.

Furthermore, different types of containers may not be compatible with some software. The Canon C100 Mark II can record in AVCHD (or MP4), but the AVCHD wraps the files in one large container. These can be broken apart, and most editing software will do this, but if it can't, then you need to import the footage into another software (for example, see Free AVCHD to Mov app). There you can convert it to different types of formats.

Whatever the file type, you can choose to change the chroma subsample and resolution at import (upscaling). For example, I would take all 8-bit 4:2:0 footage and import them as ProRes 422HQ (the highest quality of ProRes 422 chroma subsampling). If I'm shooting RAW, then I'll import the material in DaVinci Resolve, do a color grade to the footage, then export as ProRes 444HQ, then import the footage into Final Cut Pro for editing and additional grading work. The ProRes 444HQ keeps the footage at 12-bit, so I can do additional color work in Final Cut without having to go back to Resolve.

Whether you're scaling 2K footage to 4K and/or changing the chroma sample from 4:2:0 to 4:2:2 or higher, test the workflow with a few shots before committing to a particular format and/or resolution. You need to know what the end result will look like on a projector before committing to these choices.

TIMELINE

The timeline is where you place footage for editing and adding effects. You can conform a variety of different formats into one format on the timeline. It's the place where you can trim, move, slow down, speed up, add text, add film looks, etc.

FRAME RATES

You can change the speed of your footage to make it speed up or slow down on the timeline. Slow motion tends to emphasize a psychological moment and clues the viewer into dramatic moments of a film. Slow motion can be attained by shooting at a high frame rate, such as 60p or higher, then reconforming the footage on the timeline at 24p. At 60 fps, more than twice the data is being recorded than footage filmed at 24 fps.

Let's say you shoot a seven second shot at 60 fps, then place it on a 24 frame rate timeline. It will remain seven seconds and look normal until you apply the effect. In Final Cut Pro, you could decide to trim the seven second shot to a two second segment, then stretch that segment out to six seconds, slowing that moment down by three times. You could just apply the slow motion to a 24 fps shot and force the timeline to conform, but the image may fall apart (Final Cut has a modification called Optical Flow that will help prevent the image from falling apart). The higher the frame rate, the more data you receive for slowing down the footage without it falling apart. Most cameras profiled in this book shoot up to 60p. The Sony a7R II can shoot up to 120 fps (in 1280x720p resolution mode).

L-CUTS AND J-CUTS

Often, you want dialog from character B to fall under shot of character A—we hear B's dialog as we see A's reaction. If you did a clean cut where one person talks and we see her, then cut to the other person talking and see him, then we cannot control rhythm and pacing of your film. The L-cut has audio falling on the right side of the timeline, while the J-cut falls on the left side (thus the names L and J). (See Figures 5.10 and 5.11.)

FIGURE 5.10
This edit that lacks rhythm and pacing. In a screenshot of the timeline edit from my documentary, *Tracking Alewives for the Passamaquoddy*, we can see how the audio is embedded in the head shot of Asha Ajmani, with ambient sound occurring with the two clips previous to her speaking, making these three shots twenty-two seconds long. The pacing feels slow. It doesn't work.
(Courtesy Kurt Lancaster.)

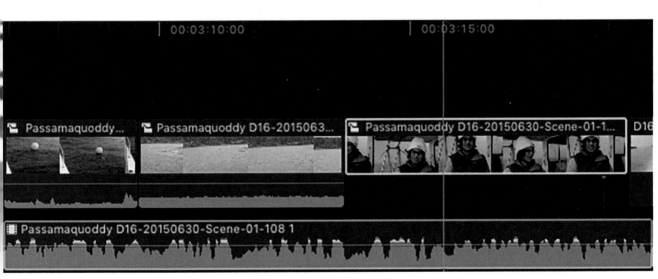

FIGURE 5.11
Using a J-cut by extending the dialog of Ajmani beneath the previous two shots, we can now feel the rhythm and pacing of the film change for the better. I've also kept the ambient audio in those two previous shots. If the ambient audio is too loud and we can't hear our subject speaking, then be sure to lower the volume of the ambient audio. The sequence is now seven seconds shorter and the rhythm and pacing feels much better. The J-cut smooths out the transition.
(Courtesy Kurt Lancaster.)

PHOTOS AND MOVEMENT

Ken Burns made photographic motion in films famous in his *Civil War* (1990) documentary series. For example, in a shot of Eastman Johnson's painting, *A Ride for Liberty: The Fugitive Slaves*, Burns starts close on the image and slowly pulls out to a wider shot over the course of nine seconds, then holds the shot for another twelve. (See Figures 5.12 and 5.13.)

FIGURE 5.12
Burns begins close on the painting so we can see some detail in Johnson's painting, *A Ride for Liberty: The Fugitive Slaves*. He slowly pulls out over the course of nine seconds.
(Ken Burns *Civil Wars*. ©1990 Florentine Films.)

FIGURE 5.13
Nine seconds later, we see the end result of the slow pull-out from Johnson's painting, *A Ride for Liberty: The Fugitive Slaves*, used as a motion technique by Ken Burns in his *Civil War* series.
(Ken Burns *Civil Wars*. ©1990 Florentine Films.)

SCREEN TEXT

Screen text can be used for lower-thirds titles of subjects talking in a documentary or subtitles for closed captioned accessibility. Choose san-serif fonts for on-screen material (these are the fonts that don't have the curly edges, such as Calibri, Arial, and Verdana), since these are easier to read on screens.

SOUND DESIGN

Sound design is half of your film—or at least it should be. If you or someone on your team do not spend a lot of time on this, your film will be weaker than it should be. Record each sound discretely in layers so that during the audio mix, you can adjust each element individually: dialog, room tone, environment, foley/sound effects, and music. See Figure 5.14.

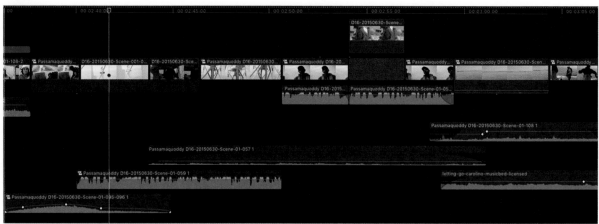

FIGURE 5.14
A segment of discrete sound design layers from *Tracking Alewives for the Passamaquoddy* in Final Cut Pro. Notice the use of nodes on the volume bar, allowing you to adjust specific segments of the volume in a clip.
(Courtesy of Kurt Lancaster.)

Most beginning filmmakers think sound design is just the addition of music, but it includes far more:

Dialog

Should be a clean recording. If dialog needs to be replaced, a sound recording studio can help with ADR (automatic dialog replacement), where the performers come into a sound proof audio studio and record the dialog on individual microphones in order to get the cleanest recording.

Room tone

The ambience of the environment the scene was recorded in, giving the editor audio to fill in dead audio spaces in an edit.

Environment

Ambient audio is probably the most important element of a sound design, for this places the viewer into the environment of the film—whether fiction or nonfiction—and more than any other tool in conventional cinema, it's the one that will immerse them into the world of your film. Take note of this and think deeply about what it means. Start listening to the environment of films (close your eyes and analyze the sound designs of scenes). You can create audio environments from several layers of sound.

Foley and sound effects

Foley artists record sound effects and environmental sounds in a sound proof sound stage room, using props and surfaces to create a variety of sounds. For example, the sound of a woman in high heels may not have reached the clarity or type of sound the director wished during the shoot. The Foley artist will put on shoes (or one of the team members) and walk on a hardwood floor in a small sound stage to get the recording desired. Sound effects may be mixed with other sounds to get the desired effect. See *The Foley Artist* at: https://vimeo.com/124053378. (See Figures 5.15 and 5.16.)

FIGURES 5.15 AND 5.16
Director Oliver Holms creates a fictionalized world of a Foley artist and a woman protagonist on-screen in *The Foley Artist*. In these two shots, there is a cut to the woman reaching to turn off her alarm (above), followed by a match cut of the Foley artist completing the action on a particular alarm clock (below), one of several he can choose from. Note the microphone placed to pick up the audio of pressing the alarm clock button.
(©2015 Feast Films.)

SOUND MIXING AND MASTERING

Once you have your layers of sound, you need to adjust the volume of each later at particular moments during the film (not just for the entire scene). Moments may include a few frames, or it might include the full scene.

Include fade-in and fade-outs of a couple of frames at the beginning and end of clips to avoid any artifact noise (an electronic pop). See Figure 5.14.

COLOR CORRECTION

Footage may need fixing if shots were over- or under-exposed, or if there is an issue with the wrong color temperature recorded. If you chose to shoot "flat" footage in-camera—a process that allows for increased exposure latitude—then you will need to adjust highlights and shadows to increase contrast and get rid of the flat look.

The goal in color correction involves making the exposure and color of footage appear even from shot to shot within a scene.

COLOR GRADING

Color grading is the process by which a colorist shapes the look and feel of the film by changing color, exposure, and applying effects, such as film emulation plugins. In my short, *Tracking Alewives for the Passamaquoddy*, after doing basic color correction I applied Koji Color's Kodak emulation 3514 film stock to the project.

(See Figures 5.17–5.20.)

FIGURES 5.17 AND 5.18
To the left, a still of the image off of a Bolex, as shot.
Color correction of the shot in DaVinci Resolve.
(Courtesy of Kurt Lancaster.)

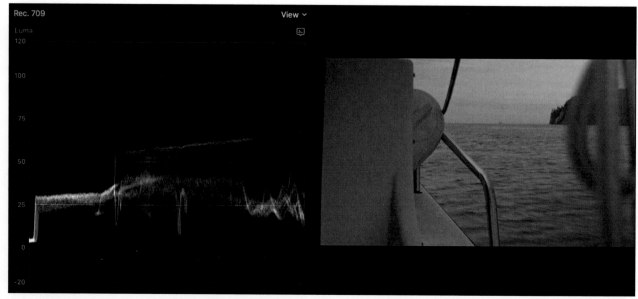

FIGURES 5.19 AND 5.20
Above, color correction before using Koji film emulation.
Below, color correction and Koji Color film emulation software. The tool allows for the use of color correction tools, such as adjusting the color temp, lift, gamma, and gain.
(Courtesy of Kurt Lancaster.)

RHYTHM AND PACING

If a short film or a scene feels too long—and yet it is of a short duration—then there's either something wrong with the rhythm and pacing or the story simply doesn't work. If it feels a bit short—when your audience is left wanting more, then you've done your job as a filmmaker.

The performance of the film's subjects, as well as the visuals and the sound design, influence and shape the rhythm and pacing of a film. In a scene, if a shot doesn't convey anything new—if it doesn't progress the story through new information, emotion, or plot point—then the shot is useless. In a film, if the scene doesn't convey information, emotion, or plot point, then the scene isn't doing its job. The editor must be in tune with the beats and rhythm of the story in order to bring it all together and deliver a scene and film with emotional impact to an audience. The director's job is to deliver the shots for the editor, while the editor in essence puts together the final draft of the film story.

In the following scene, we can feel the rhythm and pacing failing to deliver a cinematic experience to the audience.

By utilizing a variety of editing tools, the editor can reshape the rhythm and pacing of the scene and make it more compelling:

Identify the scene shift: In every scene, there should be an emotional beat where the story changes. Nicholas Proferes calls this the fulcrum, Norman Hollyn calls it the lean forward moment. It is the turning point, where the plot shifts in a new direction. It could be a new piece of information that causes a character revelation or insight that shifts the plot in a new direction or a decision a character makes (usually through escalating action or stakes). Any good director would have identified this before shooting and make sure that it's there when shooting the scene. Typically, we may find it in a close-up. If the director shot coverage (covering the entire scene in a wide shot scene master, medium shots of performers, then close-up of each performers, including cutaway shots), then the editor will usually use the close-up at the emotional turning point since a close-up captures the strongest emotion in a character. Once this point is clearly identified, make sure the editing rhythm and pacing build up to this point—don't waste a close-up on something that's isn't meant to deliver this turning point. It'll throw off the rhythm of the scene. Wrap all of the other shots and sound design elements around this moment.

Altering shot duration: You can use the trim tool to extend or shorten the duration of shots and be sure to feel how a particular shot influences the rhythm and pacing of previous and following shots. You may also speed up or slow down particular shots, if needed, although this will impact the style of the film. In either case, be sure that the shot expresses the information needed for an audience and that it is of the proper duration for the audience. A shot is too short if the audience isn't given the time to process the information contained in the shot. Extend the shot. If the shot is too long, the audience is waiting for something to happen. This will pull them out of the film.

L- and J-cuts: Explained above, this is the use of overlapping sound design and dialog elements in order lead the audience aurally from one shot to the next, providing a way to smooth the transitions from shot to shot. If the scene feels too staccato or disjointed, then try these tools.

Sound design: Environmental sounds, music, and sound effects create an immersive environment and shape much of the rhythm and pacing of a scene. Use these tools to help draw your audience into the scene.

See Figure 5.10 for an example of a scene that's feeling too long. With the application of a J-cut (see Figure 5.11), the scene feels much better. Along with the proper placement of sound design elements of ambient natural sound and music, the scene feels just right.

Still from Jamin Winans' *Uncle Jack*. ©2010. Used with permission.

CHAPTER 6

Telling Better Stories

HOW TO CREATE INTERESTING CHARACTERS

The key to finding your story is determining what your main character wants and what he or she does to get it. In a wedding video, a bride and groom want to get married; therefore all of your choices, from the look of the film to what shots you choose to shoot, must revolve around this dramatic need.

amin Winans' great Internet short *Uncle Jack* is one of the strongest short films shot on a DSLR—due to the fact that it tells a powerful story. Jack wants to escape his pursuers, while at the same time wanting to keep his niece happy by telling her a fairytale.

n summary, *Uncle Jack* takes the fairytale motif and updates it into a contemporary comedy in which a man is fleeing a crime scene chased by thugs who want him dead. An unconscious clown sits in the passenger seat of the car, while a giggling woman screams with glee in the back seat of the convertible. Bullets fly and Jack's cell phone rings. Without listening to who's on the other end, Jack assumes it's one of his cohorts, and he warns him that the plan has been compromised and to "Get out of here." The film cuts to a young girl on her bed, who quizzically says, "Uncle Jack?" He tries to ditch her, but she insists that he tell her a story because her parents are fighting and he once told her that she could call him any time when that happens. Not wanting to break his word, he tells her a fairytale, using his present predicament as the metaphor for the story. By the end of the film, Uncle Jack and his buddy in the clown suit are cornered in a costume shop, and the niece realizes what's going on and tells her uncle what to do to beat the enemy. After their defeat, Uncle Jack's niece tells him to stop gambling.

The story works well because the main character isn't just a shady character trying to avoid a gambling debt; he's a shady character who loves his niece and doesn't want to disappoint her. Good stories evolve from avoiding the stereotype that tends to drive the profit-motivated bottom line. The famed cinematographer Haskell Wexler, ASC, puts it this way:

> For me, artistic goes beyond the visual image or photograph; it's the totality of the philosophy, the ideas, the personality and the soul of people. Too often, the search for what seems to be commercial—the things that grab

people's attention—opens the door for celebrating antipersonal behavior, celebrating warfare, celebrating ways which do not elevate and serve mankind.[1]

Uncle Jack could have devolved into blockbuster violence, but Winan's takes the story to a deeper level by making Jack a conflicted character who represents something more than a stereotype. Wexler's advice extends to documentaries and news. What kinds of stories are you going to tell? The answer stems from the roots of why human beings tell stories in the first place.

HOW TO TAP INTO THE MAINSTREAM AUDIENCE'S EMOTIONAL CORE

There are probably as many reasons to be entertained by a story as there are people. The films of George Lucas and Steven Spielberg tend to resonate with a wide audience because these filmmakers understand how to shape the images and stories that carry emotional and intellectual meaning for the viewer. Storytellers with broad appeal seem to naturally craft compelling stories that meet the needs or demands of a wide audience.

When storytellers strive to create and capture images that are unique to their own personal perspective, when they're tapping into their subconscious intuition, they can inspire viewers and perhaps teach them something about how to live their lives more fully.

In *Uncle Jack*, Winans taps into larger themes and not only provides us with an entertaining but tragically flawed character, but also uses the niece as the impetus to help change this character into something better than he is. "I liked the idea that the niece was just someone listening to the fairy tale," Winans explains in an interview, "but by the end you realize she's truly part of it and ultimately the knower of all. She's part of his world initially, but by the end, he's part of her world."[2] Being conscious of when such change of character occurs is essential when crafting compelling stories—it's the hinge where your directing and cinematography revolves, since when you know where a character changes, you can craft images that highlight that change.

Whether we want to write our own scripts or shoot another's script, we should choose projects that resonate in some way with our need to tell this particular story. The art of shooting it well—shaping the look and feel of it—will be more honest and clear when we do a project that means something to us. This doesn't mean that when you choose to shoot a wedding or a commercial, for example, every moment of the work is imbued with deep psychological meaning. But a job can be more than a job when we endow it with our passionate view of how we perceive the world. Do we linger on a glance from the bride in a tight close-up when

---

[1]Fauer, J. *Cinematographer Style: The Complete Interview*, Vol. I. American Society of Cinematographers, 2008: 297.

[2]All quotations by Winans in this chapter were conducted by the author in June 2010.

One of the reason's Vincent Laforet's *Reverie* (https://vimeo.com/7151244) is powerful isn't that it was shot on a Canon 5D Mark II. It's that he opened with that romantic kiss between a couple and the guy blows it—he tries to pursue his love but loses it. The story contains power. It resonates with a universal theme of lost love, and most of us have experienced that loss in our own way. And in the hands of a good director-cinematographer, the story can be translated into powerful images that resonate with an audience.

she looks at the groom because we see in this moment a universal moment of truth … and we weld this image to the cultural belief that love can last forever? Maybe.

For Winans, the premise for *Uncle Jack* told through a fairytale lens was about shaping a point of view: "I strongly believe the world we see is a choice of perspective. Some of us see the laws of physics and some of us see magic. The fairy tale theme in a modern context was just choosing to see the typical action (cars and guns) sequence as magical instead." The perspective was shaped by the dramatic need for Jack to tell a story to his niece—not only to keep his promise, but eventually this act provides him self-realization about his own foibles and need for humility and change.

Uncle Jack and his niece—their conflicting dramatic needs that coalesce around a mutual desire to help each other out—express the core of Winans' short. How the characters react to the situation they're in defines who these characters are, and by having Jack become this father figure to his niece in her time of need provides her an opportunity to help save his life over the phone. And the dramatic needs of the characters are what an audience identifies with.

The story sets the tone and becomes the soul of the shoot. The camera is secondary. Philip Bloom, at a DSLR Hdi RAWworks Masterclass held in Los Angeles on March 6, 2010, discussed that it didn't really matter what lenses or camera you use if the content is "engaging"; it's the story that matters.

Always start with characters—from them stems the conflict, thus the drama, and the audience will more easily get caught up in the story.

> Always start with characters—from them stems the conflict, thus the drama, and the audience will more easily get caught up in the story.

Documentary filmmakers Brent and Craig Renaud have made such films as *Warrior Champions*, *Little Rock Central High: 50 Years Later*, *Taking the Hill*, *Off to War*, and *Dope Sick Love*. When asked about shooting short doc projects for the *The New York Times* after the earthquake in Haiti, they discussed the importance of finding stories that others avoid:

We love to tell stories that won't get told otherwise or at least not in the same way. In one story we produced for the *The New York Times* recently we focused on the young Haitian American Navy Corpsmen aboard the *USNS Comfort* hospital ship who have been called upon to be translators for victims of the earthquake in Haiti. With no training at all, these young men and women stepped up and became a lifeline for vulnerable Haitian patients coming aboard the ship, a foreign country really, unfamiliar and scary. The Corpsmen comfort the patients and attend to their needs, letting them know that the United States is here to help. Sometimes they tell the patients that their legs will be amputated, or even that they will soon die. Through the experience of these translators the viewer is given a totally different and interesting look at this crisis. These Corpsmen are national heroes, and had we not profiled them, very few people would have known it. Showing things like this to the world is something that makes us proud.

One of their major themes revolves around the underdog doing something that deepens the human experience. The Renaud brothers capture these moments in their projects because something within compels them to bring back stories that mean something. And at the heart of it is the story—not what camera they shoot on; not the technology—but what story they are going to tell and what characters would compellingly help convey that story.

In our long form documentary work everything is about character. We are more likely to start a project with a character we like rather than an issue or a story. The short form news stories that we produce for the *Times* are a little different, but not a lot. With these stories often we are starting from a larger concept, like the Drug War in Juárez, or the earthquake in Haiti, but whereas most news stories are dominated by a correspondent either on camera or in voice-over, we are still looking for characters to drive the story. We do use some voice-over in these news pieces because it helps focus and keep the stories short. However we use as little as possible. We believe the look on a child's face, or a gesture from a politician, uncommented on can sometimes speak worlds more than an all-knowing voice-over. (Interview with the author.)

WHERE DO GOOD IDEAS COME FROM?

I tell my writing and production students that there is only one of them in the universe, and their job is to discover their unique voice and share that with others. Good stories come from storytellers who are honest with themselves and tell a story that's unique to their voice and passions. If you are going to shoot a scene in which a couple kiss, then you had better film it in such a way that comes from how you see the world—whether that's drawn from a fantasy dream vision, a nightmare, or from real life. In either case, it's rooted in how you feel and see the world. That's essentially what good filmmakers do and helps guide them in shaping images that haven't been seen before. We haven't seen shots quite like those

FIGURE 6.1
The clever and powerful story of *Uncle Jack* revolves around fairytale themes in a few short minutes. In this shot, a Pentax K-7 DSLR is taped to the steering wheel with a wide angle lens to shoot everyone in the car. The car is set in a studio against a green screen.
Video at: http://vimeo.com/9578519.
(© 2010 Jamin Winans. Used with permission.)

in Laforet's *Reverie*. Although we've seen plenty of chase scenes in film, we haven't quite seen the one Winans gives us in *Uncle Jack* (see Figure 6.1). These scenes stem from the vision of how these filmmakers perceive the world. It's their unique voices that help provide power to those images. Then their choice of cameras and how they shape the look and feel of their scenes are coming from the right place—the story.

However, if the shots are too unique—not tapping into the dramatic action of a character with wants and needs—you may end up putting together a pretty film, but you may lose your audience. Without a solid story, you won't likely capture a large audience.

> It's their unique voices that help provide power to those images. Then their choice of cameras and how they shape the look and feel of their scenes are coming from the right place—the story.

In a personal example, when I directed a short written by a former student of mine—*The Kitchen*, set in a 1950s farmhouse—the stifling heat of August would bring in evening thundershowers. In probably every movie I've seen, the sound of thunder always occurs simultaneously with the flash of lightning. But that's not how I observed the world growing up during summer thunderstorms in Maine. There might be distant flashes of "heat" lightning with no thunder, and as it got closer, the lightning flash would always occur first, until it was right overhead. After seeing a flash, we would count the silence until the thunder to determine the approximate distance of the storm (five seconds would be about a mile). So when I crafted the sound design for this short around my experiences as a child in Maine, there would be flashes followed by moments of silence, the moments shortening as the storm intensified—and I paralleled this with the increasing emotional tensions of the film.

Winan's *Uncle Jack* "started with the idea of a character forced to stay on his phone through ridiculous circumstances and yet try to make it seem like everything was fine," the writer-director explains. "From there I asked the question, 'Who's the last person he should want to be on the phone with?' I liked the contrast of a clearly shady guy talking very genuinely and sweetly to a little kid. That quickly led to him translating his current situation into a bedtime story."

Developing Story Ideas by Michael Rabiger (Focal Press, 2006) is an essential read if you really want to tap into your original voice for finding and analyzing stories; it's useful for writers and nonwriters. In it, he presents dozens of writing exercises that will help you discover a unique voice in telling stories. "Discovering the source of your stories," he writes, "those you are best qualified to tell, means looking for causes and effects in your own life and grasping the nature of what you feel most deeply. ... it regularly produces insights that make people more accessible and interesting—both the real people around you and the fictional ones you nurture into existence." The book includes exercises on discovering your voice and influences in life, conducting dramatic analysis, and assessing the feasibility and quality of stories. It also includes a series of writing projects covering tales from your childhood and family stories, retelling a myth in a modern-day setting, telling a story based on dream images, adapting a short story, adapting a news story and a documentary topic, writing a 30-minute fiction piece, and writing a feature film.

Having taught beginning scriptwriting for years, I determined the number of good scripts in my class hovered around 20–25%. After my students began using Rabiger's book, I saw the number of good scripts increase to 75–80%. The exercises work, so, as a professional educator, I do recommend the book.

Essentially, Rabiger guides you through a series of short writing exercises that tap into your memories—whether it's a childhood memory, a story told in the family (such as about the time when my crazy uncle ...). He has you write in the present tense in outline script treatment form. In addition, he provides tools on how to analyze a script for its story structure, as well as how to assess a story for its strengths and weaknesses.

I end this section with a couple of writing exercises that should help you find your voice and begin writing stories (or choosing stories that resonate with you). The first is drawn from Rabiger's *Developing Story Ideas*, and the second presents a way that I developed to write dialog. I include examples to help jump-start the exercises.

Exercise

Discovering Stories You Should Tell and Finding Story Ideas

Modified from Rabiger's *Developing Story Ideas* (Focal Press, 2006: 25–26).[3]

"Survey of Yourself and Your Authorial Goals"

1. Describe the "marks left on you by one or two really formative experiences"—ones that were life-changing or forced you to appreciate life in a different way. It can be happy and/or sad experiences—but it should be something that moved you to experience deep emotions. Keep these notes private. They do not need to be shared.

2. "Develop two or three themes connected with the marks that this main character carries. Examples: isolation; betrayal; the high cost of pretense."

3. "Think of three or four types of characters toward whom you feel particular empathy."

4. "Develop four provisional story topics. Make all four exploit a single theme from your answer to #1," and make each topic contain a main character, explore concerns you care about, and be as different from each other as possible.

5. If you want to work on a fiction piece, write a short three- to five-paragraph story in the present tense and showing only what an audience can see and hear (you can't see thoughts, so keep the story within the main character's point of view and what the audience can see on the imaginary movie screen of your mind). Craft the story around one of these story topics. Be sure to give your main character an agenda: she has a need, desire, or want that she must attempt to fulfill. Make her do it and put an obstacle or two in her way.

Example from one of my former students:

1. Psychological marks (private notes, not published).
2. Develop two or three themes
   a. Shame
   b. Self-destruction
   c. Misdirected anger
3. Three or four types of characters:
   a. Professional career people who obtained "everything" on their own and subsequently destroyed it all on their own.
   b. Someone who lost his/her identity due to self-indulgence (Gollum/Sméagol from *The Lord of the Rings*).
   c. Children who are emotionally abandoned and therefore never feel validated in their own emotions.
4. Four provisional story topics based on the theme of self-destruction:

---

[3]This exercise was published in *Developing Story Ideas*, Second Edition, by Michael Rabiger, Chapter 3, "Artistic Identity." ©2006 Focal Press. Printed with permission.

a. A motivated career woman who is secretly plagued by self-loathing and doubt but strives to be recognized and respected.

b. A daughter pretending that she's successful, happy & healthy in order to protect her mother from the truth about her addiction to drugs.

c. A young thrill-seeker who hangs out with the Moab crowd to ride off cliffs with his bicycle and participates in various daredevil stunts—who is beginning to realize that he really doesn't care if he gets hurt or even dies.

d. An animal rights activist & stray/abused animal rescuer who ends up getting overwhelmed and is finally arrested for animal abuse & neglect.

From this, we can see how this student evolved this theme into this story outline.

Scene 1: A 9-year-old girl named Millie wakes up and pads into the tiny kitchen of a dilapidated, wooden shack, clutching a ragged teddy bear. It is 1927 in rural Oklahoma. Millie sees her mother in the kitchen, staring wildly at the dirty pots and pans strewn all over the sink and table. Millie asks her mother what is wrong. Her mother tells her that ghosts came in during the night and messed up the pots and pans after she'd cleaned them, making breakfast for themselves and leaving before anyone in the house woke up. Millie tries to reason with her mother, but her mother emphatically tells her that she heard the ghosts clanking the pans and making a [ruckus] all night long. Millie presses the teddy bear close to her chest with both arms, turns around and goes back to her room.

Scene 2: Millie comes home from school during a cold winter day and sees that her little 4-year-old brother, Jake, is curled up in the corner, writhing in pain. She runs into the kitchen to tell her mother that something is wrong with Jake. Her mother continues to hum to herself and plod around the kitchen, making some kind of imaginary dinner for imaginary guests. Millie tugs on her mother's skirt, insisting that she come now and look at Jake. Millie's mother shoos her away and tells her it's not polite to interrupt adults when they're having a conversation—even though Millie's mother is the only adult at home right now. Millie runs back into the living room to check on Jake. He is pale and holding his belly. He emits a loud moan and her mother's voice can be heard from the kitchen, telling the children to pipe down and be quiet. Millie runs back into the kitchen once more, begging her mother to please come look at Jake, telling her that he's really, really sick. Her mother stares out the window while she holds an imaginary bowl of imaginary food in one arm and stirs with an imaginary spoon in the opposite hand. Millie runs back into the living room and props open the front door. She clumsily gathers Jake up in her tiny arms. He is almost as big as she is, so she has to pull him up several different ways before she finally gets a good hold of the boy. Millie carefully steps out of the house and down the rickety wooden steps, and sets off across the fields.

Scene 3: Millie toddles across the field with her brother in her arms. She knows the general direction of town and heads for it. She continues walking with Jake, having to set him down every now and then to catch her breath, then gather him up again to keep walking. The hospital is miles away. Millie carries Jake this way all by herself for the entire journey.

Scene 4: Millie finally arrives at the hospital. Nurses notice her as she stumbles up the walkway, exhausted. The nurses run out to grab Jake and help her up. They ask her what is wrong, and she can barely breathe, much less talk. One of the nurses, after one look at Jake, picks the boy up and hurries into the building. Millie is helped inside by the nurses and given a drink of water. Millie sits on the cold, hard wooden bench and waits, her water cup emptied, her dress and face filthy with dirt and dead weeds from the fields she had to cross. She lies down and curls up on the bench.

Scene 5: Millie wakes up. A doctor is touching her shoulder, trying to ask her questions about where her parents are and how she got there. Millie rubs her eyes and gazes up at the doctor, asking for Jake. The doctor informs her that Jake had a serious case of appendicitis, and that if she had not taken him to the hospital when she had, his appendix would have burst and he very likely would have died. The doctor tells Millie that Jake must spend some time in the hospital bed and that she should go home. Millie obediently walks out of the hospital and heads across the miles of fields that lead to home.

We can see the development of an original voice in this story, one that comes from this student's unique perspective on life. We can also see the development of the three-act structure—the emotional arc mapping the change in character: the setup (the daughter notices that there is something wrong with her mother), complications (the daughter tries to get her mother to help the sick brother), climax/crisis (she takes her brother by herself to the hospital), and resolution (the brother survives).

Exercise

Writing Good Dialog

Give two characters conflicting agendas and place them into a scene that occurs in one location in one moment of time. As they speak, do not allow either of them to reveal their agenda through dialog—until the end of the scene (if at all), unless you want your story to sound like a soap opera! This will heighten the subtext—the underlying emotions and motivations of the characters—and will usually lead to good dialog. If you reveal the agenda too soon, the energy will likely dissipate quickly.

Example of dialog with hidden agendas by Margo McClellan:

```
Daytime, outside a posh restaurant on Sunset
Boulevard. PAULY is standing in front of the doorway
and lights a cigarette. He dons a tacky blue jumpsuit
and gold jewelry. A strange looking man, an ALIEN,
wearing a tailored suit that could be Armani (if it
weren't for the fish-scale-like print) stoically
walks up to Pauly.
```

                    ALIEN
Good afternoon. Please take me to
your--

                    PAULY
Hey, is that a vintage Jag?

                    ALIEN
... good afternoon. I would like for
you to--

                    PAULY
Hey man, what kind of mileage you
get in that baby?

                    ALIEN
Mile--

                    PAULY
Yeah I bet she guzzles, eh? But
who gives a crap, right? That car
is HOT.

                    ALIEN
Good ... afternoon ... I would like--

                    PAULY
You don't speak English too good,
do ya?

Pauly glances up and down the street.

                    PAULY
Hey, my girlfriend's comin' out in
a sec. She's gotta SEE this thing!
   (toward restaurant entrance)
Hey, SHEILA! Get yer ass out here,
RIGHT NOW ... you gotta SEE this!
       (to ALIEN)
Hey uh, do you have the time?

                    ALIEN
Time? I--

                    PAULY
HEEEY SHEEEILA!!!

SHEILA sprints out of the restaurant, glancing over
her shoulder. She notices Alien and smiles sweetly,
then looks at Pauly urgently.

                    PAULY
          Here, baby, c'mon—you gotta SEE

          this CAR!

Pauly grabs her arm and starts to pull her toward
Alien's "car."

                    PAULY
               (walking around the car)
          Check this OUT, man!

                    (to ALIEN)
          Hey, you wouldn't mind if we took

          it for a little spin would

          you? I'll give you FIVE HUNDRED

          BUCKS right now if you just let me

          take it around the block. All you

          gotta do is just WAIT HERE 'til we

          get back ...

                    ALIEN
          Wait ... here? You must take me to

          your--

                    PAULY
          Yeah yeah yeah I'll take you

          wherever you wanna go, foreign

          boy. After we get back.

He and Sheila exchange a knowing glance as they get
into the "car." The vehicle begins to sputter, then
starts violently flashing bright yellow and orange.

                    PAULY
               (from inside the car)
          WHAT the--

The "car" winks out of existence. Alien just stands
there, staring at the empty parking space.

                    ALIEN
          Well ... crap.

We can clearly see the two different agendas: The Alien wants directions
to the "leader," while Pauly wants to "borrow" or steal the Alien's ride and
impress his girlfriend. Although it's clear what both characters want, by having Pauly be the lead—taking charge, doing what he wants—he is able to
overcome the obstacle of the Alien character. The Alien, on the other hand,
is clear on what it wants, but its agenda is so at odds with Pauly's that it never

gets a chance—which adds to the comedic flavor of the scene. Good dialog is driven by hidden agendas.

Example of dialog with hidden agenda by Ed Crosby.

```
Will and Joe, two high school students, hang out in
the back of their school. They're smoking cigarettes.
Jennifer skips up to them.
                    JEN
          Hey Will.

                    WILL
          'Sup.

                    JOE
          Hey Jen.
Jen doesn't take her eyes off Will.

                       JEN
          Oh hey ... umm Will, how are you?

                    WILL
          Fine.

                    JEN
          Oh cool.

                    JOE
          What's goin on with you, Jen?

                    JEN
          Nothin much.

                    WILL
          Man, I can't wait to get my leather
          jacket.

                    JEN
          Oh yeah that's a beautiful jacket. It's
          gonna look really good on you.

                    WILL
          Yeah, I know, I've been saving for
          like a month but it's gonna be worth
          it. Man I'm going to look so cool.

                    JEN
          Yeah.

                    JOE
          Hey Jen did you get that note I left
          in your locker?
```

                    JEN
Huh? Uhh no ... I don't know.

                    JOE
Yeah well basically I'm going to
The Rat this weekend to see The
Unseen so I can pick you up a
t-shirt or a pin or whatever 'cause
I remember you said how you liked
them when we were talking about
bands at the pep rally.

                    JEN
What? Oh yeah that would be cool.

                    WILL
That punk rock shit, fuckin sucks.
They can't even play. Sounds like
shit.

                    JOE
It's not about musicianship, Will,
It's about raw aggression.

                    WILL
Yeah cause that's what gets girls
in the mood, "raw aggression."

                    JEN
Ummm, I kind of like it.

                    WILL
Whatever.

                    JOE
Yeah so if you want a t-shirt
They're only like 5 bucks but I can
totally spot you the cash. You can
pay me after or maybe you could buy
me a beer sometime.

                    JEN
Hmmm hmmm. Hey Will, uhhhh ...
Can you give me a ride?

                    WILL
You wanna ride in The Machine?

                    JEN
          Yeah, I love The Machine.

                    WILL
          Sure, babe. What you gonna do

          for me?

                    JEN
          Heh heh.
Jen looks at Joe who is looking at the ground.

                    WILL
          God I love that car. It's like an

          extension of my personality. It's

          like you can look at my car and go,

          "Yeah, that guy is pretty cool."

                    JEN
               (turned off)
          Uhhh yeah.

                    JOE
          That's how I feel about my 10

          speed. One look at that thing

          and the ladies go wild.
Jen laughs.

                    WILL
          What, are you serious? No chick is

          into a guy who rides a bike.

                    JEN
          Yeah, I mean how old are you?

                    JOE
          16.

                    JEN
          And you ride a bike?

                    JOE
          Yeah, that's right I ride a bike!

                    JEN
          Okay, Jesus!

They all stand around shifting uncomfortably. The
schoolbell rings.

                    WILL
          Well, school's out. Gimme another

smoke, Joe. Come on, The Machine
awaits.

>   JOE
>   (Looking at the ground)
I'm gonna walk.

>   WILL
What dude, you live like four miles
from here.

>   JOE
Yeah I know.

>   WILL
You're going to walk four miles in
those ratty tennis shoes. They're
going to fall off by the time you
get home.

>   JOE
I don't care.

>   WILL
Okay, come on, Jen.

>   JEN
Hey, you know, I just remembered
I have detention today.

>   WILL
Okay.

>   JEN
Okay see you guys later.

Jen runs off without looking at either of them.

>   WILL
She is so weird. Alright, man, have
a good walk.

>   JOE
Thanks.

Will walks off. Joe suddenly hauls off and kicks a
garbage can, then he just stands there. He turns to
walk away.

>   JEN
Joe!

>   JOE
Jen?

```
Jen walks out from behind the school.
                    JOE
          Will left already.
                         JEN
          Oh.
She looks around and fidgets.
                    JOE
          What happened to detention?
                         JEN
          Uhhh ... cancelled ... yeah they

          cancelled it.
They both stand there looking uncomfortable.
                         JOE
          Well I was gonna go ...
                              JEN
          YES!

                         JOE
          Yes?

                              JEN
          I mean what were you going to say?
                         JOE
          I was gonna go home and listen to
          records.
                              JEN
          Oh that sounds cool.
                         JOE
          I mean you could come too if you

          wanted.
                              JEN
          Uhhh sure.
They walk off together smiling.
```

The subtext is clear, and we never have to worry about feeling as though the author is spoon-feeding how we should feel about the characters or let them tell us what their agendas are. Rather, the writer lets the emotional dynamics of the characters take over as they try not to say what's exactly on their minds, and we're led into a story that is entertaining because it forces the audience to guess what's going on, and this guessing is what keeps them interested.

STORY STRUCTURE

After you have a sense of character down and what the story may be about—and have a sense of how to write decent dialog—you need to think about story structure. This story structure is mainly shaped, or caused, by the main character, whether the character is initiating the action or reacting to it. In *Uncle Jack*, Jack wants to flee his pursuers, while trying to keep his niece happy over the phone. The structure of the story comes out of his need to escape while simultaneously using the changing scenes of his escapade to embellish the fairytale he's telling his niece.

Every action has a reaction. What occurs in one scene causes what will follow. A character does this by performing actions. He engages in actions because he wants something. Uncle Jack's niece wants him to tell her a story so she doesn't have to think about her parents' fighting. Uncle Jack reacts to this by telling her a story, while he simultaneously wants to escape his attackers. Neither character is static. For one thing, if a character is static, then there's nothing to propel the story forward; there is no dramatic need for an audience to gain emotional attachment and they'll look for other stories that hook them. And second, these actions, the dramatic needs of the characters, must be arranged in a such a way as to build emotions in the characters and, by extension, the audience.

Dramatic need drives the plot—the arrangement of actions. A bride wanting to get married would be the dramatic need in a wedding video, for example. So, when we're the DSLR shooters, what actions do we need to capture that reveal this dramatic need? In fiction, the dramatic needs of the character start with the writer but continue through production and into the postproduction phase of editing. But the principle applies to nonwriters, as well. The filmmaker, whether shooting a documentary on the fly or setting up a commercial, rock video, or wedding shoot, must understand the dramatic needs of the characters and subjects to be able to deliver useful shots for the editor (even if the filmmaker is the editor!); these shots need to move the story forward.

Typical story structures follow this pattern: hook, introduction or setup of the dramatic need of the character (some may refer to this as the exposition, the minimal necessary information needed by an audience to get the story), conflict or complications to the dramatic need that rises to a climax, and finally a resolution (the dramatic need is resolved).

A hook is an incident that grabs the audience's attention right away. We're given some kind of background or context or introduction to the character or situation. There's some obstacle the character must overcome to get what she wants; this conflict builds to a crisis point or climax where the character either gets what she wants or doesn't. Finally, the resolution reveals what the character learned from her experience.

This should not be a formulaic process, but rather one that's organic, rising out of the character's needs and wants as expressed by the writer (or filmmaker analyzing the story structure of whatever piece she's planning to shoot). The emotional changes a character goes through pivot around the setup, complications, and climax. These emotional changes in character (the character arc) typically revolve around three acts.

- Act 1 presents the setup, the introduction of the characters, their background, and setting. It may introduce the conflict—the central need or want of the character coming into conflict with something, someone, or even herself.
- Act 2 presents a turn of events for the central character in her quest to get what she wants; obstacles or complications get in her way, eventually escalating to Act 3.
- Act 3 comes at the apex of the story, the climactic point representing the strongest emotional moment for the character where she must face the final confrontation, the final crisis (the wedding vows and kiss at the wedding). She either gets what she wants or she doesn't, thus resolving the story.

In the Alien/Pauly story described in the dialog writing exercise, we can even see the emotional arc of the characters in a mini three-act structure; indeed, individual scenes will contain elements of the three-act structure (but usually not the resolution, because the story continues into another scene):

- Setup of Act 1: The Alien wants directions, while Pauly checks out the Alien's ride, thinking that it's a souped-up car.
- Act 2: This act adds the complication of Pauly deciding not to just look at the "car," but to call his girlfriend out and take the car for a spin, perhaps even to steal it—rising to the climax/crisis in the next act.
- Act 3: Pauly takes the "car," leaving the Alien dumbfounded as it stands on the sidewalk as the resolution.

In *Uncle Jack*, the emotional arc of the characters look like this:

- Setup of Act 1: Uncle Jack tries to escape thugs shooting at him. His niece calls him. He tries to get rid of her, but can't, taking us to ...
- Act 2: This act adds the complication of Uncle Jack trying to tell a fairytale to his niece while he flees the car, enters a train, saves his buddy clown from falling from a building, and heads down a tunnel.
- Act 3: And they hide in a costume shop, where they are cornered by two gunman, while the niece explains to Uncle Jack how to escape the situation, thus resolving the story.

As the person responsible for setting the look of the shots and capturing them on camera, you, as the director (whether shooting it yourself or working with a cinematographer), must understand the story and know what images go where so the editor has everything needed to deliver a strong story. Gordon Willis, ASC, describes how the cinematographer "is responsible for the image. He is responsible for putting that magic up on the wall. He's the visual psychiatrist, moving the audience from here to there"[4]

If the cinematographer doesn't understand the story—the underlying dramatic needs of the character expressed over time—then how will she know what to shoot and how to shoot? This is rooted in the story. When a clearly written script maps the change of a character as he attempts to get what he wants (or even just a brief outline of the emotional change of the bride and groom in a wedding video), then it's much easier to revolve the story around a central character trying to get what he wants. If the story is vague, with a weak central character, the story doesn't move forward and the cinematography doesn't have a basis on which to shoot. Plus, you end up with random shots that might look pretty but don't move a story forward, moment by moment, shot by shot, and will likely bore an audience.

Get a script, write a script, adapt a story, or analyze and structure a rock video or wedding shoot around a story. If you can't think of a story, then modernize a fairytale and shoot it with friends. What would a short film look like if you rewrite and set the "Little Red Riding Hood" folktale in New York City or Los Angeles or a small town in middle America? Tell a story with your images.

Until you're telling a story, you're not doing cinema but simply playing around with a camera.

Let's look at an example to see how this structure can be seen in Vincent Laforet's Internet hit *Reverie* (see http://vimeo.com/7151244), shot on a Canon 5D Mark II. This short piece (97 seconds, excluding credits), tells the simple story of a man forgetting to meet a girl at a specific place. He wakes up and realizes he's late, then flies out the door, grabs flowers, and races his way to her location in his car, but misses her. Finally, the search escalates as he rides a helicopter in order to find her, but he fails. The movie ends as it began: a man sleeping on a couch dreaming about a girl. He wakes up and rushes out to try and meet her in time, but his love is gone—or perhaps it was just a dream.

Let's map Laforet's short as a mini three-act piece on the graph, as shown in Figure 6.2.

Act 1: Hook, setup of dramatic need: The man wants the woman. We see a man and woman kissing. Man on sofa, sleeping, as TV flickers light onto him. He gets flashes of images of a woman dressed in red, waiting for him. The conflict is set up: he should be there, but he fell asleep watching TV.

Act 2: Rising action, further complications to his dramatic need. The man washes his face, rushes up stairs, grabs flowers, and races through the city, looking around as he drives. The woman stands and waits. There is a series of shots of the man driving, overcoming further obstacles; he's using the GPS—perhaps he's lost. He arrives, whipping off his sunglasses, but she's not there.

Act 3: Climax/crisis/final confrontation and resolution. The girl's gone. The man's arrived too late, and the flowers drop out of his hand. The conflict intensifies. Will he find her becomes an unanswered question that drives the narra-

---

[4]Fauer, J. *Cinematographer Style: The Complete Interview*, Vol. 1.. American Society of Cinematographers, 2008.

tive forward. He sweats bullets. He drives around the city, looking for her. The sequence ends with a climactic shot of him in a helicopter as he continues to look for her. Panoramic shots of the city. The story is resolved as he realizes he's not going to find her. The short ends with him on his couch, waking up and rushing out the door—presumably the beginning of the film, or perhaps he's just dreaming about the encounter and failure to meet the girl. In either case, the story is resolved. He doesn't get the girl.

Once the story is in place, a script written, then the cinematographer—in consultation with the director—determines the look and feel of the film, before shooting begins. In smaller projects, you may be the cinematographer and the director. In either case, the story should be your guide in determining how the film should look—whether you're shooting people to provide a snapshot of a city, wedding, commercial, music video, short, documentary, video journalism, or feature.

Winans, the writer and director of the Internet short *Uncle Jack* (as well as the writer-director of 2009's independent film, *Ink*, believes that "story is everything" when it comes to narrative filmmaking. As a beginning filmmaker, he used to gravitate toward "cool shots, cool editing" without thinking too much about the story. "But after enough miserably failed films with really cool shots," Winans explains, "it became apparent that if I didn't have the script, and more specifically the story, then I was sunk no matter what I did with the camera." So as he honed his filmmaking skills, he focused on the story: "As the years have gone by, my focus has been less and less on the technical process and more and more about the script." He faced a hard lesson and realized that "filmmaking is way too difficult, expensive, and time consuming to waste on a bad script."

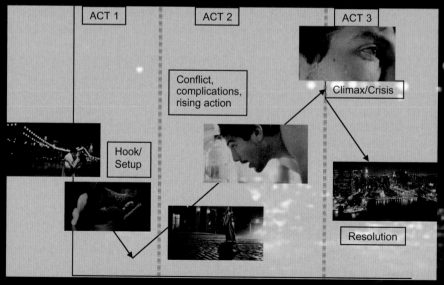

FIGURE 6.2
The three-act structure of Vincent Laforet's *Reverie*.

STORYTELLING SHOOTING EXERCISE

by Dave Anselmi

A good way to practice scriptwriting and see how what you write gets translated on film is to take a small scene from one of your favorite films and re-create it, shot by shot. Shoot a scene from one of your favorite films (make sure it's a good film that you can actually shoot—an action film with a lot of special effects may be too hard, but a good scene of drama can do the trick). By repeating the scene, by re-creating it shot-by-shot, you'll get a good sense of how good storytelling works on film. With this knowledge, you'll start to understand how to write better scripts.

Still from Zandrak's *Our Songs* for Moodsnap ©2014. Used with permission.

CHAPTER 7

Cinematic Gear on a Budget: What You Need and What it Does

You don't need to break the bank to get professional results. A basic gear package with a Canon DSLR can yield strong cinematic results. You can get professional results with minimum gear.

For some people, throwing a lot of money at a problem is the only way to find a solution—but this isn't usually the best option. Being challenged with limited gear can result in creative solutions that may actually lead to better work. The challenge arrives from the fact that when you're on a tight budget and you must put together a great looking film.

But the gear is only part of it. A person with a $1000 Canon 70D can get better results than a $20,000 dollar RED—if the person on the RED doesn't know as much about cinematic storytelling—the professional skills—as the person on the 70D. Andrew Hutcheson of Voyager Creative in Brooklyn (http://voyagercreative.com) feels that the most important element for your shoot revolves around your skills and professionalism. "The client's impression of you is all that matters, it doesn't matter how you do it. It doesn't matter where you are so much, but it's really how they see you as being valuable. Did they see the work they get from you as being professional? Is it giving them what they need?"

In the end, those facets are more important than what camera you own, for example. "Most people aren't going to be impressed by what camera you have," Hutcheson adds. "Like most dates aren't going to be impressed by what car you drive, because they're dating who you are." So, yes, you need to shoot high definition and if you can't afford the camera you want, then rent it, Andrew says. "The industry at a certain point is a renter's market."

Note: any prices listed in this chapter were based on known prices at the time this book was being written.

Hutcheson says, "you should get a piece of tech that you think is going to not just be the best thing right now, but it's going to hold up for some time." DSLRs are "perfect examples" of how "they have come a long way. There's a lot you can do to upgrade them. Shane Hurlbut, ASC, is a perfect example as to how you can really professionalize these cameras. *Escape from Tomorrow* was a feature film shot at Disney World all on DSLRs, and it was a Sundance film that got distribution."

"The point," Hutcheson adds, "is to show that it's not the tools that define the job—it's you." What skills, vision, and passion do you bring to the project? "Anyone can buy the tools, Andrew explains. He heard a story from Vincent Laforet—who helped instigate the DSLR cinema revolution by using a Canon 5D Mark II as a cinema camera. An executive for a potential job asked him, 'Why should I hire you to shoot my project, when my daughter has a 5D?'" That's a good question. "What you need to sell people on is your style," Andrew says, "the same thing that you've always had as an artist:

- What's your style?
- What's your story?
- What differentiates you from someone else?"

"In addition to that," Hutcheson explains, "you should get business cards printed. Accessorize your camera package, more lenses, more media cards, more batteries. Maybe a tripod, or maybe a shoulder rig if you're more about hand held. Monopods are the most common tools we use. And I'd make sure within all of that, find out how much it will cost you to get a website and factor that in."

Furthermore, when you invest money (or credit card) for your gear, you should calculate your return on investment. Will spending money on a RED Epic give you a return in your investment over a few years? Or does it make more sense to spend $1000 for a DSLR and accessorize it for a couple thousand more and then knowing that once you've gotten a couple of jobs, your gear is paid for? And if you need to shoot a project with a RED Epic, you could rent one.

Rather than recommending one piece of gear over another, below, I describe what features you want in a computer, editing software, camera, and audio gear that video and professionals need. Getting the cheapest PC or Apple's MacAir, for example, is not the way to go when faced with gigabytes of video data that need to get processed and edited, but I'm also making an assumption that someone wanting to shoot video as a business (or hobby) isn't going to invest $50,000 or $100,000 in getting gear. Hutcheson recommends that if you have an equipment budget of around $5,000, then the "first thing I do is buy a DSLR camera and find whichever one is the best for you at the time. You get a DSLR, you get a laptop, and you get a copy of Adobe Creative Cloud (monthly subscription), since you have access to multiple apps, from color grading to Photoshop or retouching, as well as After Effects, Audition for music, and there's a storyboard visualization software you'd want to get."

Even though I do list some lower-budget gear (such as cameras under $7500), I'm not going to provide an exhaustive list. Rather, I delve into the details explaining what some of the equipment does and what features you may want to consider when purchasing or renting certain gear. Too many shooters, for example, don't know what 8-bit compression means and how that limits postproduction work when compared to a camera that shoots Apple ProRes or a camera that shoots RAW. Therefore, the heart of this chapter is really about what features and specs you should be looking for, so when you look at a camera, you can see if it has what it takes in regards to image and audio quality and, if it doesn't, what you need to compensate for it.

WHAT COMPUTER SHOULD I GET?

The merits of a laptop and a full desktop system cannot be understated. If you're starting out and need the portability to edit or at the very least back up files in the field, you'll want a laptop. It's your choice whether you should get an Apple or PC— and that will depend on what software you want to use for editing. If you want to use Final Cut Pro, then you must get an Apple computer. Avid or Premiere, and you can choose an Apple or PC. If you want to use Sony Vegas, then it's PC only. To keep the budget reasonable, I'm not going to into much detail with the iMac Pro, but when your budget increases, you may want to go for the top of the line model if you really want serious computing power—especially if you want more 4K and RAW footage processing power.

Whatever you end up choosing, these are the kinds of specs you'll want:

- Processor
  This is what will render your projects, including special effects, and graphics. The more processors you have, the faster the render times. Quad-core processors are a minimum. Apple's MacBook Pro has a 2.9 GHz speed with turbo speeds up to 3.8 GHz in the high-end early 2017 model, but there are high end PCs clocking in at 4 GHz, and you can choose more than four cores (8, 10, and 18 in Apple's iMac Pro).

- Memory
  16GB RAM (minimum). This allows you to run more apps at once, or for video purposes, less refresh of your timeline. Some PCs and the 27-inch iMac can go up to 64GB and more.

- Graphics card with dedicated video memory
  Make sure you have a dedicated graphics card with at least 2GB of dedicated video RAM (4GB is better, but the higher this number the better off you are— especially if you're running 4K and/or RAW files). Some models I describe below, such as the PC laptop, below, contains up to 8GB or more of video card memory. (The iMac Pro can go up to 16GB of graphics processing.)

- Display
  You want this to be high, preferably 4K (not what's called full HD 1920x1080). Apple's Retina display on a MacBook Pro is 2880x1800 (in the 2017 model). I

would say this is the minimum you would want, since you need to have good real estate area on your screen when editing.

- Storage drive
  This is where all of your software goes. Hard drives spin and you want at least 7200 rpm. You can also get more expensive SSD (solid state drive), which contains no moving parts and is faster than hard drives in general. I use Apple's MacBook Pro with a 500GB SSD, which makes the bootup times fast and increases performance. All of my software goes on this main drive. However, I don't store any video or audio, here. Use dedicated drives.

- External storage drives
  Get dedicated hard drives to store your footage. We're talking terabytes, not gigabytes. The onboard base drive for your computer should be at least 500GB—this is for your software. Don't store your footage on your main drive. Use additional drives. You can get large array drives or stand-alone portable drives. If you're getting a hard drive, you'll want a minimum of 7200 rpm spin speed with a USB 3.0, eSATA, or Thunderbolt for high speed connectivity. For field drives, look at LaCie's 4T RAID drive with USB 3.0 and Thunderbolt inputs, G Drive Mobile (1T USB 3.0), and CalDigit Tuff 2T (USB-C). For large storage bays, look at CalDigit and G-Drive.

Here are some example computers you may want to consider, or at the very least use these specs as a baseline when choosing a later model (prices will stay relatively the same, but the specs will be better):

MacBook Pro (laptop)
~$3100 (early 2018 model)
Get the highest-end model with a Retina display. Anything less, and you're not getting the full power you need for editing. The lower-end models and 13-inch models are really not worth it. See http://store.apple.com/us/buy-mac/macbook-pro. Also, take note tha the new Pros contain only four Thunderbolt (USB-C) ports, so you'll need adapters to attach other devices.
- Processor: 2.9 GHz Quad-core Intel Core i7, Turbo Boost up to 3.9 GHz
- RAM: 16GB 2133 MHz
- Graphics card: Radeon Pro 560 with 4GB memory
- Storage drive: 512GB SSD
- Display: Retina (2880x1800 resolution)

iMac with Retina 5K display (desktop)
~$3100 (early 2018 model)
This is the top of the line iMac. Although the iMac Pro contains better specs, it's going to cost an additional $2000, so if you're on a budget, this iMac delivers the most bang from the buck. With the 5K display, this is one of the best computers you can get from Apple. Unlike the MacBook Pro, the iMac contains regular ports (such as SDXC card reader, four USB 3, two Thunderbolt (USB-C), and Ethernet).
- Display: 5K (27", 5120x2880 resolution)

- Processor: 4.2 GHz Quad-core Intel Core i7, Turbo Boost up to 4.5 GHz (if you're running just one app, such as Final Cut, then you could save $200 and get the standard i5 core—but if you're doing more than one, pay for the i7)
- RAM: 32GB 2400 MHz DDR4 (it can go up to 64GB)
- Storage: 2TB Fusion Drive (SSD with a normal a drive)
- Graphics card: Radeon Pro 580 with 8GB of video memory

Titan X4K PC (Windows) laptop workstation
~$2865 (early 2018 model)

Priced a bit less than the MacBook Pro, and there's more bang for you buck in this work horse from Titan Computers, including six cores. The fact that this model has a 4K display, with high memory and a strong video card makes this a great workstation for editing. As you shop around for PC laptops, take note of how the specs on this computer outperforms Apple's MacBook Pro. But also note that by putting this kind of power in a laptop, the weight of the computer comes in at 7.5 lbs (as opposed to the four pounds of the MacBook Pro):

- Display: 4K, 15.6" Samsung (3840x2160)
- Processor: Quad-core Intel i7-8700 Kaby Lake 6-Core 3.7 GHz (4.7 GHz turbo)
- WD Hard Drive: 256GB SATA III internal SSD
- Hard Drive storage: Internal SeagateFireCuda Hybrid 1TB (SSHD)
- Memory: 32GB (DDR4 2400 Mhz) (expandable to 64GB)
- Video card: NVIDIA GeForce GTX 1070 with 8GB GDDR5
- It includes two built-in Thunderbolt 3(Type-C USB port), among a variety of other ports no longer found on the MacBook Pro, such as audio, mic input, HDMI output.
- You can tailor this model with several options (see: https://www.titancomputers.com/Titan-X4K-Intel-i7-Coffee-Lake-6-core-laptop-p/x4k.htm).

Titan X199 PC (Windows) tower
~$2400 ($3400 with recommended display; fall 2017 model)

This computer is comparable to Apple's 5K iMac (and in some ways exceeds it), but the internal specs are better on this Titan. See Titan Computers for an example of how you can map out a top of the line PC. http://www.titancomputers.com/Titan-X199-Intel-Core-i7-Broadwell-E-Series-3-p/x199.htm. Specs as of mid 2017:

- Processor: Six core Intel i7-6800K Broadwell-E 3.4 GHz (3.6 GHz turbo)
- OS Hard Drive: 250GB
- Storage Hard Drive: Seagate 1TB
- Memory: 32GB (2 x 16GB) Expandable to 128GB
- Video card: NVIDIA GeForce GTX 1070 with 8GB graphics card
- Display (not included), but a recommended 4K display would be LG's 31" 4K monitor (31MU97-B) for under $1000 (see this link from Amazon: https://amazon.com/LG-Electronics-Digital-31MU97-B-31-0-Inch/dp/B00OKSEVTY).

Again, these specs are mid-2017. The secret to computer prices—high-end machines will stay about the same price; what changes are increased specs.

WHAT EDITING SOFTWARE SHOULD I GET?

There are professionals who spend too much time debating the merits and demerits of particular editing software (and cameras, for that matter). The debate tends to revolve around the big three of Avid Media Composer, Apple's Final Cut Pro, and Adobe's Premiere Pro (through their Creative Cloud service). Avid was the first and in many ways is the most stable when locking in a picture for film out, so it tends to be the most popular among feature film editors. Apple purchased Macromedia's software and rendered it into their version throughout the 2000s, making it popular among the indie film movement, who were attracted to the graphics- and windows-based Macs, but when Apple finally created their own software from scratch with the release of Final Cut X, some, who were so used to the old interface, couldn't adjust and jumped over to Adobe's Premiere, which engages a similar interface to the previous version of the defunct Final Cut 7. Fundamentally, all do they same thing—allowing you to put together a digital film comprised of digital images, audio, and graphics. If you want the most flexibility as a professional editor, you should learn how to use them all. Each one has a different interface and that's where most users revolve their arguments around, which comes down to personal taste. Then there's Blackmagic Design's DaVinci Resolve. A professional color grading software, it now offers full editing capabilities (including audio postproduction). See Chapter 5 for a software comparison chart.

WHAT YOU REALLY NEED TO KNOW ABOUT CINEMA CAMERAS

There have been more innovative and competitively priced cameras released over the past two to three years than probably at any time in the history of the industry. Canon, Panasonic, Sony have released DSLRs, mirrorless cameras, and low-end cinema cameras that can shoot cinematic quality for low costs, from full HD to 4K resolutions. Blackmagic and Digital Bolex have released cinematic cameras that shoot RAW (little to no compression), providing cinematic quality postproduction capabilities at inexpensive prices.

No matter what camera you decide to shoot on, what you need to look at is the sensor size, resolution, frame rate, type of shutter, compression codec, and audio quality—I'll describe what these mean below. Some cameras come with different lens mounts (such as Canon EF, micro four-thirds, PL cinema, C-mounts, and so forth). Whatever the lens mount, cameras will evolve every year, but lenses and audio gear don't change often—if you invest in lenses and audio, that will be more important than buying a new camera every year. In some ways, you could invest in a set of good lenses and audio gear and rent new and different cameras for different projects—maybe invest in one cheaper camera to own for small projects, personal use, and as a backup or second camera on a shoot. Later, I'll provide a chart describing the key features of several different cameras in relationship to these elements, after laying out these definitions.

Lens mount

Different cameras come with different lens mounts based on the brands of cameras: Canon, Sony, Panasonic. Some companies use other manufactuers' lenses. For example, Blackmagic Design have released cameras with Canon's EF mounts. PL mounts are standard for many cinema lenses. Micro four-thirds are used on smaller sensor cameras.

Sensor

CCD (charged coupled device) with a global shutter. High-end cameras, scientific instruments, and even older model video cameras used CCDs, but they're more expensive to make. Joe Rubinstein, who designed the Digital Bolex camera, says "the pixels that are next to each other on CCD sensors affect each other. When one pixel overflows with energy it affects the pixels around it. The pixels work together as a unit, much the way chemicals on a film plane do. We believe this gives the sensor a more organic look." There is less light sensitivity with CCDs, and due to the expense, most camera manufacturers use CMOS sensors. (The sensor for the Digital Bolex, for example, costs about $1000.) Does this mean you should not shoot with a rolling shutter camera? No. Thousands of professional projects have been shot with cameras containing rolling shutters. But you need to be aware of the conditions so you know their limitations.

CMOS (Complementary Metal Oxide Semiconductor) with rolling shutter. These are active pixel sensors. Rubinstein says that "Active Pixel Sensors read all of their pixels linearly from top left to bottom right while the shutter is open. The pixels don't store any charge, they simply read how much light is hitting that pixel at the exact moment and convert that into an electrical signal. A rolling shutter (as opposed to a global shutter) is always active and "rolling" through pixels from top to bottom. This can result in the now-familiar motion artifacts often referred to as 'jello.'" It must be noted that some manufacturers have placed global shutter options on their cameras. CMOS sensors are more light sensitive, are fairly inexpensive, and can engage in high frame rates. (See http://www.digitalbolex.com/global-shutter/.)

Sensor size and resolution

The sensor size is measured in millimeters, while the resolution of the sensor represents how many pixels are being used in a particular shot (in some cameras, such as Blackmagic's Ursa Mini, you can choose the resolution on their 35mm sensor to be 4.6K, 4K, 2K, full HD, or even less, while the Digital Bolex, shoots 2K and full HD on a 16mm size sensor). The sensor size impacts how the focal length of lenses affects how the field of view gets resolved. Photographers set the standard of the focal length against the full frame sensor, so they refer to the APS-C sensor on a 70D, for example, as a cropped sensor. Thus a 50mm focal length lens will be equivalent as an 80mm on a full frame camera (it has a crop factor of 1.6). (See http://www.abelcine.com/fov/ for a visual reference guide where you can input different cameras' field of view based on the focal length of the lens.)

Full frame

Photographers love the full frame sensor. The frame is the size of old-school 35mm film (but not 35mm cinema film!). Due to the larger sensor, filmmakers can get really shallow depth of field when shooting wide-open apertures. You don't need a full frame sensor camera and if you're going for a 35mm cinema look, this is really not the camera to get, unless you're going for its unique look—some argue that it actually provides a 65mm film look. The Canon 5D Mark III (and Mark IV), 6D, and Sony's A7s contain this large sensor.

Cropped frame

This is the APS-C sensor, which is close to the size of the S35mm sensor, has a crop frame of 1.6x compared to a full frame photo sensor. Most DSLRs are this size, including the Canon 60D, 70D, and so forth. If you're shooting with a DSLR, this is the standard for getting a 35mm film look.

S35mm

This is the cinema standard, found in the Canon C100, C200, C300, URSA mini, among others. Cinematographers consider this the standard frame, but if you want the comparison to the full frame photo sensor, then it's 1.4–1.5x (depending on man-ufacturer's size.

Micro Four-Thirds (MFT)

A smaller format found on many mirrorless cameras (such as Panasonic's GH5). Crop factor is 2x.

Super 16mm

The sensor size found on the Digital Bolex D16 and the Blackmagic Pocket Cinema Camera. Crop factor is 2.9x.

Dynamic range

The ability of a sensor to record in a range of dark to bright without losing informa-tion in the extreme ranges—the contrast ratio. If a camera has a dynamic range of 12 stops, it means that it can capture a range of detail from dark to light within this 12-stop range. If the scene is beyond a 12-stop range, then the values beyond these 12 stops will not be recorded (the darks will either go black—crushed—or the light will go all white (blown out or clipped). Typically in the digital cinema field, you'll want to expose for the highlights, since data can be recovered in the dark regions, while it is impossible with clipped shots. Some cameras can record images in a "flat" mode. These include Sony's S-curve or Canon log curves, a mathematical process that spreads the image data along the full dynamic range making the image appear flat on-screen. It's designed for postproduction work by which you pull this data out in the highlights and the shadows, recovering a larger dynamic range and allowing for greater color grading (see Chapter 3, "Exposure"). In addition, you can read general exposure data if you use a histogram, which shows the intensity of darks to lights on a scale on a camera's monitor, so you can adjust the exposure if you're clipping values in the whites or crushing the blacks. (Again, you can crush blacks and recover the data, although it'll be noisy, but if you clip the highlights, it's gone forever.) False color and waveform monitors also are used to read exposure level.

Frame rate

The film standard is 24 fps (frames per second); NTSC Television is 30 fps and PAL television is 25 fps (these are based on the electrical current rates of 60 Hz and 50 Hz cycles, depending on what country you live). High frame rates allow you to create slow motion shots (since you're getting more data and conforming it to 24fps, slowing down the images and vice versa (shooting at 16 fps, will cause a faster rate. The higher the frame rate, the slower the playback of motion. A 60 fps rate will give you a pleasant smooth slow motion. For certain scenes and shots, this is an important tool for filmmakers. Frame rates that show 23.97 or 29.97 refer to the space needed for a broadcast signal to carry an audio signal.

Shutter angle/speed

A standard look to your footage will be a shutter angle of 180 degrees or 1/48 per second shutter speed (on a 24 fps frame rate). This is half of a circle standard in a film camera as the shutter rotates, letting in half the light in a single rotation. The smaller the angle, such as 90 or 45 degrees (or high shutter speed, like 1/500), the more staccato the look with minimum motion blur, the larger the angle, such as 270 degrees (or low shutter speed, such as 1/24), the smoothness or motion blur of the look increases). (See Figure 7.1.)

Figure 7.1
Shutter angle/shutter speed. As the angle increases, you increase motion blur (or when setting the shutter speed slower) and as it decreases you get sharper edges (or setting the shutter speed faster).
(Image used under Creative Commons license 3.0.)

Shane Hurlbut, ASC, describes the shutter angle this way:

> What is shutter speed? Imagine a pie, and that pie has 24 pieces. If the film plane or digital sensor in your camera were to always to see the lens, this would be shutterless. Nothing is obstructing its view with a 360-degree shutter. To the best of my knowledge, this can only be done on digital cameras, unless you pull the shutter physically out of a film camera. At 360 degrees, you will have a lot of motion blur in your action because as an actor moves his arm or his drumstick you are seeing it on all 24 pieces of the pie. If you were to use a 180-degree shutter,

which has become the industry standard at 24 fps, you would see motion blur that we have all come accustomed to in the theater. At 180 degrees, the film plane or digital sensor at 1/50 or more exacting 1/48 sec of a second would be seeing the drumstick on 12 out of the 24 pieces. (See https://www.hurlbutvisuals.com/blog/2013/08/intensity-with-internal-camera-settings/.)

Compression

Every consumer camera and DSLRs in video mode is recorded in 8-bit H.264 codec (compression/decompression algorithm). Eight bits means there are 256 points of data per pixel and the H.264 is a compression standard that engineers created to make the image look great with the smallest file size—which means the image is compressed. It looks good in a small file size, because it is a finishing codec designed to look good as a finished product online or with Blu-ray discs. Manufacturers use these in consumer type cameras, so a lot more recording can be placed on memory cards. But they're not good for editing, since data is being shared across images. When you import these compressed files into your video editing software, the files are typically decompressed for editing, increasing the file size into Apple's ProRes or equivalent codec (4:2:2—a note about this below). This isn't really a big issue if you get the look of the shot in-camera accurate (proper color balance and exposure, for example). If your color and exposure is inaccurate, you can tweak the image just a little bit in post to correct issues, but the images quickly fall apart if you push it too far, because there's not enough data in the compressed image to recover any details. Treat 8-bit like negative reversal film stock (if you're old school).

High-end professional cameras, and some of the cheaper cameras, such as Blackmagic Design's cameras, can shoot in ProRes at different compression rates. An 8-bit compression contains 256 points of info (4:2:0 and 4:2:2), 10-bits is 1024 (4:2:2), and 12-bits (4:4:4:4) is uncompressed with 4096 pieces of data per pixel. The less the compression, the more data you get and more headroom you'll have in post to make corrections and adjust the look and feel of your project during color grading. Other cameras use uncompressed and compressed forms of RAW, providing the best quality image, but requiring a lot of recording and storage space (2K recording at uncompressed RAW will click in at about 500GB for about ninety minutes of recording).

Chroma subsampling

The eye perceives the nuance of brightness more than color. To take advantage of this, chroma (or color) subsampling compresses color information to save space. In this type of compression, there's one piece of information for luminance (brightness) and two for color (chrominance). The numbers represent the one brightness sample rate (given as a 4) and two color sample rates among a group of pixels (given as a 0—no sample; 2—half sample; or 4—full sample, no compression). All pixels get full brightness or luma values, thus these sequences always begin as 4. (When there's a fourth number 4, that represents the chroma channel for green screen work.) See Chapter 5 for more information about chroma subsampling. Here's a summary:

- 4:4:4

  All light and colors are sampled at the same rate. There is no subsampling, so this provides the strongest image for postproduction work.

- 4:2:2

  In a four pixel sample, all the luma values are used (4), but only half the color data (2:2) is used. The image is considered very good and nearly indistinguishable from 4:4:4—except when you need to do heavy post work, when the image will fall apart into blocky, noisy artifacts, and banding across colors.

- 4:2:0

  Same level of luminence, but now half the color data of 4:2:2. The image will fall apart quickly in post if you have to make changes to the image—hence the importance of getting the image right in-camera.

Below is a chart summarizing the compression scheme of the most popular types of codecs. When I use the word "typical" in the bit depth, it means that these formats can also be utilized in 8-bit modes, the data rate will simply be lower. But since 10-bit is the minimum professional standard, I will only focus on the 10-bit rates.

Resolution: Full HD, 2K, 4K

The number of pixels recorded. The higher the number, the higher the resolution. Full HD is 1920x1080 and is the current standard for Blu-ray DVDs and broadcast television. 2K is cinema quality for projection. 4K is the future. Those who are shooting 4K now will not have a large audience see their work in 4K, since most of cinema is still 2K and most television sets are full HD—although more and more televisions are being released with 4K capability. It will likely become more of a standard by 2020 or a few years later. However, there are increasingly more cameras being released that shoot 4K. There are several benefits to shooting in 4K now:

- Future proof. Store your film or project in 4K so it's ready when there's a market for it.

- Cropping a shot. The editor may want to crop an image and if you have a large area of resolution (such as 4K), then the image can be cropped or recomposed for an HD or 2K project without losing any data, such as the image going soft.

- Fixing unwanted motion in a shot. There might be a wobbly shot that allows software to fix that motion. If you're shooting in full HD or 2K, that software will share and grab data around the wobbly shots in order to fix it. If there's no space around the shot, then the image will lose some resolution, but if there's a lot of space around it, then it can pull data above full HD and 2K without losing any resolution.

- If you're doing work for Netflix, HBO, among others, 4K production is required.

CODEC	Bit depth	Data rate at 1080, 24p	Storage space at 1080p	Uses
4:2:0 (H.264, AVCHD, MPG-4)	8-bit	18Mb/s	20GB/hr	Finishing for web streaming and Blu-ray DVDs, and not for professional work. If shooting, nail proper exposure and color in-camera. Most lower end cameras record in this format. Very little post work can be applied before the image begins to fall apart.
ProRes 4:2:2 LT	8- & 10-bit	82Mb/s	37GB/hr	Shots must be accurate in-camera (proper exposure and color balance). Use if extra recording space is needed. Not recommended for professional work.
ProRes 4:2:2	8- & 10-bit (typical)	117Mb/s	53GB/hr	A professional codec, but the look should be nearly accurate in-camera, since there's not a lot of headroom in post for color and exposure correction (although there is some wiggle room).
ProRes 4:2:2 HQ	10-bit (typical)	176Mb/s	79GB/hr	A professional codec, but the look should be nearly accurate in-camera, since there's not a lot of headroom in post for color and exposure correction (although there is more wiggle room than the normal ProRes mode). Use this for LUT work.
ProRes 4:4:4	12-bit (typical)	264Mb/s	119GB/hr	A professional codec with plenty of headroom for postproduction work, including the use of LUTs and green screen work.
ProRes 4:4:4 HQ	12-bit (typical)	396Mb/s	178GB/hr	A professional codec with a lot of headroom for postproduction work, including the use of LUTs and green screen work.
Avid DNxHD 4:2:2 80	10-bit (typical)	80Mb/s	33.6GB/hr	Similar to ProRes LT. Shots must be accureate in-camera (proper exposure and color balance). Use if extra recording space is needed. Not recommended for professional work.
Avid DNxHD 4:2:2 115	10-bit (typical)	116Mb/s	73.71GB/hr	Similar to ProRes 4:2:2 HQ. A professional codec, but the look should be nearly accurate in-camera, since there's not a lot of headroom in post for color and exposure correction (although there is some wiggle room).
Avid DNxHD 4:2:2 175	10-bit (typical)	176Mb/s	48.7GB/hr	Similar to ProRes 4:2:2 HQ. A professional codec with plenty of headroom for postproduction work, including the use of LUTs and green screen work.
Avid DNxHD 4:4:4	12-bit (typical)	352Mb/s	147.8GB/hr	Similar to ProRes 4:2:2 HQ. A professional codec, but the look should be nearly accurate in-camera, since there's not a lot of headroom in post for color and exposure correction (although there is more wiggle room than the normal ProRes version).
CinemaDNG (compresssed raw)	12-bit	Varies based on compres-sion level	Varies based on compres-sion level	A professional codec for cinema work, leaving a lot of room for postproduction work. Saves a bit more space compared to uncompressed RAW. Use for green screen work and heavy LUT application.
CinemaDNG (uncompresssed raw)	12-bit	357 Mb/s	500GB for just under 2 hours at full HD.	A professional codec for cinema work, leaving a lot of room for postproduction work. Saves a bit more space compared to uncompressed RAW. Use for green screen work and heavy LUT application.

Audio quality

Don't skimp on audio. Poorly recorded audio is the number one killer of a project. For this reason, you must be able to see levels on a meter and listen to the audio being recorded on headphones. Either you're doing this or you're hiring a sound recordist to do this. There are not shortcuts to good audio. Some settings to keep in mind:

- 24-bit audio should be the standard (as opposed to many cameras still using 16-bit recordings)—more data gives you more headroom in post. It doesn't matter if it's 48 kHz or 96 kHz, just as long as you have headroom in post.

- XLR inputs are a must, which results in low interference, low impedance. It's the professional standard. If your camera doesn't have it, then you'll want a field mixer and/or recorder with XLR connections, resulting in the recording of audio separate from audio on-camera. One-eighth-inch inputs found on many DSLRs, the C100 with the top handle removed, and the Blackmagic Pocket Cinema Camera are high impedance, which results in picking up more noise, and are not used by professionals (it's OK to use such mics for reference audio).

If your camera doesn't have good audio recording, use an external audio recorder to get strong and clean audio. It's best to have a dedicated sound recordist, but when you can't, dedicated audio recorders will give you better audio than what the camera provides.

Metabones Speedbooster

DSLRs and the lower-end Blackmagic cameras (such as the Cinema Camera or Pocket Cinema Camera), as well as the Digital Bolex (with the micro 4/3 mount), can greatly benefit from the Metabones Speedbooster. It's a lens adapter that increases the field of view and the aperture speed of lenses. The Digital Bolex, for example, is a difficult camera to get a zoom lens that starts wide. With the EF to BMPCC model, you can place a Canon 17–55mm zoom lens (with a simple modification) and get the equivalent of a 10–32mm lens with a 1 2/3 increased aperture stop. In addition, some of the adapters accept a 5V battery from a mini-USB on the side of the adapter. This allows you to change the f-stop of the lenses that use automatic controls (good for cameras with passive Micro Four-Thirds mounts (such as the Digital Bolex). See http://metabones.com for more information.

Cameras	Canon 80D	Canon 5D Mark IV	Canon C100 Mark II	Canon C200
Lens mount	Canon EF	Canon EF	Canon EF	Canon EF
Recommneded starter lens	Canon 17–55mm f/2.8 (~$800) and 50mm f/1.8 (~$125)	EF 24–70mm f/4 (~$1000) and 50mm f/1.8 (~$125)	Canon 17–55mm f/2.8 (~$800)	Canon 17–55mm f/2.8 (~$800)
Sensor type	APS-C (~S35mm)	Full frame	S35	S35
Resolution (video mode)	1920x1080p (full HD)	4096x2160p 1920x1080p (4K and full HD)	1920x1080p	4096x2160p 3840x2160p 2048x1080p 1920x1080p
Crop factor (to photo full frame)	1.6x	1x	1.39x	1.39x
Histogram	Yes, but not while recording.	Yes, but not while recording.	Yes	Yes
Waveform	No	No	Yes	Yes
Max frame rate (frames per second)	60	30@4K 60@1080p 120@720p	60	60@4K 60@3840p 60@2K 120@1080p
Shutter speed or angle	Speed	Speed	Angle and speed	Angle and speed
Audio input	1/8" minijack	1/8" minijack	1/8" minijack and XLR	1/8" minijack and XLR
Audio quality	16-bit	16-bit	16-bit	16-bit
Headphone jack	No	Yes	Yes	Yes
Recording media	SDHC	SDHC and CF	SDHC (2)	SDHC and CFast
Bit depth	8	8	8	8, 10, and 12
Codec and max bit rate (Mb/s)	H.264 90 w/MOV wrapper 30 w/MP4 wrapper	H.264 500 w/M-JPEG (4K) 180 w/MOV (60fps 1080p) 90 w/MOV (24fps 1080p) 30 wMP4 (24fps 1080p)	H.264 28 w/AVCHD 35 w/MP4	1GB/s w/Cinema RAW light)@4K 150Mb/s w/MP4 @4K (UHD) 35Mb/s w/MP4 @2K and full HD
Log mode	No	Canon Log, as an add on	Canon Log	Canon Log and Canon Log 3
Additional notes	Powerful for the price.	Good 4K camera.	Best bang for the buck if you do not need to shoot in 4K.	Wide pixel pitch for better low light capabilities.
Cost	~$1200	~$3500	~$3500	~$7500

Camera	Blackmagic Design Pocket Cinema Camera	Blackmagic Design URSA Mini 4.6K Cinema Camera	Blackmagic Design Production Camera 4K	Sony PXW-FS5 XDCAM
Lens mount	Micro Four-Thirds	Canon EF (among others)	Canon EF	Sony E
Recommneded starter lens	Panasonic Lumix 12–35mm f/2.8 (~$900)	EF 24–70mm f/4 (~$1000) and 50mm f/1.8 (~$125)	Canon 17–55mm f/2.8 (~$800)	Includes 18–105mm f/4
Sensor type	Super 16mm	S35	S35	S35
Resolution	1920x1080p (full HD)	4608x2592p 4096x2304 (4K 16:9) 4608x1920 (4K 2.4:1) 3072x2560 (3K anamorphic) 2K and full HD	4000x2160p (compressed raw mode only) 3840x2160p 1920x1080p	3840x2160p 1920x1080p
Crop factor (to photo full frame)	2.88x	1.39x	1.39x	1.39x
Histogram	Yes	Yes	Yes	Yes
Waveform	No	Yes	Yes (with an output cable, but not in-camera)	No
Max frame rate (frames per second)	30	60	30	30@4K 60@1080p
Shutter speed or angle	Shutter angle	Global shutter angle	Global shutter angle	Angle
Audio input	1/8" minijack	1/8" minijack	1/4" jack	XLR
Audio quality	16 bit	24 bit	16 bit	24 bit
Headphone jack	Yes	Yes	Yes	Yes
Recording media	SDHC	SDHC and CFast (2)	SSD	MS/SD (1) SD (1)
Bit depth	8, 10, 12	8, 10, 12	8	10
Codec and max bit rate (Mb/s)	220 w/ProRes 4:2:2 HQ Lossless and compressed CinemaDNG	513 w/CinemaDNG @4K 62.5 w/ProRes 444XQ @1080p	CinemaDNG ProRes 4:2:2 HQ 1920x1080p	100 w/XAVC Long @4K 50 w/XAVC Long @1080p 24 w/AVCHD @1080p
Log mode	Film mode	Film mode	Film mode	Sony S-Log3 Gamma
Additional notes	Need to rig this camera. Batteries die fast. Audio is weak.	The shoulder mount, top handle, and viewfinder are not included in the base price. The pro version has a base price of $6000; the 4K model base is $3000.	Best bang for the buck if you need to shoot in 4K. Needs a rig. Audio not strong. Research the right SSD.	
Cost	~$1000	~$5000–7500	~$5000	~$6250

Camera	Sony Alpha7R II Mirrorless	Panasonic AU-EVA1	Panasonic Lumix DC-GH5
Lens mount	Sony E	Canon EF	Micro Four-Thirds
Recommneded starter lens	Sony FE 24–70mm f/4 (~$1200)	Canon 17–55mm f/2.8 (~$800)	Panasonic Lumix 12-35mm f/2.8
Sensor type	Full frame photo	S35	Micro Four-Thirds
Resolution	3840x2160p 1920x1080p	5.7K 4096x2160p 3840x2160p 2048x1080p 1920x1080p	4096x2160p 1920x1080p 6K anamorphic
Crop factor (to photo full frame)	1x	1.39x	2x
Histogram	Yes	Unknown	Yes
Waveform	No	Yes	Yes
Max frame rate (frames per second)	30@4K 60@1080p	60@4K 120@2K and 1080p 240 (with 4:3 sensor crop)	60@4K 180@1080p
Shutter speed or angle	Speed	Speed	Angle and speed
Audio input	1/8" minijack	1/8" minijack	1/8" minijack and XLR
Audio quality	16-bit	24- and 16-bit	16-bit
Headphone jack	Yes	Yes	Yes
Recording media	SDHC, SDXC Memory Stick Pro Duo	SDXC (2)	SDHC SDXC
Bit depth	8	10 and 8	10
Codec and max bit rate (Mb/s)	100 w/XAVC S @4K 50 w/XAVC S @1080p 24 wAVCHD @1080p	MOV (10-bit 4:2:2) H.264/MPG-4 150 bitrate (max)	400 w/4:2:2 (all-I) @4K
Log mode	Sony S-Log2 Gamma	V-Log and V Gamut	V-Log
Additional notes		Claims to capture a color space larger than film. Built-in stabilization.	A lot of features in this camera. Additional equipment: get the XLR hot shoe adapter (~$400).
Cost	~$3000	~$7300	~$2000

LENSES

Different focal lengths of lenses determine the psychological impact on an audience. For equipment, I'm including a starter lens suggestion in the camera table. In the lens table, I'm including the low end Rokinon prime (or fixed focal length) cinema lenses, since these are the best buy. They are not as rugged as high end lenses, so you will want to treat them with care. If you're looking at zoom lenses, be sure to get one that contains a fixed aperture along the full focal lenth range of the lens. In either case, you're looking for focal lengths, speed, and whether it's a zoom (adjustable focal length) or prime (fixed focal length lens).

The speed of the lens refers to how open you can set the aperture (given as an f-stop number), which lets in more light (the wider the opening, the less light you need). The smaller the f-stop number, the more open or faster the lens is. For example, f/2.8 is considered a fast lens, while an f/4 or f/5.6 is considered slow. Inexpensive zoom lenses will have changing speeds on their lenses, so getting a fixed aperture zoom lens is important, but they are more expensive. Also, cinema lenses are rated with T-stops, which are the same as f-stops, but it takes into effect the loss of light going through the glass, so the T-stop is accurate, while the f-stop is a mathematical rating that doesn't take the transmission quality of the glass into effect.

Rokinon Cinema lenses	Cinema lenses are expensive! Although they need to be handled with care, the Rokinon cinema lenses are decent starter cinema lenses and they come in a variety of mounts from Canon to Sony. Take advantage of some of these lenses that come in kits, because you'll save money.	
Lens mount	Canon EF, MFT, Sony E & alpha	
Focal length (mm)	16, 24, 35, 50, 85, 135	
Exposure range speed	16 and 135 = T2.2–22 24, 35, 50, 85 = T1.5–22	
Minimum focal distance and cost	16 = 7.9" (0.2m) 24 = 9.8" (0.25m) 35 = 9.8" (0.25m) 50 = 17.7" (0.45m) 85 = 3.6' (1.1m) 135 = 2.6' (0.8m)	~$350 ~$550 ~$500 ~$450 ~$300 ~$600
Filter thread size	16, 24, 35, 50, 135 = 77mm 85 = 72	
Focus ring	Manual	
Aperture ring	Manual	

MICROPHONES

Without good sound, you do not have a viable project, and your work will never be perceived as professional. While viewers may forgive a subpar image, they will never forgive poor sound. Most cameras with XLR inputs can record clean audio, as long as you record a clean and strong signal—which usually means someone monitors the audio with headphones and observes the meters for a −24dB to −6dB range to make sure the signal doesn't clip, and allow plenty of headroom in post.

A note about foam windscreens—these come with nearly every mic and they're designed to help reduce pops for people who pop their Ps and Ts when speaking. They're not windscreens. You'll want a dedicated windscreen, and if you're really fighting wind, then get a blimp-style windscreen. Microphones are covered in more detail in Chapter 4, so here's a brief summary:

- Shotgun
  These types of mics can sit on the camera with a shockmount (to absorb handling vibration sound), pistol grip, or boom pole. These directional mics may be utilized to pick up dialog from the direction it is pointed (and always point them at the subject's mouth for the strongest signal) and ambient sound that it is pointed at.

- Lavalier
  A clip-on mic designed to pick up dialog from a person talking. Good for documentary work, especially if the subject is moving around.

- Camera mic
  Never use a built-in camera mic as primary audio (use only as reference audio that you will replace with an external audio recorder and microphone).

Furthermore, different microphones use different pickup patterns. Keep the mic less than 2 feet (no more than 3 feet) from the subject's mouth.

- Omnidirectional
  Audio is picked up from all directions like a sphere. Many lavaliere mics (clip-on mics for interviews) are omnidirectional.

- Cardioid
  A heart-shaped pattern where audio is recorded mainly from the front, but also some from the side. It'll pick up ambient sound from the sides, while utilizing the strongest signal from the front. Use for dialog.

- Hypercardioid
  The audio signal is picked up mostly from the front with very little from the sides and rear. Directional mic used to pick up audio/dialog from the direction it is pointed.

Microphones	There are not many alternatives to cheap microphones. You need something that's durable, can provide clean recordings, and give professional sound. Below are some budget mics.			
Model	Rode NTG2 Shotgun mic	Audio-Technica AT8035	Rode VideoMic Pro	Sennheiser G3 wireless lavaliere mic
Notes	A quality budget microphone that can be powered by one AA battery or with phantom power. The Rode NTG-2 sounds nearly as good as a Sennheiser shotgun for half the price. You will want to get a windscreen and a shockmount that you can attach to your camera so you can use this as a run-and-gun mic—which is good for picking up ambient sound. You can get away using it for interviews if you are close to your subject.	A strong directional shotgun mic. Uses a single AA battery or phantom power. Hypercadiod designed to minimize audio coming in from the sides and rear—strong directional mic.	If you're using a DSLR, Blackmagic Pocket Cinema Camera, or a Canon C100 with the top handle off—a camera without XLR inputs—and you need good audio along with portability in the field, Rode's VideoMic Pro will give you usable sound in a crunch. At the very least, if you have a separate sound person and want better backup sound than a camera's built-in mic, then get the Rode. Uses a 9V battery. For 1/8" mic inputs. Get the extra windscreen.	This lav mic kit is rugged. When it comes to lav mics, getting a cheap one isn't worth the effort. There are better ones that are more expensive, but this is the best midrange "budget" wireless on the market. The receiver can mount onto a camera's shoe mount, allowing you to feed the XLR wire into your camera.
Cost	~$270	~$270	~$230	~$630

PREAMP FIELD MIXERS

While many people record audio with a microphone attached to their camera—and if they're shooting solo this may be their only option—there are field mixers with dedicated preamps that will provide the best sound in the field. Most of them will have at least two XLR inputs, so professional microphones can be attached. Some of these preamp mixers may be attached directly to a DSLR, for example, since DSLRs, the Blackmagic Cinema Camera, the Blackmagic Pocket Cinema Camera, do not contain XLR inputs. Because these devices are dedicated to audio, they'll also contain better and cleaner amps than those found in most cameras. With the multiple input XLRs, shooters may connect a lav and shotgun mic on two separate channels—the lav dedicated to an interview, for example, and the shotgun mic dedicated to recording ambient audio and acting as a backup to the lav. It will also include phantom power, which will power microphones that do not have batteries (but will also shorten the device's battery life).

AUDIO RECORDERS

Most professional shoots utilize a sound recordist who will have both a field mixer and an external audio recorder. They may also plug an XLR line into the main camera so it receives the field mixer's feed. There are many field recorders on the market. Be sure to set the recording to 24-bits at 48 kHz (or 96 kHz), so that there's more headroom in post. Make sure the levels hit between −24dB to −6dB. A dedicated sound person is best, because they can monitor the audio and adjust it if the levels get too low or high. Most devices also contain limiters preventing you from accidentally clipping audio.

Audio mixers and preamps	These are best utilized when you have a dedicated sound person capturing audio, but some models allow you to attach them to your camera. If you do not have XLR connectors on your camera (which is the case of DSLRs and some of the lower end Blackmagic cameras), then it is recommended that you hire a sound person or get one of these devices below. They not only provide XLR inputs, but they also contain preamps and limiters that will help you to record strong audio and prevent over modulation (or clipping).			
Model	Zoom H6	Tascam DR-70D	Sound Devices MixPre-D field mixer	Azden FMX-42u field mixer
Recording format	wav	wav	NA	NA
Bit depth	16 and 24	16 and 24	NA	NA
Input/output type	4-XLR/TRS combo jacks 1/8" headphone jack	4-XLR 1/8" headphone jack	2-XLR in and out 1-1/8 in and out 1/4" headphone jack	4-XLR in and 2-XLR out 1-1/8" out 1/4" headphone jack
Recording media	SDHC	SDHC, SDXC	NA	NA
Battery type	4-AA	4-AA	2-AA	6-AA
Notes	Includes the ability to hook up different types of microphones. Manual control of levels.	This is a combined four-channel mixer and recorder designed to be attached to the bottom of a camera. Includes plate adapter for camera's tripod. Tends to eat up batteries fast. Manual control of levels.	Includes a TA mic level output for inputting into DSLRs. Includes studio grade transformer-balanced XLR for unclippable peak limiters. At an additional cost, an adapter attaches to a camera's tripod.	Four-channel field mixer (not a recorder) with limiters, 48V of phantom power. Includes a 10-pin camera return so high quality audio can be recorded in-camera.
Cost	~$350	~$300	~$990	~$550

VIDEO FIELD RECORDERS

You'll want a video recorder if your camera doesn't record in a 10-bit or 12-bit codec. Nearly every low budget camera records in a compressed 8-bit codec that could lead to unprofessional results. The video field recorders will circumvent the compression through the camera's HDMI 10-bit output, providing professional 8- to 10-bit 4:2:2 codec (some recorders will do 12-bit). Most will record in Apple's ProRes or Avid's DNxHD codecs.

Video field recorders				
Model	Blackmagic Video Assist	Blackmagic Video Assist 4K	Atomos Ninja Flame 4K and Shogun Flame 4K	Convergent Design Odyssey 7Q+
Screen size, resolution, and brightness	5" 1920x1080 350 nits	7" 1920x1200 350 nits	7" 1920x1200 1500 nits	7.7" 1280x800
Recording format (max level)	ProRes 4:2:2 HQ DNxHD 220	ProRes 4:2:2 HQ DNxHD 220	ProRes 4:2:2 HQ DNxHD HQX Shogun also includes DCI raw 4096x2160 (with supported cameras only)	4K (UHD) @10-bit ProRes 4:2:2 HQ 2K 1080p @12-bit ProRes 4:4:4 2K 1080p 10- and 12-bit in DPX raw
Max frame rate (fps)	60	30@4K (3840x2160p) 60@1080p	30@4K (3840x2160p) 60@1080p	60@4K (Sony FS5, FS7, FS700) 240@2K (Sony cameras)
Bit depth	10 (8 w/certain cameras)	10 (8 w/certain cameras)	10 (8 w/certain cameras)	10- and 12-bit
Input type	HDMI and 6G-SDI	HDMI and 6G-SDI	Ninja: HDMI Shogun: HDMI and 12G-SDI	HDMI (8 bit 1080p60) 6G-SDI (12 bit 4K)
Recording media	SDHC, SDXC	Dual SDHC, SDXC	SSD (2.5")	Dual SSD (2.5")
Audio	2 channels of audio embedded in HDMI or SDI Headphone jack Audio meters	2 channels of audio embedded in HDMI or SDI 2 mini XLRs Headphone jack Audio meters	2 channels of audio embedded in HDMI or SDI Mic minijack input 24-bit Headphone jack Audio meters Shogun also includes 2 XLR (with included breakout cable)	2 channels of audio embedded in HDMI or SDI Mic minijack input Headphone jack Audio meters
Features	Touchscreen. Includes focus peaking, histogram, and zebra overlays.	Touchscreen. Includes focus peaking, histogram, and zebra overlays.	Touchscreen can be seen in the bright sun. 10-bit monitor for color accuracy. Includes LUT support. Includes 60i to 24p 3:2 pulldown.	Touchscreen. False color. Histogram. Waveform monitor. Focus assist. (RAW support may require an additional $1000 fee.)
Cost	~$500	~$900	Ninja: ~$800 Shogun: ~$1000	~$1500

TRIPODS AND MONOPODS

You need stable shots. A lot of beginners and amateurs think that they can hand-hold their camera and get good-looking shots. Very few people can pull off a strong handheld shot, so a locked-off tripod shot is best, because it shows control. Be sure to get a tripod that contains a fluid head and a half-ball leveler, so you're not adjusting tripod legs to get your tripod level. The half-ball leveler will allow you to loosen a bottom handle to the half-ball, adjust it quickly, then lock it off, when it's level.

For cost, stability, and portability, the monopod with legs is one of my favorite film-making tools, especially for documentaries. It allows you to get into tight spaces and provide camera movement.

Tripods and monopods	Stability is important, so relying on handheld is not the way to go. Carbon fiber tripods are light and strong, but tend to be more expensive.			
Model	Manfrotto XPRO 500US monopod with fluid video head	Benro A48FD monopod	Manfrotto MVH500AH fluid head with 755XB tripod	Induro carbon fiber tripod
Height max	60" 20.2" (closed without head)	64.6" 22" (closed without head)	65" 25" (closed without head)	54" 21.3" (closed without head)
Notes	This is my favorite tool for documentary work. You can get stability with the pull-out legs, which can lock in place.

Movement from the ball joint at the base for pan and push-in/pull-out shots (as well as tilt with the head).

The feet are removable. | Similar to the Manfrotto. You can get stability with the pull-out legs, which can lock in place.

Movement from the ball joint at the base for pan and push-in/pull-out shots (as well as tilt with the head).

Get the Manfrotto MVH500AH video head for ~$150. | Standard tripod with half ball for leveling. | Induro's carbon fiber tripods do not disappoint. The price doesn't include the head. It's light, the legs drop when you twist the locks.

Get the Manfrotto 502HD head with 75mm half ball for leveling: $171. |
| Cost | ~$190 (~$255 with head) | ~$90 (without head) | ~$450 | ~$360 (not including head) |

SLIDERS AND JIBS

Provides for cinematically smooth tracking shots without needing to set up a track on the ground. Get a slider that attaches to a tripod. Make sure the movement reveals something in the shot—that it helps tell the story, rather than providing movement for the sake of movement. Change the way the camera faces, rotating it along the axis to get parallel tracking shots and perpendicular push-in and pull-out shots.

Jibs or small cranes will attach to your tripod and will allow you to do vertical up and down movements as well as pushing in and pulling out from a shot.

Sliders and jibs	For inexpensive cinematic motion (if you can't afford a dolly), sliders that sit on tripods are a good way to go when on a budget. The jib attaches to a tripod, providing crane movement up and down and push-in/pull-out motion.		
Model	Edelkrone SliderPlus	Cinevate Inc 32" Duzi Camera Slider	Kessler Crane Pocket Jib Traveler
Length/reach	17.2" length 24" travel distance on tripod 12" on the ground	32" 24" (closed for travel)	72" horizontal reach from the fulcrum 62.3" vertical movement 27" (collapsed for travel)
Notes	This slider uses a unique technology that provides extra reach when mounted on a tripod, proving 2 feet of slider travel. There are smaller and larger models, but this size can fit in a backpack. Sliders typcally need a tripod head, so factor that into your cost.	This slider utilizes an onboard flywheel for providing inertial dampening, which results in additional stability and smooth slides. Sliders typcally need a tripod head, so factor that into your cost.	For true cinematic motion a jib is an essential tool for independent film-makers. This portable jib will do the trick for low budget projects. This rig will support only up to 10lbs, so if you're using bigger cameras, you may need to upgrade to a larger rig. You will likely need to get a quick-release mounting plate and a carrying case, which will increase the budget. The jib attaches to a tripod, so you will need one that's large enough to support the weight. Kessler Crane makes one for ~$600 (which does not include a head).
Cost	~$500 (without head)	~$500 (without head)	~$500

GIMBALS

For full stabilization handheld mode that allows for fluid movement, use a three-axis gimbal for pan, tilt, and roll. Essentially the powered system is a gyro allowing for smooth shots and stability even while running.

The camera needs to be balanced for weight, including lenses and batteries. It is recommended that you set up a separate audio system so it doesn't add weight and get in the way.

These gimbals also include a transmitter so pan and tilt can be operated remotely. Unless you also have a remote follow focus, you will want to set the focus to a deep depth of field, since it will be too difficult to adjust focus manually.

Gimbals	The gimbals listed below offer a variety of weight limits so be aware of the total weight of the camera, including battery, lenses, remote follow focus, external microphone, cage, etc. You may need to strip down your camera to the basics to meet the weight limitations.		
Model	ikan EC1 Beholder	DJI Ronin-M Gimbal	CAME-ARGO
Weight limit	4.5lbs (2kg)	8lbs (3.6kg)	6.6lbs (3kg)
Notes	For small cameras Includes double grip handle.	Includes double grip handle.	Includes double grip handle.
Cost	~$850	~$1000	~$800

FIELD HARD DRIVES

Having a good hard drive in the field (along with a laptop) is essential for backing up data as you shoot. When a card fills up, dump the footage onto a hard drive (two, for a backup is a good idea). Three of the hard drives below are portable and are powered by a laptop. They're designed to resist damage if dropped. The Caldigit Tuff is also dust proof and water proof.

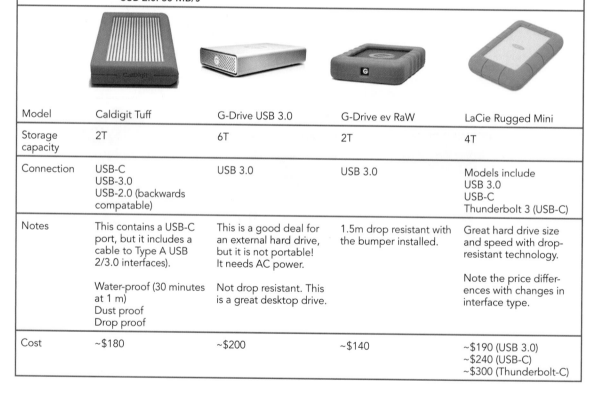

Field hard drives	You need a hard drive that's fast. The spin speed should be a minimum of 7200rpm and have a connector that's USB 3.0 or better, such as a thunderbolt line or eSATA connection. Portable SSD drives are an option, but I do not include them in this list due to their high expense (over $400 for a 500GB SSD drive). Speed of hard drives. Throughput data rates: • Thuderbolt 3 (USB-C): 387 MB/s • RAID: 240 MB/s • USB 3.0: 130 MB/s • USB 2.0: 60 MB/s			
Model	Caldigit Tuff	G-Drive USB 3.0	G-Drive ev RaW	LaCie Rugged Mini
Storage capacity	2T	6T	2T	4T
Connection	USB-C USB-3.0 USB-2.0 (backwards compatable)	USB 3.0	USB 3.0	Models include USB 3.0 USB-C Thunderbolt 3 (USB-C)
Notes	This contains a USB-C port, but it includes a cable to Type A USB 2/3.0 interfaces). Water-proof (30 minutes at 1 m) Dust proof Drop proof	This is a good deal for an external hard drive, but it is not portable! It needs AC power. Not drop resistant. This is a great desktop drive.	1.5m drop resistant with the bumper installed.	Great hard drive size and speed with drop-resistant technology. Note the price differences with changes in interface type.
Cost	~$180	~$200	~$140	~$190 (USB 3.0) ~$240 (USB-C) ~$300 (Thunderbolt-C)

SMARTPHONE CINEMA

Yes, the time has come where smartphones—when rigged up properly and installed with the right apps—can deliver cinematic images. From Lindsay Walker's experimental short, *The Courage Closet*, to David Darg's and Bryn Mooser's short documentary, *The Painter of Jalouzi*, produced for RYOT Studio (both profiled in the Introduction), it's happening. Below is a list of gear and software for you to try out the cinematic potential of your smartphone.

I'm not going to include smartphones, here, since models change every six months or so and I'm not going to debate the quality of a Samsung over an iPhone, for example. If you're interested in smartphone cinema, it's like you already have a smartphone. Below are some of the recommended geart to turn it into your own microcinema package.

Smartphone cinema gear	You need the right software and you need the right smartphone, and the later models will deliver on higher-quality images than earlier models. And you want high-capacity memory, since it's unlikely that you'll be hooking up an external hard drive to it. The iPhone 7, for example, contains up to 256GB of memory, optical image stabilization, f/1.8 aperture, 4K video recording at 30 fps and 1080p up to 120 fps. The iPhone 8 will contain even better specs. Wireless charging will need to become standard, since many of these lenses are not designed to be attached to a case.			
Model	olloclip 4-in-1 Lens Set for iPhone 6	olloclip Macro Pro for iPhone 6	olloclip Telephoto for iPhone 6	Moondog Labs Anamorphic Lens Adapter
Features	Includes fisheye, wide angle, 10x, and 15x macro lenses. https://olloclip.com/	Provides 7x, 14x, and 21x macro lenses for detail shots. https://olloclip.com/	Features 2x telephoto lens, as well as a wide angle, a 10x macro, and a circular polarizing lens. https://olloclip.com/	For those who want more than the standard HD 16:9 widescreen, but 2.4:1. http://moondoglabs.com/
Notes	Cannot be used with a case. The lenses fit on the camera, naked. Be sure to get external batteries for your phone for long shoots. For all models of the iPhone 6. Additional lenses available for the iPhone 5 and 7.	For those who want to get really close to their subject and portray detail shots.	1.5m drop resistant with the bumper installed.	Great hard drive size and speed with drop resistant technology. Used in the film *Tangerine*.
Cost	~$80	~$70	~$120	~$175

Smartphone cinema gear (continued)

You'll need some of these additional accessories to kit out your smartphone and make it cinema-ready.

Model	Freefly Movi Gimbal Stabilizer	Steadicam Volt	Multimedia iKlip	Kodiak 2.0 Power Bank	FiLMiC Pro app

Features	This is essential if you want your shots to move smoothly through space. http://gomovi.com/	A gimbal stabilizer from Steadicam. If you're going to do smartphone cinema, you'll need this or the DJI Osmo. The collapsible design folds in for portability. https://tiffen.com/steadicamvolt/	Wireless audio receiver with built-in preamps, an XLR input, gain control, and phantom power. It plugs into your smartphone, giving it professional audio quality recording. For those who need to get good audio attached to the camera. http://ikmultimedia.com/products/iklipav/	6000 milliampere hour (mAh) battery with USB connection to charge your phone while shooting. (This should lasts about six hours on a full charge under optimum conditions.) https://outdoortechnology.com/products/kodiak	Provides control of focus, exposure, white balance, zoom, focus peaking, zebra stripes, false color (for exposure control), audio meters, shutter speed, frame rates (1-240 fps for slow motion shots), a data rate of 100mb/s at 4K and 50mb/s at 1080p, and audio control. http://filmicpro.com/
Notes	This is one of the most advanced and powerful tools you can get for your smartphone. It comes with its own app and it includes five different shooting modes for cinematic shots.		This will not attach to a gimbal stabilizer. You can attach this to a tripod. If you plan to record audio separately and sync up your clips in post, then you don't need this accessary.	Rugged silicone wrap for drop protection and it is waterproof when closed or water resistant when open. If you're doing long shoots, get several of these.	You really can't do smartphone cinema right without this app.
Cost	~$300	~$200	~$180	~$50	~$15

Dear Tom
https://www.youtube.com/
watch?v=O8GLOYVgPkA
Film by David Tembleque.

Still from David Tembleque's *Dear Tom*. Used with permission.

CHAPTER 8

David Tembleque: Blackmagic's Pocket Cinema Camera in *Dear Tom...*

Some filmmakers fictionalize their lives. Others engage in essay films and talk about their experiences as we look at footage. David Tembleque relies on visuals with strong composition and use of natural light. He then adds a woman performing a break-up on a phone message. Is a it fiction? Is it real? It's real.

"Dear Tom was a real love story that I lived with someone some time ago," Tembleque says on his site. He dated her for several months and he filmed some of their private moments together. But then it was suddenly over. "One day I woke up and she was gone, leaving a goodbye voice message on my phone. What you see is our real story," he adds.

And the woman reading the break-up letter? It's the Ex. "The girl in the film and the narrator is herself. There are no actors, no budget, and no lightning. It was filmed with a camera of the size of a hand and a lot of love."

Tembleque loves the camera that literally fits in your pocket—and it's not a cell phone, but Blackmagic Design's Pocket Cinema Camera (BMPCC).

The film earned awards and screened around the world, from New York to Paris, from Istanbul, Turkey to Orlando, Florida. For a film with no budget, Tembleque learned an early lesson in filmmaking—the story (along with some good-looking shots) is the most important element. The themes of lost love are universal and resonates with audiences.

Tembleque started taking pictures after his father bought him a DSLR when he was fifteen. He hasn't stopped. And he is also passionate about cinema and comic books. "Photography, cinema, and comic books have always been my passions," he says. "While the first one allows you to portrait the reality and bring it to the people," he adds, "the other two allows you to imagine stories and make them real."

Tembleque started to make cinema more real or more seriously with his short *Dear Tom*. He works as a filmmaker for the fashion company, Zara. In fact, he made a few short films as a student, but he never went to film school. He did study audio-visual communication at Complutense University of Madrid in Spain, but he really started teaching himself after he graduated. "I have been continuing my studies in photography, editing, color correction, and cinematography" by taking online courses, tutorials online, and then practicing, he explains. If his self-teaching using online resources is his post-bacc, Tembleque feels that "Working in Zara as a fashion filmmaker has been my master's degree, giving me hundreds of hours of shooting," he tells me.

Some of his strongest influences include the Hong Kong cinema great, Wong Kar-wai, and his cinematographer. "I was very shocked, influenced, and quite obsessed with Wong Kar-wai films, including *Chungking Express* (1994) and *In the Mood for Love* (2000), and also with his cinematographer, Christopher Doyle." Doyle, an Australian who was never trained in cinematography, helped shape the look of new Hong Kong cinema. (See Figures 8.1–8.3.)

Tembleque loves Doyle's and Wong's crafting of "intimate situations, the saturated colors, the ambient, the neon lights of Hong Kong, the Asian culture, the way the

FIGURES 8.1-8.3
Shots from Wong Kar-wai's *Chungking Express*. Notice the colors, lighting, shadows, and composition—all designed to emotionally convey the story, visually. Cinematography by Christopher Doyle. (©1994 Jet Tone Production.)

characters live, the absolute modern and trendy use of wide shots and sequence shots." Watching these films, he adds, "made me want to naively go and film at any cost." But he was never literal in his source of inspiration. "There are hundreds of people copying Wong Kar-wai's style," he says, "so I tried to adapt it to my own style and make something very different."

We can see some use of colors and composition inspired by Doyle's cinematography in Tembleque's *Dear Tom* and *What If*. (See Figures 8.4–8.8.)

But getting that look in-camera can be tricky. It helps to shoot in RAW. In addition, with his background in photography, Tembleque realized that the ability to do post, to shape of the look through color grading, he discovered his personal style. Without the bit-depth of RAW, it's difficult to pull off, he says.

FIGURE 8.4

Tembleque keeps an eye out for colors in natural light situations in order to add impact to his films and here we see elements of the Wong Kar-wai influence. We see the couple lit by television screens, ambient light in the restaurant, and a light from the table in *Dear Tom*.
(Image courtesy of David Tembleque. ©2015 David Tembleque.)

FIGURE 8.5

Natural light on the train brings out the blues and yellows as Tembleque composes his partner leaving on a train in *Dear Tom*. (Image courtesy of David Tembleque. ©2015 David Tembleque.)

FIGURE 8.6

Colors pop in this still from Tembleque's *What If*. (Image courtesy of David Tembleque. ©2017 David Tembleque.)

"I wanted to make the cinematography very personal based on my own photography style," he tells me. "Filming video in RAW gives me endless possibilities for retouching. And not just a random LUT (preset look-up table) that everyone can use. I love saturated colors and the vintage look with film grain."

While most cameras shoot in a normal video space known as Rec 709, providing an in-camera look that's accurate, shooting in log (or flat mode), is better for dynamic range, Tembleque explains. "It gives you much more opportunities and range for color correction. You notice that pulling up the shadows and recovering the highlights" (see Chapter 3). When he does use Rec 709 for normal image mode, it's only for "making something where the image color is not extremely important or in cases that the color has to be very natural like fashion shows."

I wanted to make the cinematography very personal based on my own photography style.

FIGURE 8.7

Natural light at a restaurant shows off Tembleque's strong composition and colors in a found space in *Dear Tom*. (Image courtesy of David Tembleque. ©2015 David Tembleque.)

The ability to color grade—shaping the final look of the film in post—is a key aspect of the filmmaking process for him, especially in personal projects. "When I have a personal project," he explains, "it's important to me that I try to film in RAW in order to engage in the maximum opportunities to color correct later and make something really special, visually."

But it never really comes down to the camera. The personal may be recorded by the camera (and nearly any camera would do), but one of the reason's Tembleque avoided setting up lights reflects his desire to let the lighting, emotions, and situations of the scene stem from natural moments. "I really love the natural shots where you can feel that the character and the person are the same," he says. "She laughs, cries, and plays naturally, without acting or posing at all. It was very important for me to get these kind of shots to show the real love between a couple and have it touch the audience. You realize that she is doing it for real, not as an actress."

This reality comes through by the intimacy of the camera, but it also helped to get her used to the camera, keeping it ubiquitous in the relationship. By using a "real partner," he contends, she was open to "showing her real feelings at any time." In addition, by "using the camera at all times, she got used to it and ended up acting normally." The combination of these two factors—and adding a bit of a Wong Kar-wai visual style—helped him shape an award-winning film.

FIGURE 8.8

One light splashes across the top of the woman, as the rest of her falls into darkness in *Dear Tom*. (Image courtesy of David Tembleque. ©2015 David Tembleque.)

POSTPRODUCTION WORKFLOW

Tembleque's postproduction workflow reflects this. Most of the time, his process includes using Premiere Pro CC. Even though he's used DaVinci Resolve, he "finds it a little bit messy and complicated," so he gravitated towards Premiere, which allows him to "change simple things like brightness, contrast, highlights, and shadows."

LUTs (or look-up tables)—a predetermined look utilizing color space tools—allow him to play with the visual feel of the film project. "My favorite LUTs by far are the OSIRIS LUTs, which works for almost every type of footage that you film, not only flat footage but also normal Rec 709 films. This LUT can be found at: https://www.colorgradingcentral.com/osiris/.

Tembleque feels that Film Convert is a good tool for beginners to play with, which can provide an "interesting look" pretty easily (see https://www.filmconvert.com/).

A final step Tembleque discussed includes the application of film grain to the footage in order to help create "a more cinematic look." He likes Gorilla grain (see http://www.gorillagrain.com/).

For his day job as a fashion design filmmaker, Tembleque shoots with a Red Raven camera and the DJI Ronin gimbal stabilizer, but for his personal projects, he likes the intimacy of the Blackmagic Pocket Cinema Camera and the use of ikan's Beholder gimbal designed for small cameras. At the time, the BMPCC worked for him ("It was an amazing camera"), but he feels it's old technology that's being replaced by "a lot of new cameras hitting the market", especially cameras shooting in 4K." He feels that there is no "perfect camera," but if it existed it would be the smallness of the mirrorless camera, take good stills, and shoot 4K video in RAW or ProRes 444 up to 120 fps, with internal three-axis stabilization, contain a full frame sensor or one no smaller than Super 35mm or APS-C, and be able to use any lens made by any company.

The importance of 4K shooting includes the ability to crop and re-scale your shots if your final output is full HD (1920x1080p). "Even if you export the film to 1080 and we watch everything in 1080 normally on internet and TV," Tembleque argues, "it's not the same as shooting an original 4K image to work with. It allows you to crop and rescale your shots." In addition, even when downscaled to 1080, the 4K image origination "increases the definition, the sharpness, and the details—they're much more incredible," he adds.

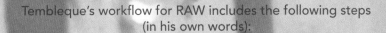

Tembleque's workflow for RAW includes the following steps
(in his own words):

When I film on RAW I use another method for the final color correction. It's a bit messy but you can get amazing results.

- First I chose a frame of every shot and open all of them with Lightroom.

- I color correct it with Lightroom, which allows you to retouch it as a normal RAW in photography. You can also download hundreds of plugins for Lightroom with amazing looks, work as a base with them and then make the corrections:

  - VSCO cam (http://vsco.co/store/film)
  - LIGHTGRAM (http://www.lightgram.com/) (where you can get amazing vintage looks).

- Then, when I have color corrected one RAW frame (one single picture) of every take that I am going to use, I export them as DNG, so the program saves the parameters of the retouch.

- Then I open After Effects and import the DNG, which automatically opens the Camera Raw with the picture and the color correction that you saved before. Then I save the presets with the Camera Raw.

- Finally I open the entire take as "sequence of images" in Camera Raw and load the presets that I have saved.

- Save the .XML of the .DNG that you color corrected with Lightroom and paste it in the folder of the RAW sequence to load the presets.

- Be careful with the noise. If you put noise with After Effects, you will get noise as a still image instead of a moving one. It happened to me in *Dear Tom* and it's a very rare effect. I didn't want to correct it, as part of my training process to see how to evolve over time.

Fragments
http://vimeo.com/120850943
Agency: The Delivery Men
Story: The Delivery Men
Cast: Jessica Perrin, Dietrich
Schmidt, Diane Perella, Walter Allan
Director: Joe Simon
DP: Joe Simon
Writer: Hussain Pirani
Executive Producer: Brent Ramsey,
Canon Camera
Producer: Gina Gatto
Casting Director: Sarah Dowling
Hair and Makeup: Misha Fruge
Gaffer: Derrick Mitchell
Grip: Chris York
Production Assistants:
Katie McGaha, Derek Fuller
Editor: Hussain Pirani
VFX: Graham Hutchins
Color: Joe Simon
BTS Camera: Tyler Gorrell

CHAPTER 9

Joe Simon: Canon's C100 Mark II in *Fragments*

by Dana Beasley

Like most love stories, *Fragments* begins with a spark.

But this is more than your figurative flame ignited between sweethearts. This blaze, rather, takes the form of a literal sparkler illuminating the opening scene. Set against a black night, the fire crackles beneath soft, female narration—gradually revealing a newlywed couple drifting in slow motion beneath a glimmering arc.

It's then that the flashbacks begin—highlighting the most cherished and earliest moments in this couple's journey; "When time slows down," the narration goes, "there is time to wander into the past."

Filmmaker Joe Simon and his production company, The Delivery Men, drafted an initial script for *Fragments* after being approached by Brent Ramsey of Canon to create a film that showcased the C100 Mark II. As Ramsey explains, "Having just completed a 'traditional how-to-shoot-a-wedding video,' I pitched Joe on the concept of shooting a short film around a 'country wedding theme' that might inspire wedding video shooters to upgrade their equipment to achieve more cinematic results." Joe loved the idea. Canon would sponsor the project, showing off the new capabilities of the C100 Mark II:

- new ergonomics and accessories
- ual Pixel Auto Focus (FACE AF)
- new codec
- new slow motion capabilities.

The end result is a three-minute fictional short that utilizes a variety of technical applications and artistic approaches to visually and emotionally convey the couple's romance. "It's this whole time-shifting story of this person's life," said Simon, who served as director and director of photography for the film. "Basically, at the very end, you see that they're an old couple now, and you see that they're looking at the photo from their wedding as they reminisce through all those times when they first met and their courtship" (see Figure 9.1).

This poignant production differs dramatically from what first led Simon toward film work in the early 2000s. As a former professional BMX rider, Simon used a Sony Digital8 camcorder to record himself and his friends doing tricks—these "antics with the kids," as he puts it, ignited his passion for filmmaking. "When you don't have anybody paying you to do something," he says, "you learn how to love it for what it is." Once this interest was solidified, the self-taught filmmaker's repertoire quickly progressed to live event videos and commercial productions. By 2004, Simon was a full-time filmmaker, and in 2010 he established The Delivery Men, a full service Austin-based production company specializing in commercial, narrative, and documentary work.

Regardless of genre, Simon has found a love—even an "addiction"—in the filmmaking practice. "It's one of those things that you have to love doing in order to continue, because it's never easy. I love the creation aspect." he says. But this creation, and subsequent execution, is rarely an individual effort. Simon cites collaboration as part of what propelled his filmmaking career, especially in the narrative realm. "I've been doing this for a long time," he says, "but I could have been farther along if I had pushed it earlier—I was so content just working by myself or with a really small team, and not letting go of the control. It takes a lot of people to make a good product. You can't do everything yourself."

Excluding Simon, the film crew for *Fragments* consisted of an assistant camera, two grips, a production assistant, and a producer. It was all hands on deck, as the group had only two weeks to develop and workshop the story; create shot lists; and prepare props, locations, and camera equipment. Then, they filmed the short over a period of just two days. "It takes a really amazing team to pull off a film like this

FIGURE 9.2
Teamwork is important in putting together the short, *Fragments*, in a timely manner. "It takes a really amazing team to pull off a film like this in the amount of time we did it," says director Joe Simon.
(Image ©2015 The Delivery Men. Used with permission.)

in the amount of time we did it, and with the amount of different setups we had to do," said Simon, in a *Fragments* behind-the-scenes video. "Everybody is doing lots of different jobs, and that's kind of part of being in the smaller production world, is that you wear a lot of hats to make things happen." (See Figure 9.2.)

Ramsey says that he "encouraged Joe to produce an inspiring product during our first phone call, not just a promotional film." For Ramsey, the film, sponsored by Canon, was designed "to be inspirational to artists." With the film being shot on a C100 Mark II, the real promotion would "come from the behind-the-scenes photos and video, where the camera and lenses and the technology would be promoted," Ramsey explains. From the start it was a collaboration between a corporate entity and the filmmaker.

After finalizing pre-production details, they filmed *Fragments* at a scenic ranch on the outskirts of Austin, Texas. The story features a dreamlike series of flashbacks, from running through a field of grass, to late-night stargazing in the bed of a vintage, baby-blue GMC.

Generally, Simon considers himself a "naturalistic lighter," a quality demonstrated through his clever use of daylight bounce and diffusion, as well as practicals. "I walk into a space and I see what it looks like naturally, and what I can do to enhance that," says Simon. "It's that whole approach of 'What does this actually

FIGURE 9.3

An HMI light was set up outside a window to provide an illusion of natural light of a window imaged in Jessica Perrin's eye. (Joe Simon. ©2015 Canon USA, Inc. Used with permission.)

look like in real life?' What would it look like just to have this conversation with this person in this room?"

This approach also has many benefits for filmmakers working with limited resources. As Simon explains, the lower your budget, the more important it is to use the time of day to your advantage. "A lot of the time you'll have that sun coming in and it'll bounce off the floor and help create some light, or have that shaft of light coming through the window to create a sharp edge," he says. "Interior wise, you could just use bounce or flags to control that. It's fairly simple, but you have to work a little bit quicker because you only have the sun." Given the light sensitivity of modern cameras, practical fixtures, such as lamps or other on-site light sources, can also serve as good key or fill lights to add contrast to shots. (See Figure 9.3.)

A prime example of this crafty use of practicals is the nighttime truck scene, which Simon cites as one of his favorites. This moment features the couple stargazing in the back of an old GMC, their faces softly lit by bouncing only the glow of a flashlight off the pages of a book they are holding.

For added depth and texture, Simon instructed Dietrich Schmidt to breathe heavily, the condensation making visible the beam from a flashlight (see Figures 9.4 and 9.5). In the wide shot, the camera's ISO was set to 20,000 in order to capture the light of the stars above, while the side of the truck itself was lit using a pair of 300 watt Low Pro lights.

FIGURES 9.4 AND 9.5
Joe Simon lights the scene at night with a flashlight in *Fragments*.
(Images ©2015 Canon USA, Inc. Used with permission.)

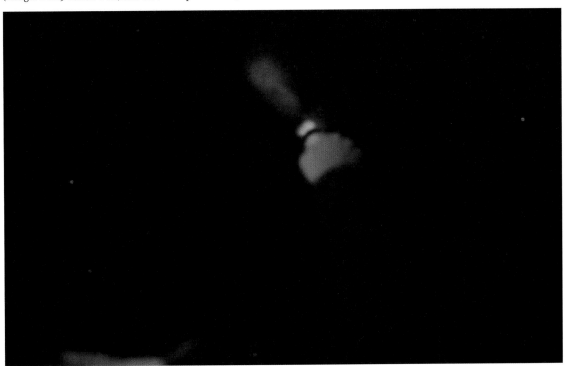

FIGURES 9.6 AND 9.7
Joe Simon flaps a scrim to push haze in the room. Image (©2015 The Delivery Men. Used with permission.)

The haze adds texture to the scene, as can be seen in the background of the shot from *Fragments*, below. (Joe Simon. ©2015 Canon USA, Inc. Used with permission.)

This isn't the only instance of staged atmospheric effects. Simon explained that "haze" is used for nearly every indoor shot—a technique that allows the camera to capture the movement of air by distributing a fine, even mist that diffuses light and creates depth and separation. "It's not about making it foggy," says Simon. "It's being able to visually see the air, and being able to see that air gives you layers" (see Figures 9.6 and 9.7). Creating layers is also achieved through the use of foreground elements, or "looking from one space to another." This is demonstrated when the couple runs through a grass field from the vantage of the house's second-story window. For this sequence's exterior shot, Simon used the C100 Mark II's auto-focus capability on a 100–400mm lens to track the pair running in the field toward the camera. Simon says the camera's grip-relocator easily adjusted the autofocus, to either track objects manually or automatically as they moved across the frame. He relocated the camera's grip unit with Zacuto Zgrip Relocator as part of Zacuto's Recoil shoulder rig used on the project.

The film has a few distinct looks: the wedding exit is smooth (filmed using a Freefly MoVI M5), while the pre-wedding flashbacks were done using a Zacuto Recoil shoulder rig to authenticate the movement of point-of-view shots, making it "a little more raw," says Simon (see Figure 9.8). He explains that the way a film-maker frames a shot, including lens selection, sends a subconscious message to the viewer, offering insight into a character's emotional state.

FIGURE 9.8
Joe Simon mounts the C100 Mark II on a MoVI M5 for a pull-back shot in *Fragments*. (Image by Brent Ramsey. ©2015 Canon USA, Inc. Used with permission.)

"Nearly every shot in the flashbacks was at 50mm," Simon says. "Being that a lot of those were point of view—looking from the girl to guy and back to the other—we're looking through their eyes. The view of your eyes is 52mm, so it's as close as you can get to that." The depth of field also communicates a lot to the audience, Simon explains: "Are you trying to hide something? Are you trying to show something? Shallow depth of field is a great tool for making someone feel alone, and it's so special when you have a little bit of a wider shot—say medium, to medium close-up—and you have it very shallow and you can't see anything else around them. It feels very isolating." (See Figures 9.9 and 9.10.) Simon generally sets his f-stop between f/2.8 and f/5.6, to provide shallow depth of field to most of his shots. Filming f/8 and up, he warns, causes a noticeable loss of production value—or makes a project feel too "video."

For further separation, there were different color grades added in post-production. The wedding exit scene was fairly standard—a C100 Canon Log with the look-up table (LUT) on top of it. For the flashbacks, Simon used a flatter grade with less saturation, then added grain to offer texture and achieve a more vintage look. The final—contemporary—scene, therefore, is more saturated.

FIGURE 9.9
Jessica Perrin and Dietrich Schmidt as the young couple in *Fragments*. In the medium wide shot, we see a deep depth of field, with the older couple in the background in focus, providing a scope of the space and characters.
(©2015 Canon USA, Inc. Used with permission.)

FIGURE 9.10
In the close-up, Simon opens up the aperture, creating a shallow depth of field, so our attention is fully on Perrin's expression.
(©2015 Canon USA, Inc. Used with permission.)

During pre-production, Simon was careful to ensure that all of the flashbacks connected, so each transition—including cleverly utilized match cuts and body wipes—would seamlessly take the viewer to the next scene. One sequence begins with the couple on a camping trip, where a collapsing tent segues to a bedsheet being flapped over the lens. The couple is then shown in a bedroom having a pillow fight—the feathers spilling out from the cases subsequently transitioning into fire embers from a campfire, then fire from the wedding sparklers (see Figures 9.11–9.13).

Simon's directing style also allows for added fluidity within the shots themselves. When it comes to blocking, he says he prefers to let the talent make it their own: "I've found that the more involved and the more collaborative everybody is, the more they feel their input is important, and they'll take that to heart." These approaches to cinematography and talent–filmmaker interactions allow the production to take on a more organic quality.

FIGURE 9.11
Jessica Perrin and Dietrich Schmidt's pillow fight in *Fragments*. As the pillow hits Schmidt's face, Simon cuts to the planned transition, below.
(©2015 Canon USA, Inc. Used with permission.)

FIGURE 9.12
Instead of feathers popping out of the pillow, the planned transition cuts to sparks from a campfire.
(©2015 Canon USA, Inc. Used with permission.)

FIGURE 9.13
From the campfire the film cuts to the sparks from the wedding sparklers. These types of transitions are deliberate throughout the film and aids in visual storytelling through cuts.
(©2015 Canon USA, Inc. Used with permission.)

In terms of technical specifics, the film was shot in Canon Log, something Simon recommends to achieve a more cinematic look that captures the full dynamic range of the C100 Mark II's sensor. Shooting in Rec. 709, he says, will produce blown-out highlights or too-dark shadows, and generally lower contrast. When shooting, however, Simon prefers looking at false colors to monitor exposure by using a smallHD 702 or 502 monitor. He says he judges everything off the Rec. 709 LUT, because it better indicates what the image will look like in post-production.

In general, Simon says, when faced with an 8-bit codec camera, you can run into banding issues—where you see layers of color contrast bands in the sky, for example. The 8-bit is most noticeable on any sort of solid color, like a wall or the sky, so you risk seeing banding if you're inside shooting an interview in front of a solid-colored wall. When you have a lower bit depth, there's only so much it can handle when pushing or pulling exposure or altering color in post before it falls apart. It can get worse when compressed again for web output. This is why getting the exposure and color in-camera accurate is important.

In Simon's capable hands, the C100 Mark II never ran into any banding issues, Ramsey remarks. "I thought that not only did the camera perform as expected, but in Joe's capable hands, it truly exceeded expectations," Ramsey adds.

If you're shooting for the big screen, the 8-bit compression may become a bigger issue since the larger screen of a theater will exaggerate any potential flaws. The Delivery Men still shoot many projects, including *Fragments*, in 2K resolution instead of 4K. Full HD is just shy of 2K, and the C100 Mark II is limited to full HD (1920x1080). Although 4K does offer more capabilities in post-production, such as cropping or stabilization, this selection typically comes down to media management, as 4K data takes up significantly more drive space than 2K. "Ultimately, I'd shoot 4K as much as I could, just because it gives you options," says Simon. "But I don't think it's necessary."

It's been over two years since *Fragments* was first produced, but Simon says the Canon C100 Mark II is still one of the best low budget cameras available, especially concerning battery life and the color it captures, particularly skin-tone renditions. "The nice thing about Canon cameras is they work out of the box pretty simply," he says. "It has peaking, it has waveform, it has zebras—it has all the tools that are handy, and the screen is big enough that you can actually see what you're doing. You could shoot a whole project on that if you had to, and it's going to look nice."

And that's just what Simon and his crew have done. In the end of *Fragments*, the wedding flashback dissolves into an old, x-tone photograph being held by the now-elderly couple (see Figure 9.14). The narration continues in the background: "Spoken words can fade—it's how you felt that lasts a lifetime. It's irreversible, eternal. It's a moment that stays still—forever."

In many ways, a great film behaves the same way. The visual storytelling, the words, the shapes of the scenes, all come together to hopefully leave a lasting impression on the viewer—maybe not in an obvious way, but in the way the audience subconsciously experiences the story through the transitions, lighting, or lens choices determined before filming even began. It's this unglamorous work that Simon says you have to love doing, because it ultimately pays off: "You're learning, you're evolving, you're fixing things, and you make this final product that you can sit back and watch and feel proud of," he says. "You're starting with nothing, and then you end up with a story."

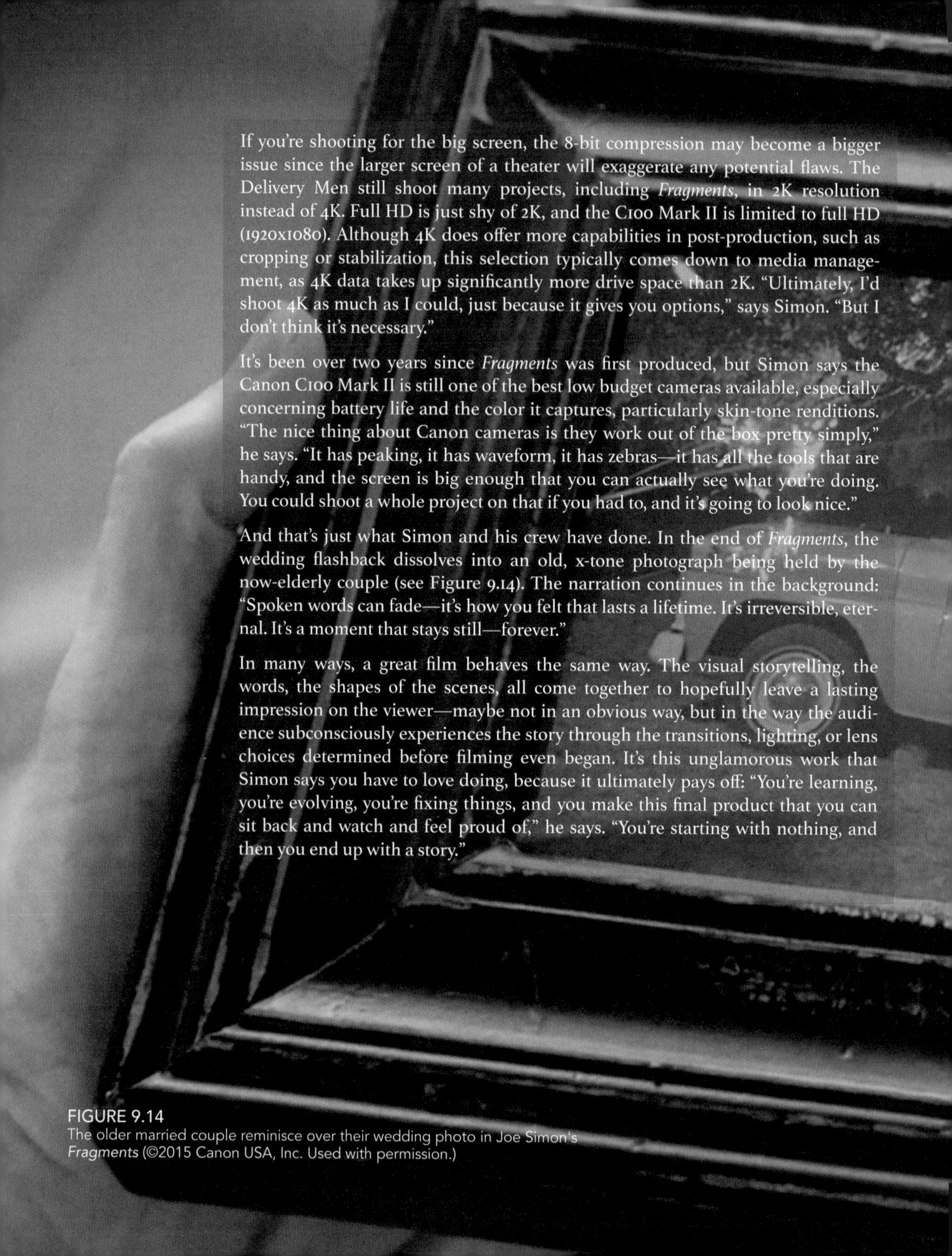

FIGURE 9.14
The older married couple reminisce over their wedding photo in Joe Simon's *Fragments* (©2015 Canon USA, Inc. Used with permission.)

CHAPTER 10

Philip Bloom: Canon's 7D in *A Day at the Races*

MEETING PHILIP BLOOM*

Bloom, hailing from England, arrives late at Venice Beach's famed Sidewalk Café, where you can find a Louis L'Amour hamburger on the menu, as well as homeless teens with their dogs intermingling with circus act characters roaming along the boardwalk. But he's always jolly and can win you over in moments with his charm. Bloom came out of the ranks of Sky Television in England. He begged to be a camera operator and actually found his break when a sound-crew member left. He filled the opening and Bloom says he "learned to shoot from some of the best cameramen I've ever worked with." He also learned to work efficiently and quickly by shooting news. "I would have to say that some of the greatest training for people to learn to shoot fast and shoot efficiently is to work news. Because you really have to get stuff done fast," he notes. "I will walk into a room and it is almost like a Terminator-style scan," he quips. "I'll look around the room and within about 30 seconds I will put any additional lighting where the subject is going to be and where the camera is going to be." He stayed with Sky Television for seventeen years, traveling the world producing documentaries for his last three years at Sky. "It was great fun," he smiles.

FIGURE 10.1
Still from *A Day at the Races* directed by Philip Bloom, showing off his trademark close-up of people's faces.
(©2010 LumaForge, LLC. Used with permission.)

> Some of the greatest training for people to learn to shoot fast and shoot efficiently is to work news.

---

*Author's note: Although this interview occurred in 2010, I've decided to keep it in the third edition due to Bloom's significance in helping forward the DSLR cinema movement professionally, showing other potential filmmakers his tips and approaches. This story reveals how he utilized high-end cinema cameras on a short

FIGURE 10.2
Still featuring Ishan Tankha from a 90-second spot, *Voices of Change* directed by Lucy Campbell-Jackson and shot by Philip Bloom on a Canon 5D Mark II. Note Bloom's oblique composition capturing the depth in the shot. (©2009 Greenpeace.)

After leaving Sky, he went independent. And found DSLRs. But he first balked at their potential. He tossed the Canon 5D Mark II aside. After seeing some footage over the summer of 2009, he began to change his mind. "Initially I thought the weaknesses outweighed the strengths, but by progressively using them, and with new cameras coming out and more importantly with new firmware coming out, it feels like it is going the other way and the strengths are outweighing the weaknesses," Bloom explains.

Bloom shot some projects with it, including a commercial for Greenpeace (see Figure 10.2). He quickly became one of the foremost gurus of DSLR cinema, even hired by Lucasfilm to show the Lucas team the cinematic potential of the cameras and then later brought onto the set of *Red Tails* (2012) to shoot some plates and pickup shots with Canon DSLRs.

"When you see them on the big screen, you can understand why Lucasfilm is so amazed by these cameras," Bloom explains, "and the whole industry is so interested in buying them because filmmaking is an expensive business and a big part of that is cameras and big parts of that [are] the amount of crew that is needed."

Philip Bloom's Greenpeace commercial, *Voices of Change*, directed by Lucy Campbell-Jackson: http://vimeo.com/6695584

"Behind the Scenes on Lucasfilm's *Red Tails* with the Canon DSLRs": http://vimeo.com/11695817;

Skywalker Ranch: http://vimeo.com/8100091

Bloom admits he's not an expert in the design of Canon lenses or the technical aspects of how everything works inside the camera, but he does say, "I'm just very passionate about using them and I use them prolifically and that is why people come to me. They come to me because of my experience."

He's distinctly known for a style that captures intimate portraits of people's faces, a style that strikingly echoes with the composition of George Caleb Bingham's *Mississippi Boatman* (see Figure 10.3). And for *A Day at the Races*, the Cooke lenses add compositional strength to Bloom's project.

But what is more interesting is how some of Philip Bloom's images from *A Day at the Races* (including many shots from his people series), captures a similar style and composition to that of Bingham (see Figures 10.3 and 10.4).

Although I don't believe Bloom has studied Bingham's art, many cinematographers do study art, and what Bloom instinctively conveys is a keen concept of composition that echoes what a master painter does with composition—all of which provides cinematic strength to his HD videos. Bloom's shots not

FIGURE 10.3
George Caleb
Bingham's *Mississippi
Boatman* (1850).
(Courtesy of National
Gallery, Washington,
DC.)

FIGURE 10.4
Philip Bloom captures
emotion with a close-
up in *A Day at the
Races*.
(©2010 LumaForge, LLC.
Used with permission.)

only convey the compositional sensibilities of an artist (such as Bingham's work from
160 years earlier), but they also engage what good artists always do—capture the
essence of humanity in moments of unvarnished truth, the rawness of the human
condition filtered through the artist's eyes with aesthetic prowess.

SHOOTING WITH CINEMA LENSES

In early 2010, Neil Smith, founder of the digital post house Hdi RAWworks asked Philip Bloom to come to Los Angeles and shoot *A Day at the Races* as a proof-of-concept piece—that the Canon 7D can be utilized as a cinema camera by fitting it out with Cooke lenses (S4i; see Figure 10.5). These lenses are meant to be rented, unless you have an extra $20,000 lying around. "As a serious professional post house, the first time I came across DSLR cameras I totally pooh-poohed them," Smith laughs. "I thought we would never use them. They would never be used in cinema projects."

Neil Smith hired Philip Bloom not only to shoot a short with a 7D fitted out with Cooke cinema lenses, but to present a master class workshop at The Lot in March 2010. It was a way to prove how these cameras can be utilized by a small crew and still attain a cinema look for film projects. It's a way of "making things simpler and more streamlined. And that's certainly [... what] these cameras are very good at doing," Bloom says.

FIGURE 10.5
A Canon 7D, fitted with a PL mount, sports a $20,000 Cooke lens. (©2010 LumaForge, LLC. Used with permission.)

Bloom explains how he initially conceived the story with Neil Smith. "He wanted the majesty of the horses through the morning mist running on the race track," Bloom remembers. But "the longest lens I got was 100mm" and there was no mist. "Filming horse racing with one camera and the longest lens [at] 100mm, you aren't going to get much," Bloom remarks. "I was expecting longer lenses, and I didn't get them, so as soon as I saw the lenses I had, I completely changed the plan. I said, OK, we are going to do the detail behind the racing. We are going to capture the life around the racing instead of the racing itself."

This became the story—an immersion into the environment surrounding the horse races, such as the stables, rather than the race, itself.

RETROFITTING THE CANON 7D

Hot Rod Cameras (hotrodcameras.com; Illya Friedman, President) designed a PL mount for the 7D, allowing professional filmmakers to mount cinema-type lenses, such as the Cooke modeled in *A Day at the Races*. Bloom utilized two Cooke S4 lenses, 25mm and 100mm, as well as a modified Tokina 11–16mm. Bloom loved the way the images with the Cookes turned out. "What a gorgeous image these lenses give you," he explains on his blog. "Yes it was a lot more fiddly and time consuming using these lenses with a mattebox for NDs than my normal 'run and gun' setup but it was worth it. The images ... speak for themselves!"[1]

---

[1]Bloom, Philip. "Shooting 7D PL with Cooke Lenses for Saturday's LA Masterclass." Philipbloom.com. (http://philipbloom.co.uk/2010/03/04/shooting-7d-pl-with-cooke-lenses-for-saturdays-la-masterclass/)

ON LOCATION

Bloom shot in and around horse stables at Hollywood Park for two and a half hours; then he and his team shot for a couple of hours at Santa Anita racetrack. It was a 5:00 a.m. shoot. Smith explains, Bloom "shot only in available light. He captured some beautiful images of the race horses being put through their morning training before sunrise and then in the afternoon at an actual race at the Santa Anita track."

The only shots where they used the mic were with the interviews and the man playing the trumpet. All the ambient noise was recorded in-camera, including the shoveling of the hay (see Figure 10.6). If the level is low enough, editor Jeremy Ian Thomas says, "it's good enough" to use in the project. However, if the levels are too high, "then you hear that kind of tin can feel," Thomas adds. (Which is why recording on a separate audio recorder is preferable.)

FIGURE 10.6
You can hear the scooping of the hay beneath the music track in *A Day at the Races*. The audio for this shoot was recorded on-camera. (©2010 LumaForge, LLC. Used with permission.)

Despite the fact they didn't get long lenses for the initial plan of shooting a race, Bloom felt it worked in his favor by covering the backdrop of the races so that they could focus on the people setting up the event, the ones working in the stables. "That is the kind of thing I do anyway," Bloom explains. "We had the horses in there as background and that worked so much better. I was really happier with it."

Jeremy Ian Thomas, the editor of the piece, was on location with Bloom, who explained to Thomas that the story "wasn't going to be about the majesty of the horses, but the life swirling around the horses, and that there's this whole other world" where "the horses are actually innocent bystanders in a much more human" story, Thomas says. "It's not really about the horses. They're beautiful and humble and quiet, but around them is a whole industry of gambling, and Philip and I were very cognitive of that early on in the storytelling. He and I were looking at each other like, 'We need to stay here in the stables.'"

But Neil Smith originally "wanted to go shoot the horses running," Thomas explains, "but Philip said, 'Let's stay here' [in the stables] and I agreed with him. 'Let's stay here and let's capture the light here, and then we'll move on to the horses.'"

Thomas continues, "Anybody who [watches] it will see that the horses are quite out of focus in a lot of it. They're behind the people, and it's more about the life around it, and I thought that was brilliant" (see Figure 10.7). Thomas pauses. "Horses are great and I think horses are amazing, but there's been a lot of movies and documentaries about horses, but there hasn't been any, that I've seen, about the life around the race horses. And I thought that was pretty cool."

FIGURE 10.7
A woman poses in front of a horse, revealing the shallow depth of field in natural lighting of the Canon 7D in *A Day at the Races*.
(©2010 LumaForge, LLC. Used with permission.)

Philip Bloom remembers arriving at "the ungodly hour of 4:30 a.m." They started with Mike Mitchell, a trainer at the Hollywood stables. Bloom remarks on his blog how he has a "family in the racing business in England, and the people working in the stables are generally young blonde students (huge sweeping generalizing there!)," but at the Hollywood stables, "they seemed to be Latin American guys with *massive* filmic moustaches. Much more fun for me to film, as people know I tend to film interesting-looking people than the obvious pretty ones!"[2] And one of Bloom's signature styles is to gravitate toward the close-ups of these faces (see Figures 10.1, 10.7, and 10.13).

For most of his previous projects—and all of his personal ones—Bloom typically edits. But due to the time constraints on this project, he passed off the task

[2]Bloom, Philip. "Shooting 7D PL with Cooke Lenses for Saturday's LA Masterclass." Philipbloom.com. (http://philipbloom.co.uk/2010/03/04/shooting-7d-pl-with-cooke-lenses-for-saturdays-la-masterclass/)

to Jeremy Ian Thomas of Hdi RAWworks. "It is so nice to see someone else take your work," Bloom says, "and Jeremy was so tuned in to what I wanted. It worked brilliantly."

After dumping the footage into the computer, Thomas crosses his fingers and says he "hopes this footage is good"—and he speaks from being one of the people on location that day. "I hope we didn't mess up," he laughs. He's seen Philip Bloom's work and knows what he's looking for. "I like Philip's editing style," Thomas says, "but it is different than mine, and I thought, 'OK, I don't want to go too far left field and have to re-edit it because he doesn't like it.' So I kept in mind what Philip might want to see." But when it came to pacing the film, Thomas took "a lot of liberties."

Thomas did not want to mimic Bloom's work found in much of his personal short DSLR projects. "His stuff tends to be dissolves—long dissolves, beauty photography of trees and deserts and stuff, and I wanted this to feel more narrative—like it was building and building and building," Thomas remarks. "I wanted it to feel a little more hypnotic," while at the same time sticking "pretty close to what [Bloom] was used to seeing."

Bloom explains how he is drawn to "real people's stories. That's my favorite. I like real people, just telling about their life. Because everybody's got fascinating stories to tell." Although not in-depth character studies, the stories Bloom creates tend to revolve around people's faces and the environment they're in.

One of the images that stood out to Thomas included a shot "where you see something spinning, and you don't quite know what it is yet, and then the horse comes in frame. I knew that was going [to] be either the opening shot, or one of the opening shots, because I thought it was nice. I liked the abstract feel of that. And then the horse shows up and you go, Oh, OK, it's—and then we go wide, and you see the whole stable" (see Figures 10.8–10.10).

FIGURE 10.8
Jeremy Ian Thomas originally conceived this abstract object motion as the opening shot of the film. It appears about 30 seconds into *A Day at the Races*. (©2010 LumaForge, LLC. Used with permission.)

FIGURE 10.9
As the shot proceeds, it goes a bit wide and we see a horse.
(Still from *A Day at the Races*. ©2010 LumaForge, LLC. Used with permission.)

FIGURE 10.10
A full wide shot reveals the horse tied to an exercise carousel.
(Still from *A Day at the Races*. ©2010 LumaForge, LLC. Used with permission.)

FIGURE 10.11
Philip Bloom eyes a shot in *A Day at the Races* on a Marshall monitor attached to the Canon 7D.
(©2010 LumaForge, LLC. Used with permission.)

Thomas explains how he edited in "my mind where I thought shots would go" as he "was watching that [scene] when [Bloom] shot it" (see Figure 10.11). Thomas says that's what he does when he directs a project. "I edit in my mind. When we shoot, I already am piecing it together."

Thomas feels that color grading is a process that should begin with the cinematographer. "If you're working with a good DP like Philip," he says, "you're lucky, because you're starting out with a really good color palette to begin with." Whether DPs realize it or not, Thomas believes they are "being drawn to the color of an image a lot of times, even more than a composition." In the case of *A Day at the Races*, what Bloom shot contained "heavy, heavy color tones already," Thomas observes. "Every image he grabbed had something in it already that I liked" as a colorist. "So I would either enhance what was already there, or I would dial it back if there was too much of it. Some of the stuff inside the stalls was too yellow, so I would have to dial the yellow back and bring some more earth tones beneath the yellow" (see Figure 10.12).

FIGURE 10.12
A shot from inside a stable, which for Jeremy Ian Thomas was too yellow, so he, as the colorist, "would have to dial the yellow back and bring some more earth tones beneath the yellow," he explains.
(Still from *A Day at the Races*. ©2010. LumaForge, LLC. Used with permission.)

But this process isn't always easy, especially with some other DPs who are not looking at colors. "When you're not working with someone like Philip, and there's not a lot of color, you have to really make the DP look good, [as if] he saw that color already," Thomas explains. "But all I really did with *A Day at the Races* was keep the skin tones intact by doing a desaturation of the skin tones, and then I would saturate everything around the subject, because the colors were already so beautiful. There were these really nice greens, mid-level greens, and there were these really beautiful pink hues across the mid-tones at the stables. And there was a nice yellow, and some pink." When he saw a person in a shot, Thomas said he "would make sure their skin tones were right. But everything around them was popping, and colorful" (see Figure 10.13). Overall, he felt that it was "a really good grading experience."

In the end, Bloom was happy with the project. He gave some notes to Thomas after seeing the rough cut, and additional changes were made. Bloom wouldn't have chosen the particular piece of music for the piece and would have taken a different approach for the final edit, he explains, but he admits that "it's always great to see how someone else interprets your work."

Bloom also enjoyed using the Cooke lenses on the 7D, but at the same time, he adds, "I honestly feel for the type of shooting that I do, like this piece, that using Canon or Zeiss lenses would have been just as great."

FIGURE 10.13
The colors would "pop," as Jeremy Ian Thomas explains in observing *A Day at the Races*. He would make sure the skin tones were correct and then bring out the colors by saturating them a bit. (©2010 LumaForge, LLC. Used with permission.)

Neil Smith was pleased with the work that Bloom and Thomas did: "When we screen the movie in our theater," Smith boasts, "people are truly amazed at what Philip was able to capture with the low-light capability of the 7D and with a documentary style of shooting." In short, Smith explains, "the real purpose behind the film was to show how DSLR cameras can be used to help creative filmmakers tell their stories, easily and cheaply without sacrificing production value."[3]

[3]Cheap when compared to the cost of high-end cinema cameras. The lenses, however, are not cheap, but this film shows that a modified Canon 7D can utilize an expensive lens package that can be rented without having to use a full-size cinema camera.

Art of the People by Kiril Kirkov
http://vimeo.com/210451837

Kiril Kirkov: Documentary Intimacy with the Canon 5D Mark III in *Art of the People*

Kiril Kirkov is patient. As a photographer he'll wait for hours to get the right shot. For example, while in the Grand Canyon he saw a California condor sitting on a cliff. He approached it and waited. And waited. He wanted a shot of the bird flying. Four hours later, it took flight. And the photo would earn Kirkov awards. (See Figure 11.1.)

Kirkov grew up behind the Iron Curtain in Bulgaria and used to tour in a folklore dance company around the world. He migrated to the United States and got a job at the Grand Canyon. He later enrolled in classes at a community college in Flagstaff, Arizona, where he fell in love with anthropology. He completed his bachelor's degree at Northern Arizona University, while also earning a minor in filmmaking. He's trained as a visual anthropologist, he says, which allows him "to combine my training as an artist, as a stage choreographer, and my photographic sense of composition and light."

FIGURE 11.1
Patience was the key in capturing the flight of this California condor at Grand Canyon National Park.
(©2015 Kiril Kirkov. Used with permission.)

VISUAL ANTHROPOLOGY

"I have always been fascinated by human cultures," Kirkov explains, drawing on his folklore dance background. But he's also interested in the idea of mass movements of people. "What happens with people when they move around? I'm interested in this question, because of my own experience as a migrant." During the democratic development throughout Eastern Europe, he witnessed first-hand "how one social system becomes changed by a totally different reality." This experience "enriched" him, he adds. It "expands your horizon," and this observation of change propelled him into visual anthropology.

Visual anthropology—tied to filmmaking training—benefits the filmmaker in different ways. Fundamentally, it allows him to help people. Kirkov sees "visual representation of social issues as an important contemporary tool" in trying to solve problems. "In the field of anthropology, when you work with people, usually you are trying to solve social issues, or to understand behavior, behavioral patterns, interactions, and all kinds of social developments," he explains. "Filmmaking gives you this opportunity" in a visual way.

While a student, Kirkov volunteered as a filmmaker at a charity fundraising event with Native American artists. "They painted live, and they would sell the painting on open auction," he explains. "I would be a volunteer filmmaker to cover this event. And we just became friends." It became an important step for his project.

Kirkov describes how the collective, Art of the People, "is an amazing and creative way of supporting painters within their community." These Native artists face such challenges as "living in the middle of nowhere," having to drive long distances to get to art shows, and making a living. "This takes an enormous effort," he says. "So instead of wasting time and money, these guys work together as a team. They support each other, and every single one of them benefits from this communal approach." He found that aspect fascinating, because "this collectivism is not typical," he adds. "Usually, in the art world painters work alone, especially in Western societies."

So when Kirkov entered his senior year in college, he had to do a capstone or thesis project in anthropology. Because he loves filmmaking, he decided to do an ethnographic film—a type of documentary utilizing observational cinema techniques— for his project. In this type of filmmaking, no questions are asked in an interview. Conversations may spontaneously happen, but the filmmaking process is about observing and filming behavior and actions as they unfold in real time.

"In an observational documentary you follow an event as it develops," Kirkov says, and that's a challenge. It impacts lives. "This process of documentary filmmaking generates never-ending change of realities, and creation of new ones, because of our presence in the field." Fiction is much easier, he says, because you create a reality from a script. "Actors have assignments how to behave," he adds. But in observational documentary, there are "no such assignments; they just behave as they are," he says, and that includes unpredictable moments and emotions. "They develop this behavior, with ups and downs, positive and negative emotions." And as a documentary filmmaker you "have to capture the story" as it unfolds. "If I don't capture it, I am not good," he adds.

At an initial meeting, Kirkov met some of the Navajo artists from the Art of the People collective at a coffee shop. "We spoke about my education, and I just asked the guys if there is a way to help each other, and to create a documentary film project about Art of the People that can benefit them, and can benefit me, in terms of covering the requirement for a capstone project."

In that meeting at Kickstand Coffee, the founder of Art of the People, Bahe Whitethorne, Sr., told Kirkov that he loved the idea for the filmmaking project, "because we need visual representation of who we are. That would serve us big, definitely.

We need to be better presented before potential clients, supporters, colleagues, art festivals, and so forth." That was the beginning of the whole idea.

When Kirkov talks about helping the art collective create a film about Art of the People, Kirkov's discussing a collaborative form of filmmaking that shares "power" with the filmmaking subjects—they have as much say about what he can shoot and what is in the film as he does. "I explained to these painters about my collaborative methodology, and the rules I follow, which include the rules of ethics, respect, and equality, lack of power of the producer (or filmmaking through equal power)." These elements also help define what an ethnographic film is—and it will still convey a story through edits.

"It's not a recording of an event," Kiril says. He learned about ethnographic filmmaking from visual anthropologist Sarah Elder, who created *The Drums of Winter* (1988), a film about how the Yup'ik Eskimo dance is ingrained in the culture of the community. One writer explains how it "blurs the boundaries between verité methods and participatory filmmaking, resulting in an intimate, collaborative portrait of the creative and spiritual aspects of Yup'ik life."[1]

By following this process of filmmaking, Kirkov feels he can "show the reality behind the work, or how the process really happens," he says. In this case, the reality is about Navajo art. "The painters were very happy with this approach, they appreciated it," Kirkov says with enthusiasm. "And we spent five fantastic months working together, helping each other with every single component of the production process." It wasn't a constant five months, but the filmmaking was spread out over that period of time. He built close bonds with their families. For example, when his assistant got sick, he asked Elaine, the wife of one of the painters, Randall, to help with audio recording. He trained her and she did it.

STORY CREATIVITY

As for the content of the documentary project, Kirkov explains how the group decided to emphasize the number four, a sacred number for the Navajo people. "We chose four painters, four locations, the painters would share four stories, and they will paint four paintings, live, before the camera," Kiril says. This approach became the structure of the film. "We chose three iconic locations in northern Arizona, important and significant for the Navajo Nation," he adds, "plus one art studio—the studio of the founder, Bahe Whitethorne, Sr."

As a filmmaker, Kirkov feels that a "good story, of course, comes first." But as a professional photographer, "I always prefer to work with good light," he smiles. In fact, more than anything else "light is fundamental" to filmmaking. He prefers to shoot during the golden hour for outdoor cinematography, but sometimes "there is no other way" to get the shoot completed, he says, so "you have to go and shoot right away." That occurred during the shoot with Bahe Whitethorne, Jr. at Wupatki National Monument. "There was no way to wait for a golden light," Kirkov complains.

---

[1] Miller, Cynthia. "Ethnographic Documentary Filmmakers Sarah Elder and Leonard Kamerling: an interview." *Post Script*. #27.1. 22 September 2007.

"It was terrible. But we did the shoot anyway, because that was the deal, and we had no choice." To compensate, he applied neutral density filters and polarizers in order to make the light "acceptable." (See Figure 11.2.)

FIGURE 11.2
When faced with bad light, such as bright sun daylight, Kirkov compensates by applying neutral density filters and polarizers in order to make the light "acceptable." Navajo painter, Bahe Whitethorne, Jr. paints the sacred mountains. (©2017 Kiril Kirkov. Used with permission.)

When he shoots, Kirkov's creative choices involves four steps:

1. Light
2. Interesting compositional choices
3. Emotional shots (these tend to be close-ups)
4. Contextual shots (these tend to be wide)

Although light and composition stem from his photographer's eye—now his cinematographer's eye—Kirkov feels the emotional shots captured through close-ups are fundamental to documentary and ethnographic filmmaking. "We need intimacy, when we talk about emotion, we need emotional depth" he continues, because that's how you reach an audience. "You don't do that with wide shots," he contends, which are used to provide spatial context.

BUILDING BRIDGES

However, getting close-ups in this type of filmmaking isn't easy. The producer-director should be on camera, since observational cinema dictates that the camera is an extension of how the filmmaker feels and perceives their subject. But in order to get close to a filmmaking subject using this approach, it is only "achievable by knowing your subject," Kirkov states. And that's where the anthropological training helps him as a filmmaker. "You have to spend time with them. It is a part of the creative process, the process of discovery and building trust," he adds.

Furthermore, this approach would not work if he "had nothing in common with the painters," he adds. "They would not be so open with me." How did he build this trust? Not only volunteering at the fundraiser, but also volunteering at a charter school focused on Navajo students (grades K–8). "I taught Native children media literacy, basic filmmaking techniques, and photography" for two years. The first year he worked as an intern for NASA through their space grant, an outreach project where he taught students astrophotography at Lowell Observatory in Flagstaff.

"So I taught the children of the Navajo painters," Kirkov explains. "They know me on a personal level." And that builds bridges of trust. It not only creates a form of "equality," he adds, "but also a sense of comfort in terms of showing emotion on camera as it is—not pretending, not playing this emotion." And this last point is the most important for him, because you may be a creative filmmaker, but if you're not using the process of "building bridges" and creating trust with who you're filming, then "it won't matter," because the film will lack sincerity. (See Figures 11.3–11.9.)

FIGURE 11.3

A close-up of Keno Zahney reveals intimacy as he contemplates his work.

(©2017 Kiril Kirkov. Used with permission.)

FIGURES 11.4 AND 11.5
Keno Zahney paints at Horseshoe Bend in Arizona. In order to get close to a documentary subject using this approach, it is only "achievable by knowing your subject," Kirkov says. And that's where the anthropological training helps him as a filmmaker. "You have to spend time with them. It is a part of the creative process, the process of discovery and building trust."
(©2017 Kiril Kirkov. Used with permission.)

FIGURES 11.6 AND 11.7
Strong visual portrait of Navajo artist Bahe Whitethorne, Jr. at Wupatki National Monument. Kirkov's belief in the close-up allows for emotional intimacy to come through, visually.
(©2017 Kiril Kirkov. Used with permission.)

FIGURES 11.8 AND 11.9
A big close-up of Bahe Whitethorne, Sr. as he paints in his studio. Detail shots and expressions of the face and eyes conveys the heart of a story, Kirkov feels. A monopod allows him to keep a stable shot as he reaches in close with his lens and moves it again for a different angle and height.
(©2017 Kiril Kirkov. Used with permission.)

Kirkov stresses that this isn't a one-off. You don't just earn someone's trust when filming. You have to maintain that trust throughout the preproduction, production, and postproduction cycle. "You have to prove the quality of this acceptance every time you communicate with your subject," he says. "You have to work hard on this; it's not a single action—building trust and then from now on, 'Oh, we are good ....'" Why? Because there's "always a risk of misinterpretation or misunderstanding, just like in any other human interaction," he explains.

Because it's so key in creating intimate documentary work, Kirkov emphasizes that, "You have to work for this. And if you rely only on your skills as a technical pro, you will fail, that's it. You have to be a psychologist, and you have to really be there, in the field, with everything you are, literally." Indeed, as a filmmaking psychologist, "You have to expose yourself, too," he adds.

In his most recent project, Kirkov found during his research phase about refugee integration in The Netherlands, that he would receive such questions as, "Who you are and why do you want to do this? What is your motivation?" And you have to have the right motive. "If you don't have it," he stresses, "then you don't belong there as a filmmaker."

COMPOSITION

With the Canon 5D Mark III, Kirkov uses Canon's workhorse L-series lens, 24–105mm f/4. Although it's not very fast, Kirkov says, it does the job well. "It's not the fastest lens, but it works, because it covers pretty much everything from a relatively wide shot, to normal, to short telephoto." He also uses the Canon 16–35mm f/2.8 L lens for wide, environmental, and establishing shots. For example, he says, "in the title shot in which we see a blurred image of Randall, and a big horizontal tree— that's shot at about 17–18mm. It is a wide shot of a green forest, and a painter working in the deep background. This is achievable with nothing else, but a wide lens. It emphasizes the environment." (See Figure 11.10.)

In addition, Kirkov likes to film in "long takes, but I also film lots of takes." What he means by takes is not the same as in fiction, where a director will ask for different takes of the same action in order to get a better shot or performance. In this case, he takes a lot of different shots around the same action. For example, in the sequence with Bahe Jr. painting at Wupatki, "we spent six hours, filming non-stop," he states. But the edited sequence is only three-and-a-half minutes long. During the shoot, "I cover the texture of his brush; I emphasize close-ups of his face; the seriousness of his statements through strong emphasis on his eye, the texture of his skin, and so forth." With a variety of shot sizes and camera angles, he finds he has a lot of choices during the edit.

Another one of his creative approaches to filmmaking involves his background in choreography and stage performance. "I've spent over twenty-five years doing this," Kirkov says, "pretty much all over the world. And after this career I needed to practice another kind of art. I decided to get into photography." He would extend his

FIGURE 11.10
Kirkov utilizes a wide angle shot (17–18mm) in the title sequence of the film. "We see blurred image of Randall, and a big horizontal tree," Kirkov says. "It is a wide shot of a green forest, and a painter working in the deep background." (©2017 Kiril Kirkov. Used with permission.)

compositional skills as a photographer to his filmmaking.

"The rules of composing a scene in choreography are similar to working with components within a photographic frame," Kirkov argues. "There's little difference in composing an action on stage and finding a composition through a lens," he adds. "That's why I was very attracted to taking photographic images. The compositional laws and rules are the same in filmmaking, just twenty-four frames per second."

SOUND DESIGN

So in *Art of the People* the story is about painters. This indicates what needs to be filmed. "What is important for the painter?" Kirkov asks. It's the brush and what it does on the canvas." A person not filming with intimacy might just record a medium shot of the painting, but the close-up is more important. And sound. "One of the techniques I deployed was the use of a boom mic behind the canvas, so when they paint, you can hear the sound of the brush, moving on the surface," Kirkov explains.

"When you combine this sound with the texture of the canvas, with a close-up shot of this moving brush, that's strong. This approach says, 'This is what I do as an artist.'" As the painting unfolds, he feels that the process is magical. "This is the magic they create, because for me this is magical," so it must be captured in a way to show and hear the magic. (See Figure 11.11.)

Since the process is magical for Kirkov, it's easy to film someone painting. Shooting

FIGURE 11.11
Recording the sound of the brush against the texture of canvas combined with "a close-up shot of this moving brush, that's strong," Kirkov says. "This approach says, 'This is what I do as an artist.'"
(©2017 Kiril Kirkov. Used with permission.)

a medium shot of the painting and a reversal angle on the painter's face—that's not filmmaking. "If you don't put this painting in its context, you lose a quality of the storytelling as a filmmaker," he explains. What does he mean by this? It's not only the detail shots, but the sound. "The real quality is not the painting. It will go on the wall, and the audience will be able to see it. But in filmmaking we talk about the process of creating it. And to make it powerful, you better put in the effort and work with professional level sound recording. That brings the real depth. If you don't have the sound, you have nothing."

Kirkov explains how the people in a documentary "move around. They don't stay still, and it's good if we can record the sound of their movement." That not only conveys another level of realism, but immersion into the filmic world of the subject. "When a viewer sees a forest, it's good to hear some forest sounds at the same time.

If the scene is put in a sterile sound environment—with no ambient audio—people will feel how wrong it is on a subconscious level."

FAVORITE SHOT

Kirkov's favorite shot in the film is a slow panoramic shot where "the sun is going down; there is a forest; the camera is moving from right to the left, and on the left is Randall Wilson, relaxing. That was the moment of him talking about the fifth process of creating a painting in the Navajo way. This is the relaxing moment, before he started again." It shows and reveals his philosophy as a painter, and as a Navajo. "While he was explaining this," Kirkov says, "you see the slow movement of the camera under the gentle evening light, and then a comfort and a little smile on Randall's face, showing that he is happy by his work from today, and he is ready to relax, and to regroup himself toward the next project." (See Figure 11.12.) He feels that this is a "strong" shot, "because everything is in harmony. His feelings and his

FIGURE 11.12
Kirkov's favorite shot involves strong composition and light. It also conveys the theme of Randall. "His feelings and his message are within the context of the gentle low light. The day is about to end soon, the painting is done, Randall is done and ready to relax; everything is going to relax in order to get ready for the new day. There isn't much sound involved in this scene, but its visual potential is strong."
(©2017 Kiril Kirkov. Used with permission.)

message are within the context of the gentle low light. The day is about to end soon, the painting is done, Randall is done and ready to relax; everything is going to relax in order to get ready for the new day. There isn't much sound involved in this scene, but its visual potential is strong."

TECHNICAL CONSIDERATIONS

Another technical consideration doesn't deal with composition, but about postproduction. The Blackmagic Video Assist Monitor (a field monitor that records a video signal from the HDMI output of the Canon 5D) is one of the most important tools for the filmmaker shooting in the compressed 8-bit world of low budget camera gear. The 10-bit capabilities of the recorder allow for deeper color correction.

Kirkov feels that the Canon 5D Mark III conveys a strong color scheme of Canon. It reflects in some way a bit of RAW photography. "When we talk about footage I definitely prefer the Blackmagic files," he says. "The quality is higher; the color depth is visibly better. I can immediately recognize the texture of the color, when comparing. There are also more creative options for edit in terms of color grading and contrast improvement."

Another important tool, besides the Blackmagic Video Assist, is a monopod, the one that pans, tilts, pushes in, and pulls out with a small footprint. For the kind of films Kirkov creates, it is more important than a tripod. "It gives power of freedom to the filmmaker," Kirkov explains. "It makes the camera stable, but you still can move around." And for documentary work it's important to change positions in order to find new angles and shot sizes. "In documentary you have to be fast, you have to change shot sizes, camera angles, and height really quickly. There is no time to lose in order to capture the right moment." Furthermore, "changing the height of the camera is vital. Sometimes you want to emphasize hand gestures, so you put the camera in low. The viewer would be much more attracted by this kind of a shot. The hands become the emphasis, the main subject. The monopod allows you to shoot "strong dynamic shots," he stresses.

From living behind the Iron Curtain with very little freedom, Kirkov has adapted to a new way of life as an anthropologist and filmmaker. His subjects—the people he connects with—find freedom of expression through his own freedom found through the lens of a camera.

CHAPTER 12

Po Chan and Shane Hurlbut: Canon's 5D Mark II in *The Last 3 Minutes*

SUSHI WITH SHANE HURLBUT, ASC*

Shane Hurlbut, ASC, is a tour de force. We sit at a sushi bar in Malibu Beach as the darkening spring sky brings out twinkling stars. It's been a long week shooting a short fiction written and directed by collaborator Po Chan, with fifteen-hour shoots the norm, a demanding task for a low budget film for Canon in a bid to show off the 5D Mark II's capability as a cinema camera. Exhaustion ebbs around Hurlbut's eyes, but his effulgent passion for cinematic storytelling, his jovial flare of expression, isn't tempered by fatigue. He insists that I try yellowtail touched by cilantro and fire sauce—which sums up his enthusiasm for life. "It's killer," he remarks with a laugh. He knows when to party and is quick to laugh on set, but sometimes impatient with those not firing as fast as he is.

Shane's unfailing work ethic grows from being raised on a farm in upstate New York. "I was on the tractor at eight years old. I'd wake up in the morning around 5:00 a.m., and I'd get on the tractor. Then around 7:00 a.m., I would come in and grab some breakfast and head off to school. My day would not end there. I'd practice sports after school, and then it was time to get back on the tractor, where I'd work till 10 or 11 at night." When did he have time to complete his homework? "Well, my dad welded this bookstand [onto the tractor] so I could read while I was driving it." His mother was a sixth grade teacher, who became president of the teacher's union. "I grew up seeing my parents work very hard and have a passion for what they did."

---

*Author's note: More than any other professional cinematographer, Shane Hurlbut, ASC, championed the use of DSLRs in professional filmmaking at its birth. This chapter remains in the third edition as a historical reference of how a master cinematographer approaches visual storytelling with a DSLR.

Eli Jane in *The Last 3 Minutes*. ©2010 Hurlbut Visuals. Used with permission.

His parents, with what "little they had," were willing to pay for college, Shane says. "I wanted to make sure I didn't spend their money foolishly, so I initially chose a junior college to make sure my career choice was something that I wanted to do with my life." The first year he studied radio. "I loved it." The second year "was TV and I loved that even more." In high school, his focus had been all about sports, and Hurlbut earned B grades. "College was different because I was passionate about what I was learning and graduated magna cum laude with a full scholarship to complete my studies."

But his motivation to earn better grades didn't just revolve around his work ethic. There was a girl, Lydia, whom he'd known since he was three. They started dating when Hurlbut was in tenth grade. She went to Simmons College in Boston, a move that was encouraged by her parents to separate them because this was the first serious guy she had ever dated. He says, "I remember walking in to the guidance counselor's office at Herkimer County Community College and [saying], 'Help me to find the best film school in Boston!'"

"I went chasing after the girl," he laughs. Hurlbut enrolled in Emerson College in Boston and studied mass communication, but switched to film after helping out a hometown friend from USC, Gabe Torres, who shot a project over a summer break in Aurora, New York, where they both had grown up.

"I worked on Gabe's project and fell in love with film. It was so different from TV, and I thought, 'My God, this is it.' So I went back that next semester, and I changed everything I had from TV and mass communication to film, and then I did a four-year film degree in one year."

After graduating from Emerson and getting engaged to Lydia, Shane thought that getting a job would be easy after college, since he had all of these contacts. That false sense of security quickly faded after every job opportunity was met with, "You need more experience." His parents knew what was best and insisted that he get any job just to get hands-on experience in the workforce. He swallowed his pride and worked at a film rental house in Boston, where he had formerly worked as an intern. "I started out packing trucks, and within six months I was running the whole lighting and grip department." But he realized that Los Angeles was the place to be for high-volume film production.

He convinced Lydia that they should leave both their families on the East Coast and move to California. She got a job at Children's Hospital, Los Angeles, when there was a nursing shortage and they helped pay for the move. "I got a job at Keylite, a rental house, and it worked really well because I worked my way up the ladder just like I did in Boston," Shane explains. "Three months later I started on the movie *Phantasm II* [1988]. It was an amazing experience because it changed the way I thought." At first, he didn't plan to be a DP. He wanted to be a storyteller, a director. Lighting wasn't his first priority. But it all changed in a flash of inspiration. Shane worked as a grip truck driver on the movie, and one day was racing a flag to the key grip when his friend Brian Coyne, best boy electric on the project, asked him if he would be scared when sitting in the theater with the lighting that was being done on the crematorium set. "Brian said, 'Look, there are no shadows. You can see every nook and cranny in this place. Where is the mystery? It's just not scary.' Snap! A light bulb went off in my head, and from that point on, everything I looked at was light. That was 1988." Shane fell in love with cinematography. By 1991, he shot his first music video. "Then I became a commercial cameraman in 1994 and then shot [my] first feature in 1998."

Hurlbut was offered *The Rat Pack* (1998) for HBO as his first feature. That break came when director Rob Cohen had seen a Donna Summer music video that Shane shot for Rob's film, *Daylight* (1996). He was thrilled with the visuals from that music video and decided to take a chance on Shane. Hurlbut went on to receive a cinematography award nomination from the American Society of Cinematographers.

Hurlbut's approach to cinematography is to observe what's around him. "I just looked at light wherever I went ... I think the best lighting comes from just observing. Then, when I am asked to bring a director's vision to life, I pull from a variety of personal experiences and incorporate those visual references in my head into my lighting."

The Last 3 Minutes became a project where Hurlbut wanted to showcase the cinematic capabilities of the 5D Mark II. "I wanted to have the opportunity to show Canon what the Hurlbut Visuals Elite Team and I could do with the 5D in a short narrative piece.[1] Lydia negotiated the deal with two Canon departments: education and marketing. The behind-the-scenes segments were just as important to Canon as the footage itself." They worked out the timing, gave Hurlbut the 24p firmware update, and presented it at the National Association of Broadcasters in Las Vegas in April 2010.

PO CHAN'S STORY: FROM HONG KONG TO HOLLYWOOD

The story of *The Last 3 Minutes* revolves around a weary 68-year-old office janitor who dies from a heart attack. His life passes before his eyes, and he lives through memories, both regrets and celebrations, starting from when his wife left him and then going back in time to when he was born. Typically, when there's a story about someone's life flashing before his eyes, Hurlbut explains, "It's always the perfect light and it's always at sunset. And that's awesome, but we wanted to take this very mundane man" and show his "absolutely dead existence." But beneath this surface, there are "many layers behind his life, and those layers are extraordinary," revealing choices made, good and bad, that led to the present moment.

The inspiration for the story came from Po Chan, the writer and director of the film, reflecting her own philosophy about life. She explains, "I believe that life is like a big circle. We are all born innocent, and no matter how many right or wrong

[1] Elite Team members include professional filmmakers embracing DSLR technology who work for Hurlbut Visuals for specific projects: Chris Moseley, Derek Edwards, Tim Holterman, Rudy Harbon, Mike Svitak, Darin Necessary, Marc Margulies, Bodie Orman, Dave Knudsen, and John Guerra (see bios at http://www.hurlbutvisuals.com/team.php).

Hurlbut's approach to cinematography is to observe what's around him. "I just looked at light wherever I went. ... I think the best lighting comes from just observing. Then, when I am asked to bring a director's vision to life, I pull from a variety of personal experiences and incorporate those visual references in my head into my lighting."

things we have done, how many wrong decisions we have made in life, at the last minute, right before death, we will again become innocent." She infused this theme into her film, a theme that she feels comes from being born and raised in Hong Kong. "I grew up in the Eastern culture, surrounded by Buddhism philosophy. We believe everything comes in full circle—what goes around comes around. It's like yin and yang, so to speak."

Besides the concept of the story, the second most important element in this film for Po is the music. She explains: "I think our memory is like the annual circles of a tree. The new memory will grow on top of the older one; as we grow older, our memory layers will grow thicker. I believe that the memory of music is in the core layer of our memory, especially the music that we heard when we were children. So the music in this film is the representation of the core memory of my main character." Po turned to a friend for bluegrass music suggestions "because my main character was born right after the Great Depression." After listening to over 1,000 tracks, one caught her ear, "Across the Wide Missouri," a traditional American folk song about a roving trader in love with the daughter of an Indian chief. Timothy Godwin, a talented musician and friend of the Hurlbuts, listened to the song for inspiration and then created the soundtrack for *The Last 3 Minutes*.

Po enjoys the shift from living and working in film in Hong Kong to the United States. "When I was growing up, I was taught to follow the rules, not the dream," she explains in her Cantonese accent. "When you finish school, you go find a stable job and make money. It never occurred to me to become a filmmaker, even though I always loved film. And I remember my very first film I saw in the theater when I was little; it was *Close Encounters of the Third Kind* (1977). I fell in love with that film; it blew my mind, and then I realized that it completely transformed my life in that two hours."

Like Hurlbut, Po had one of those Hollywood moments, where her experience with watching *Close Encounters* would come full circle years later. "I remember we did a job with Mr. Spielberg, and I was so shy, 'O My God, it is Mr. Spielberg, the director of *Close Encounters of the Third Kind*, right?' So I was hiding in a corner, and all of a sudden he walks up to me, and he asks me what I do ... and I said, 'Oh, I am a camera assistant for this job.'

"And he said, 'What do you want to do?' That is what he asked me, and it came out of nowhere—Mr. Spielberg walked up to me and just asked me this question.

"And I said, 'I want to be a director, I want to be a filmmaker,' and he put his hand on my shoulder and said, 'Don't give up, girl.' I just stood there frozen, thinking God has sent him here to tell me that. And you know what? I will not give up."

As for the process in writing the story for *The Last 3 Minutes*, Po explains how her creative brain works. "Most people like to capture interesting things or ideas by writing them down. I don't. I purposely don't write them down. The reason is that I want it—whatever the entity is—put in my brain and this machine is going to mold it, change it into something else. Or combine it spontaneously with other random events I grabbed two days ago. It works better for me that way. Once I have the core concept, the rest of the detail will come to me naturally, because they are all in my brain, filtered, molded, and ready to go. The most important thing is I already have feelings for all of them because they have been living in me. We breathe, we eat, we live, and sure, we will die together."

Hurlbut has collaborated with Po Chan on about nine different movies, he says. He met her on the set of the HBO series *Deadwood*. Hurlbut was hired by HBO to shoot some promo pieces for the show. "And so Po was driving the producer from Beverley Hills out to the set," Shane remembers. "I saw her dropping the producer off and I wondered, 'Who is that?' I'm starting to line up a shot inside the set, and I remember her coming through the swinging doors, walking over while I was doing a shot and questioning why I chose a particular lens."

"I turn to the producer and said, 'Who is this person?'"

"'That's Po Chan.'"

"'What does she do?'"

"'Well, she's from Hong Kong; she loves film. She loves it, breathes it.'"

They hit it off—Shane respects fearless and direct people. He hired her as his assistant, and they became collaborators. In *The Last 3 Minutes*, a script that Po wrote in one day, he talks about how "she had incredible vision in the way she worked with actors and designed the shots. She was very thorough with storyboards and a treatment that was so detailed. It made my job very easy."

SHAPING A POINT OF VIEW PERSPECTIVE

So the story evolved into a script treatment that's bittersweet. Hurlbut emphasizes that we see William's life in three minutes: "the girl that got away, the best friend who dies, the celebration of different life events. We see the tender moments, the sad moments, but [the flashbacks] didn't have to be perfect, and the light didn't have to be perfect." For example, in the sunset scene, "it's much more from a sense of how he would see it from his memory." Visually, Hurlbut wanted to "capture the emotion of each character through William's eyes"—from his point of view with the use of the small format Canon 5D Mark II.

What amazes Hurlbut the most is how the small-form factor of the camera allows him to get the kinds of shots he could never do with a 35mm cinema camera. "Never before have we been able to cinematically do a helmet cam, do something that really puts the viewer in a first-person perspective," Hurlbut emphasizes. "And that's what this camera really has enabled me to do. Tonight, we were on the beach, and my camera assistant is wearing the helmet and he is able to look at her and caress her arms, and then she turns and runs into the ocean. We start on a close-up of water dripping off one strand of her hair into a wide shot of her running on the beach" (see Figures 12.1–12.4).

Hurlbut explains that, for first-person perspective, the Canon 5D Mark II "is the device to do it. We used depth of field to make it filmic, and we took the audience on a life ride." Po Chan explains how "I do not want the audience just watching the film. I want them to be able to feel the film. I want to enable the audience to feel what I feel. All the elements in this film, from the casting and the music to the wardrobe; from makeup (the choice of lipstick) to the hairstyles and hair colors; from the patterns and textures of the set dressing pieces to the looks of the crystal itself, are all carefully chosen so that they all work in harmony to tell the story."

LIGHTING THE BEDROOM SCENE

FIGURE 12.1
Shane Hurlbut looks through the Canon 5D (with a Z-Finder), the camera attached to a helmet worn by camera operator Bodie Orman, as they set up a shot on the beach with Eli Jane. Director Po Chan leans in screen right, with producer Greg Haggart observing in the background. An assistant uses water from a water bottle to moisten Eli's hair, for the close-up of water dripping off her hair.
(Photo by Kurt Lancaster.)

FIGURE 12.2
First-person perspective from William's memories of stroking his girl's arm as water drips from her hair, from *The Last 3 Minutes*.
(©2010 Hurlbut Visuals. Used with permission.)

FIGURE 12.3
Actress Eli Jane looks into the camera to engage a first-person perspective of William looking back at his memories in *The Last 3 Minutes*.
(©2010 Hurlbut Visuals. Used with permission.)

FIGURE 12.4
Actress Eli Jane, who plays the love of William's life, coaxes him on by looking at the camera in a first-person perspective in *The Last 3 Minutes*.
(©2010 Hurlbut Visuals. Used with permission.)

In one scene, after the main character's wife decides to leave him, she packs her bags and heads out the door. There is a dress lying on the floor. William goes over to pick it up, and time slips back into a memory of when, according to Chan's treatment, he sees from his point of view, "his wife wearing the same dress. She seductively takes off the dress and crawls under the sheet with William …"

Hurlbut explains how he wanted to keep that scene "very intimate," but at the same time not make it look like a romantic "setup," such as turning "the lights all down, and make it candlelit with soft focus—edgy. Everything's dark, and now I'm going to take my clothes off. That is the exact opposite of what I wanted to convey here."

By avoiding the temptation to go for the moody "perfect light," Hurlbut crafted a scene where "the lights were on. It's nighttime and they just got back from an evening out, and she's still in her dress and he's reading a book. She's coming in, and starts to play with him. So the lights are up, he's reading, then all of a sudden we're in a strip tease scene. That's what I wanted to convey. Out of nowhere the guy is reading his book and all of a sudden looks up, and he's got a beautiful woman in front of him with the dress she just wore out to the movies and now she's taking it off."

To tell this story visually, Hurlbut explains, "You start close, start on that beautiful face. She walks away from the camera; she starts to perform a striptease act for her husband. You create that suspense where you think you're going see her but the sheet flies up into frame and blocks your view; then all of a sudden she slinks up under the sheets into a rocking close-up and tells William that she loves him" (see Figures 12.5–12.7).

FIGURE 12.5
Actress Eli Jane presents a seductive look to the camera, starting "close," in Hurlbut's words, "on that beautiful face," in *The Last 3 Minutes*. (©2010 Hurlbut Visuals. Used with permission.)

FIGURE 12.6
Hurlbut says, "She starts to perform a striptease act for her husband. You create that suspense where you think you're going see her strip, but the sheet flies up into frame and blocks your view." (*The Last 3 Minutes* ©2010 Hurlbut Visuals. Used with permission.)

FIGURE 12.7
Hurlbut continues, "Then all of a sudden she slinks up under the sheets into a rocking close-up and tells William that she loves him."
(*The Last 3 Minutes* ©2010 Hurlbut Visuals. Used with permission.)

Hurlbut feels that this is one of those scenes where it feels shorter than it really is. "No matter how much Po and I tried to cut that scene down to fit within her eight to ten-second window," we couldn't do it, he says. "When I was watching it happen [during the shoot], I thought it was eight seconds" long, but the actual take was thirty-two seconds. The final edit has it at twenty seconds. "That's when you know you have something great," Hurlbut smiles, "because when it feels shorter than it really is, you know you've struck a nerve."

LIGHTING WITH SPECIAL EFFECTS AND BLOCKING NOTES TO AN ACTOR IN THE VIETNAM WAR SCENE

In the Vietnam War scene, William discovers his wounded buddy dying in the middle of explosions. Hurlbut did not want to mimic the style found in *The Thin Red Line* (1998), created by John Toll, ASC, nor did he want to reinvent what Bob Richardson, ASC, did in *Platoon* (1986).

"These guys really knocked the genre out. What I wanted to convey was the sense of the audience being immersed in the action and using debris mortars to change and filter the sunlight," Hurlbut explains.

He continues: "We start with an explosion, and he goes down for cover. He gets up, realizes his friend's been hit, and he runs to him. We blow off this huge mortar explosion, because I wanted the world we've seen—this backlit sun dappled through the trees—to go completely overcast, forcing a mood change." (See Figures 12.8 and 12.9.)

FIGURE 12.8
"We positioned spot fires to add color, we sent debris mortars into the air to diffuse the sun, and we used lawnmower smoke to cover up the brown tones in the scene that were not realistic to a Vietnam jungle," Hurlbut explains in this sequence from *The Last 3 Minutes*.
(©2010 Hurlbut Visuals. Used with permission.)

FIGURE 12.9
Actor Alex Weber raises his hand in the midst of explosions in *The Last 3 Minutes*.
(©2010 Hurlbut Visuals. Used with permission.)

"So in an instant, you have a beautiful backlight, completely soft ambience, and when the explosion goes off and he starts moving towards him, the sun is taken out," Hurlbut says. "It goes dark. The tonal range changes, dropping four to five stops in the lighting. And the camera did so well digging into the shadow areas. And then the sun comes back out once the explosion subsides."

Hurlbut explains how he collaborated with the special effects team to light the scene. "We positioned spot fires to add color, we sent debris mortars into the air to diffuse the sun, and we used lawnmower smoke to cover up the brown tones in the scene that were not realistic to a Vietnam jungle." (See Figure 12.10.)

FIGURE 12.10
The special effects crew sets up the spot fires around actor Alex Weber, used to help light the scene in *The Last 3 Minutes*. Pyrotechnic gear and supplies in the foreground, with crew to the right.
(Photo by Kurt Lancaster.)

While working on Terminator Salvation, he learned about different mortar explosions, including trapezoids, flash pods, and a square pan. "You start to understand the terminology," Hurlbut says, "and then you use it to your advantage for lighting. I wanted to take the sun away. So with one explosion it went away. And then it comes back right as William's friend died. The timing was just perfect; it was like a sunray from heaven during the death sequence" (see Figure 12.11).

In the rehearsal for this scene, Po Chan explains the importance of a love letter to actor Alex Weber, who plays William's best friend in the Vietnam War (see Figure 12.12).

FIGURE 12.11
Actor Alex Weber provides his last look at his friend, William, who promises to give his last letter to his friend's love in a point-of-view shot from *The Last 3 Minutes*. Hurlbut explains how, as the sun lit the actor's face and the smoke cleared, "The timing was just perfect; it was like a sunray from heaven during the death sequence."
(©2010 Hurlbut Visuals. Used with permission.)

FIGURE 12.12
Director Po Chan gives Alex Weber advice on how to reach into his pocket in *The Last 3 Minutes*.
(Photo by Kurt Lancaster.)

Po says to him, "Now you're trying to reach the letter. Which pocket will you go in and take it out? You look at it; then you're gone." That's the physical action she relays to the actor. She then layers this with an emotional note: "You're expressing the feeling of the last minute [of your life]. The blood is gone. No pain. Your soul is slowly running out of your body."

Po explains that the "the letter is the most important element in this scene. The scene that comes after this scene is the night before when he is writing a letter to his girlfriend, where they're hunkered down in the torrential downpour; and this letter represents everything that he is going to lose right now, everything that is very dear to him. It's important for the audience to know that at the last moment in his life all he remembers is the letter that he needs to send to his girlfriend. And this contains all the heart and soul of this young soldier and his life."

Po rehearses the blocking—the actions of the actor as he performs his character. She clarifies the action until it's clear that the character dying wants his friend to pull the letter out of his pocket. She then tells him what the character is thinking of when looking at the letter. It's written to "the woman you love the most. Envision her in front of you. Know that after this moment you won't see her anymore. I want you to feel that moment and then say, 'I want to go home.'"

After another take, she clarifies the action even more. "When you say, 'I want to go home,' stiffen your neck, take a deep breath." They run the scene, Po sitting in excited anticipation as she engages her entire body as she watches the scene. She squeezes the actor's finger as a way to indicate when to let go his breath. After several takes, they set off the explosions, executing the scene. Po exclaims with glee after the explosions, like a child opening a present at Christmas and getting what she's anticipated.

"I'm so happy right now; you have no idea," she says, as I ask her to comment on the latest take. "It's almost like when I'm writing [the] script at home it is just OK; it's all in my imagination. But, all of a sudden it is all in front of me. It's just so beautiful. Yeah, I almost want to cry."

Po Chan lives in the moment when rehearsing, when watching the actors live her characters' lives: "Every moment when I'm looking at my actor even in rehearsal, even through the monitor, my whole world is there. So every single inch of my skin, my muscle, is there. I'm not me anymore, I'm not Po anymore, I become one with my scene. That is my way to truly feel what I want for the scene."

So the detail of grabbing for the letter, of letting out the character's last breath, involves something more than just dying, or enacting a death scene, Po explains. "I want—," she sighs, searching for the words. "It's funny because to people, it's death; it is very physical. To me, death is very soulful. It is very spiritual. Life and death [are] something other than physical, to me. So what I was looking for earlier from Alex is how I want to see him suck his soul out in that last breath."

Although Po is clear she's never been in a war, she feels a strong connection to death. "My family was not very well off, and I witnessed many deaths in my family. Then I came to this country all by myself without friends and family." The theme of regret is palpable throughout the film—not only her regrets in life, but, she adds, "the regrets that belong to someone very close to me and knowing how painful it was for that someone. Because somebody you love so much and you embrace everything that is, knowing that person has to go through the pain of regret—and it is really hard, when [there's] nothing you can do and just helplessly witness it."

Getting the timing right throughout the production is an arduous task, because all the scenes—except the opening—require one take in order to maintain the point of view Hurlbut and Po Chan need for the scenes. "When you do takes that are all in one, it requires everyone to be perfect," Hurlbut explains. Typically, when you do a scene, "you do a close-up and then you do a wide shot, and you do a medium, then do a reverse. You get the performance in three, four, five takes, no problem, and you're onto the next setup. But when the camera has to be the wide shot, the reverse, the close-up, the medium shot, and the spin-around all in one, you have to translate all that into one shot." So, Hurlbut explains, "The actors' timing, my camera movement, the lighting, and performance all have to be in sync. It's nothing you can edit around. If you don't use all of it, you don't have the scene."

It's also a challenge because the scenes are so short. "Trying to do something like this when you have eight to fifteen seconds to engage the audience, inflict the emotion, and identify with a character—that's a lot to do in eight seconds," Hurlbut laughs as he eats another piece of sushi.

THE BATHING SCENE

One of Hurlbut's favorite scenes is the bathing scene. Originally, Po had written a scene about the mother measuring the height of William as a child, but Hurlbut says they just couldn't find a location for it; nothing worked. "It just didn't fit." So the bathing scene "was something spontaneously created in a location that didn't really lend itself to the surroundings of the house where we were shooting. But we found an angle with trees in the background and sheets blowing on the line. The mom was so beautiful. She had that 1940s face of being on the farm and having survived rough times. It was a wonderful, playful scene with the splashing water, playing with her son and wiping his face. It was a very special moment" (see Figure 12.13).

The setup of the scene included a washtub full of water with the camera handheld by Shane Hurlbut (see Figures 12.14–12.17).

FIGURE 12.13

Actress Rachel Kolar bathes baby William in *The Last 3 Minutes*. "She had that 1940s face of being on the farm and having survived rough times," Hurlbut says. "It was a wonderful, playful scene with the splashing water, playing with her son and wiping his face." This scene was shot at ISO 160 with a Canon 35 mm L series lens, f/5.0 with a color temperature set to 5200 degrees K. (©2010 Hurlbut Visuals. Used with permission.)

FIGURE 12.14

Shane Hurlbut handholds a Canon 5D Mark II as director Po Chan gets ready to splash water onto actress Rachel Kolar (off-screen)—the camera becoming baby William's perspective of his mother.

(Photo by Kurt Lancaster.)

FIGURE 12.15
Shane Hurlbut watches the playback of a take on a field monitor (off-screen). An assistant is ready
with a reflector board in the background.
(Photo by Kurt Lancaster.)

FIGURE 12.16
The field monitor observed by director Po Chan and cinematographer Shane Hurlbut.
(Photo by Kurt Lancaster.)

FIGURE 12.17
Actress Rachel Kolar waits by the bathtub as Shane Hurlbut and Po Chan observe a take on the monitor in the background, screen left. Elite Team member Derek Edwards practices pulling focus. A reflector screen right is used to light Rachel's face with reflected sunlight.
(Photo by Kurt Lancaster.)

In the end, William dies, and the crystal rolls out of his hand. But for Po, the scene of death is more than just an ending. "The last breath of a human life means a lot," she muses. "The whole story is the last three minutes of this man's life; everything flashes back in front of him. That last breath is not just physical breath—it is the breath of the soul and the heart and the spirit of this person. So I wanted it really perfect at that moment, the right physical reactions with the eye line. Everything had to hit the right mark."

LESSONS LEARNED AND SCREENING RESULTS

Because the project was sponsored by Canon, Hurlbut used Canon lenses, but he was accustomed to utilizing prime lenses with a focus ring that stops, rather than the endless focus ring found in Canon glass. He admits that, "Initially, I was not a big fan of this glass because of the resolving power of their wide angle lenses and the endless focus ring. I made the wrong lens choices on the first day of the Navy SEAL movie [*Act of Valor*] and never looked back." However, he has since changed his mind. "Twelve months later and having completed a lot of research and development, we were able to solve both of these problems when using the Canon lenses with a new remote follow focus system," Hurlbut says.

> **BEHIND THE SCENES OF *THE LAST 3 MINUTES***
> Elite Team member Tim Holterman shot and edited a series of short documentaries on the making of *The Last 3 Minutes*. See http://hurlbutvisuals.com/blog/tag/the-making-of/.

Hurlbut was also pleasantly surprised by the results of Canon's L-series lenses. "I was blown away with the contrast, color, and resolving power of the 35 mm, 50 mm, 85 mm, and the 100 mm Canon macro lenses. They became my go-to lenses on the short and gave me more latitude in the under exposed areas, much more than the Zeiss. The image was creamy but sharp" (Hurlbut Visuals, "Inside Track Newsletter" March 31, 2010).

The Last 3 Minutes was placed online in April 2010. Between April 7 and April 28, 2010—in a period of three weeks—it received 146,000 plays on Vimeo. The work was also presented at NAB in Las Vegas later in the same month. Hurlbut attended NAB and discussed his experiences with the 5D Mark II to an overflowing crowd on the Canon showroom floor in the large convention center exhibit hall.

A few of the standout responses on Vimeo include this post: "The video completely took my breath away ... I was captivated for the whole thing and didn't come back to the real world until it was done. Excellent work. I wish to be as good as you are one day."

D. M. Daly: "Wow ... magical. Thanks for sending shivers my way, great feel!!!"

Chris Bishow: "My wife is making fun of me because I'm teary eyed, but it's probably the best piece of work I've seen with a DSLR. You owe me a tissue."

NAB 2010 became the first public screening for *The Last 3 Minutes*, and the website became a place for Shane and Po to receive written feedback. "The responses have been overwhelming, touching, and amazing," Hurlbut says. "I feel honored to have worked with Po, the Elite Team, and every person involved with the project to deliver such a heartfelt short. The story struck a nerve because it transported you on a journey through William's life, which initially appeared simple on the surface but as the memories unfold, so does the complexity of the piece. The 5D Mark II was the best tool to bring this vision to life."

Shane also realized that NAB 2010 was different. It was focused on the 5D (as well as 3D film and television): "It should have been called 5D-NAB because nearly every vendor had one—whether it was equipment to move it, monitor it, rig it, lens it, post it, color it, edit it. You name it," Hurlbut emphasizes.

But having this film projected on a large screen, first at Hdi RAWworks, and then at Laser Pacific, was the biggest reward in seeing how the look and feel of the camera paid off for this short: "What I saw could easily [have] been on a sixty-foot screen," Hurlbut remarks. "I was so impressed with the image quality, color, and contrast. The only minor snafu was a little rolling shutter when I ran into the ocean due to camera vibration. Other than that, the HDSLR technology performed beautifully. This is another perfect example of a concept and story that never could have been told with this first-person intimacy without the Canon 5D Mark II."

Director Po Chan told one story where she said a Vietnam vet contacted her after seeing the film online: "You have written a wonderfully moving story. Congratulations, I expect to see your name on many more movies in the future. Everyone needs to know the technical side, but the genius lies in your creative brain. Just look at all the work and good things that spring forth as your story is born and becomes of age. You get a gold star for good work!" After receiving this, she noted how deeply touched and grateful she was for this message.

It's what filmmaking's all about.

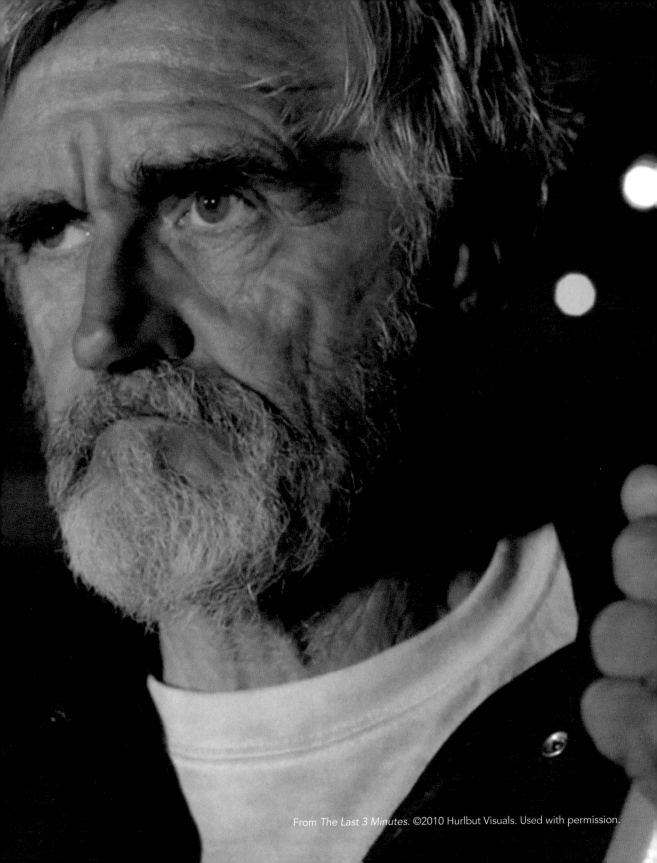

From *The Last 3 Minutes*. ©2010 Hurlbut Visuals. Used with permission.

Unmasked
https://vimeo.com/218933679
Film by Sam KJ

In this shot, the strength of Panasonic GH5 comes through in bright sunlight. "Instead of trying to chip away at the immense amount of exposure we were dealing with," cinematographer J. Van Auken explains, "I recommended going the opposite direction, and staging 4x4 mirrors around to provide key and back lights to up the contrast ratio from the broad fill we were getting off the floor, and compensate on camera with heavy ND filters." (Still from Sam KJ's *Unmasked*. ©2017 Sam KJ. Used with permission.)

CHAPTER 13

J. Van Auken: Filming Action with Panasonic's GH5 in *Unmasked*

Cinematographer J. Van Auken started making films as a child, after his grand-mother bought a video cassette camera at a garage sale and gave it to him when he was twelve. He says he never really stopped playing around with it. But profes-sionally, he's been working as a cinematographer for over ten years. His skills span from working as a director, writer, editor, cinematographer, and colorist.

VISUAL STORYTELLING AND THE AUDIENCE

This begins with the shot itself. "Every shot, every setup, I ask the director, 'What is this about? What is this supposed to do?'" It's fundamental to visual storytelling, because each filmic shot should express a purpose for the film in a simplistic way, Auken says. "It has to be simple and distilled," he adds. It shapes the "through-line of every shot we do."

It's easy to get overly complex and overthink the shot, but Auken feels that the shot "doesn't have to be a grand treatise on anything." It should be as simple as "This is where he sees the danger," he explains, "or this is where she apologizes." By making sure shots "reflect the simplest form of that idea," then the story becomes visual in the shot.

And by keeping the shots visual, simply conveying what the function of the shot is, you will communicate that meaning to an audience. "They are the other half of this equation," Auken states. He feels strongly that "filmmakers aren't filmmakers until they put the audience before themselves."

The communication of the film to an audience is relayed through the visual story-telling of shots, but there's also the deeper meaning of why the film is being made. "Who are you making this for, and why would they want to see it?" Auken asks. He shot many films and some of them are well crafted, but the producing team gave no thought about how an audience would react. "I have worked on some extremely well made projects that no one, under any circumstances, would freely choose to watch," he explains.

So if the filmmaker does something for personal expression or deep meaning it may actually fail if the audience isn't taken into consideration, Auken notes. "The film you enjoy making, the film you think is important, or the film that you think you did the best work on are meaningless without a respect and consideration for the audience," he adds.

The short action film, *Unmasked* (2017), which he and his camera operators shot on a Panasonic GH5, did factor in an audience. But it was a specialized audience. "*Unmasked* was a special case," Auken states. "It was both a commercial for and demonstration of a new camera ostensibly for the company manufacturing it." Panasonic wanted to show off the features of their new camera and hired the director Sam KJ, who brought on Auken to serve as the DP.

"There again is the most important thing: audience," Auken says. Panasonic essentially wanted a film that showed off its strengths—such as the internal anamorphic lens capability, 10-bit internal recording, v-log for expanded dynamic range, internal stability for handheld moving shots. But those strengths could be mentioned in a review—there are many "test" videos and reviews on the web about this camera.

Auken goes back to the fundamental question about who the intended audience is for their short, *Unmasked*. It's a simple answer, he says. "Camera people want to see what a camera can do." The director and writer made sure the script contained material that would show off the strengths of the camera, Auken explains.

The film would be set in locations and express actions that would push the limits of the camera. "We agreed to basically stage the action in places and lighting situations that would push the camera in ways that a very specific audience would be looking for," he says. "High contrast, outdoors in full sun to stress the dynamic range and highlight handling. Lots of fast lateral moves to push the rolling shutter of the sensor. Limited color palette with isolated areas of very high saturation to show off the color separation of the codec." (See Figure 13.1.)

> Pushing the limits of the Panasonic GH5 involved the following choices:
> - high contrast to see how it holds dynamic range
> - outdoors in high sun for how it exposes the highlights
> - fast lateral moves to see how it handles rolling shutter issues
> - limited color palette and high saturation testing color separation
> - in body stabilization for camera movement
> - to show off the anamorphic capabilities.

These technical considerations were something the director does very well, Auken explains. "Samuel, the director, and I have been working very closely for many years and developed a shorthand when we worked. Sam is an extremely technically proficient director, and so was more than aware of what the piece should accomplish on that front from the beginning." So these script choices involved including the expectations of the filmmakers as the audience and, by extension, the potential buyers of the camera (fulfilling the needs of Panasonic, who funded the project).

So the script involved the creation of a fight scene in three different locations: a rooftop, stairwell, and a large empty warehouse containing large windows. The fight scenes would convey nonstop action and very little character building, which is fine, since Auken and the rest of the team specifically knew their potential audience and meet the needs of Panasonic's desire to show off the features of the film.

FIGURE 13.1

Shot from *Unmasked*. Notice the details in the highlights on the clouds and on the surface of the roof. The Panasonic GH5 also allows for internal anamorphic.

(Cinematography by J. Van Auken. ©2017 Sam KJ. Used with permission.)

COMPOSITION

Going back to Auken's idea to keep the visual storytelling concepts simple for an audience to "get" the message or meaning behind the shot, composition is the tool of cinematographers to make this communication as clear as possible. "A fight scene is much like any other in that all you're really doing is supporting and clarifying the relationship between characters with framing," he adds, "so we approached it the same way you would in any other scene with multiple diametrically opposed characters."

With many characters involved in the fight scene, conveying high energy and powerful stunt work, a strong stunt coordinator was needed. They chose Michael Lehr, who worked on such feature films as *Logan* (2017), *John Wick: Chapter 2* (2017), and *The Fate of the Furious* (2017). For Auken, the stunt coordinator was key. "They knew just the right way to cover certain actions, and we followed their lead. Never, ever be too strong-headed to not defer to the judgment of someone who's both experienced and passionate."

As part of the composition, movement of the camera is key. "Movement, to me, is just as integral a part of composition as framing and lens choice," Auken argues, "and the choice on how or if to move is critical to conveying the subtext of a scene." In this case, Auken says that the theme of the story of *Unmasked* involves a "man-vs-world type conflict." To convey this theme as subtext through composition, Auken "framed our protagonist to be alone and surrounded, and always in a tenuous standing in relation to the larger 'mass' of opposition" (see Figures 13.2–13.4).

Furthermore, the camera should never move for the sake of movement or a "cool" shot. Camera movement should never be wasted, he adds. "An unmotivated move is just an expensive distraction."

Auken's approach to camera movement involves utilizing what he calls, "Grid theory." It involves "movement that deals with the given 'energy' of a shot and its relation to how I'd like the audience to feel at that moment," he explains. But no matter what it's called, he feels that "it's all relative to the character on-screen, their movements, and motivation." Once you nail that blocking, he "ideally" wants the "camera movements" to "always be congruent with them."

The grid theory, Auken explains, involves the idea that "the more 'grids' you move through in three dimensional space, the more energy is conveyed. So for the sequences in *Unmasked* where we wanted to ratchet up the energy, we tried to move through more than one dimension or axis at one time." This involves moving the camera by "adding a slight curve or push to lateral moves, or a slight raise or drop to the push-ins."

ANAMORPHIC

A key feature in the Panasonic GH5 includes its internal anamorphic lens capability, allowing low budget filmmakers to shoot at a 2.4:1 widescreen ratio at 6K. The micro four-thirds sensor—much smaller than the standard S35mm sensor, actually is an advantage for anamorphic shooting, according to AnamorphicStore.com (see https://www.anamorphicstore.com/gh4-gh5-anamorphic-lens/). They explain this feature:

> 2x anamorphic lenses, due to their strong anamorphic effect, generally require pairing with longer lenses to avoid vignetting. On full frame, this can be a challenge.

> But on micro four-thirds cameras, this is an advantage. Effectively, your 2x anamorphic lens is "cancelling out" your 2x crop factor. Many more lenses can be used with smaller sensor cameras.

FIGURES 13.2–13.4

To convey the theme of subtext through composition, Auken "framed our protagonist to be alone and surrounded, and always in a tenuous standing in relation to the larger 'mass' of opposition," as seen here in a sequence of three shots.

(Cinematography by J. Van Auken. ©2017 Sam KJ.)

See Figure 13.5 to see how a 50mm lens "becomes a full frame look with 2x anamorphic."

Auken decided to use Kowa anamorphic prime lenses for shooting *Unmasked*. They "were chosen both for budget reasons, and because they exhibit a lot of signature anamorphic lens character to telegraph themselves to an audience who would be looking for those hallmarks."

FIGURE 13.5

A 50mm lens on a 2x anamorphic shot.
(Image courtesy of AnamorphicStore.com. ©2017. Used with permission.)

The Kowa's, Auden explains, "exhibit a lot of the distortion and bending inherent in anamorphic lenses more often. Corner softness and tendency to flare, especially veiling glare, are also common. If you're looking for pristine, they're not your first choice, but for the more budget conscious, they are excellent performers." This gives the film a bit of a retro look.

Auken did praise the GH5's "ability to record just a section of the sensor to allow for the full 2.0x squeeze of anamorphics." He considered this a "very nice" feature, since "many digital camera don't have that, and you may end up in a situation where you have to heavily crop later to maintain the aspect ratio. The GH5 handled it very well internally."

However, Auken groans, "the camera couldn't desqueeze the preview, so to keep from losing our minds we had external monitors/recorders attached to do that." Countering AnamorphicLens' claim, he feels the micro four-thirds sensors are "absolutely the wrong sensors to use for anamorphic." He says, "They're far, far too small to make use of the range of focal lengths available." Because anamorphic lenses can't deliver wide focal lengths (40mm was the widest they go in *Unmasked*), the small micro four-thirds sensor "massively limits our wide framing options," he feels, while "a 35mm full gate size sensor would be appropriate, as that's the size all anamorphics were designed to cover and work with." Because of the limitation of the number of wide angle lenses that cannot be used on a micro four-thirds mount, Auken believes this is "outright crippling to a lot of productions, and so I don't advise it." (See Figure 13.6.)

FIGURE 13.6

Kowa Prominar anamorphic lenses used on the Panasonic GH5.

(Courtesy Radiant Images. https://radiantimages. com/lenses/35mm-pl-prime/anamorphic/429-kowa-prominar. Used with permission.)

LIGHTING

When testing for dynamic range capabilities of a camera, shooting outdoors on a sunny day is always a challenge—no matter the camera. As a beginning cinematographer, Auken would fiddle with his lighting setups, taking time to tweak the look to get it just right. It was a compulsion, Auken states. "I've long since grown away from the compulsion to tweak endlessly." The solution? "Simplify your setups. Start with asking where the light would be coming from in the first place, and use the hell out of what already exists. I have a reputation for being very fast, and that's only because I keep it very simple."

Grip gear for the project was "nothing crazy or fancy," Auken says, "just heavy Matthews stands and mounts with fat HMIs stacked on top. Mirrors were for the roof, since we didn't have heads large enough to compete with full broad sun."

Of course the rooftop would be the most challenging for lighting the shoot. "The rooftop was the most interesting piece for lighting," Auken explains. "We knew we'd be in hard broad sun, and the surface we were on was a flat white, giving a lot of return."

With a complex choreographed fight scene, they couldn't simply shoot on one side of the roof and control that light from that position. They needed the full 360 degrees for the movement. "We were physically moving around too much to work in small negative fill options, and we were seeing 360 degrees much of the time, so close sources were completely out," Auken says about their choices.

But for Auken, cinematography is about problem solving. He enjoys solving problems in real time, and "being able to see the results of those solutions on the monitor."

"There's something special about the feeling of having a novel idea," Auken says, "trying it, and seeing it work."

The solution in this case came down to reversing the problem. "Instead of trying to chip away at the immense amount of exposure we were dealing with," Auken explains, "I recommended going the opposite direction, and staging 4x4 mirrors around to provide key and back lights to up the contrast ratio from the broad fill we were getting off the floor, and compensate on-camera with heavy ND filters." A difficult problem that a less experienced cinematographer may have made overly complex. (See chapter opener image and Figure 13.1.)

Auken was happy with the results. "In the end, it gave it a slick feel, and didn't limit our movements, so it went a long way in letting the choreography shine."

It's rare for cinematographers to use a camera, which is a surprise to many students learning the craft. So when they get the chance, they love it. One day, one of the camera operators ran into "car trouble that morning and I got to step in for about ten minutes," Auken says. "There's an extremely short shot where the main character looks down and over a railing and runs away. I just like it because it was the only one I got to operate myself." (See Figures 13.7 and 13.8.)

Auken says that it was the first shot of that day, "so there was a bit of technical trickery going on to match from the previous day's shoot. The handheld rig was somewhat complex with a body vest and supporting arms attached to a kind of fig rig and wireless system. I felt like a space marine for all of ten minutes, and it was very simple; quick pan, tilt up, cut."

He does appreciate his camera operators (they used two cameras) and they built up camera rigs for them. "I couldn't be hands on, and that was a bit alien to me," Auken says, because he's used to working on smaller projects where he can be the cinematographer and operator at the same time—common on low-budget, small crew projects.

POST WORKFLOW

For postproduction, the key element was to get the flat v-log into something that looked beautiful in post. With flat images recorded in a 10-bit codec, the postproduction team had headroom to tweak the image into different looks. "The director and I had kicked around a number of different ideas for looks in preproduction, really spanning the spectrum from old Kung Fu films to *John Wick*." In the end, they went classic. "We ended up taking a lot of inspiration from some Kodachrome slide film scans we looked over, and edged that look gently into the log footage."

The process Auken took in grading Panasonic's v-log is no different than grading "any flat log workflow," he says. "First I do a first-light pass, making absolute black black, and raising the highlights to absolute white, just barely touches 100 IRE on the scopes." He sets the white balance and black balance. Auken uses the scopes for this process, not the image. The next step he calls the "'second-light,' where we apply the look we're going for, like adding a luma curve, and then pushing highlights and shadows around on the color wheels." The final step involves adding "special effects light, a tilt-shift lens look, or noise cleanup."

FIGURES 13.7 AND 13.8
Auken reveals a quick shot of our hero hoping to make a quick escape, but looks down the stairwell and sees the strength of his opposition growing.
(Cinematography by J. Van Auken. ©2017 Sam KJ.)

As for whether or not cameras should shoot 4K or higher (or even lower), Auken just wants a standard. "If agreeing upon 4K as a standard for capture and presentation will allow us to drop resolution as a talking and selling point for cameras and workflows, then I'm all for it." He feels a lot of potential filmmakers waste their time "obsessing over an increasingly irrelevant technical aspect for so long." Anything else doesn't really matter. "I really don't have the patience to have the same conversations dozens of times a year about something that affects the final product so marginally."

Auken likes to be busy shooting films. He does not like the downtime between projects. He likes to stay busy. "I can't stand not doing something," he explains. One project that kept him busy was his favorite: The feature film *Revelator* (2017), a film he wrote and directed (see http://www.revelationmachine.com/).

ADVICE ON BUDGET LIGHTING

Use the largest sources you can get and run on house power, and then spend your time and money on light modifiers: silks, softboxes, chinaballs. With limited means, get very, very comfortable modifying the cheapest light you can afford, instead of putting money on fancier sources.

STEPS FOR GRADING FLAT LOG FOOTAGE

1. Make absolute black black

2. Raise the highlights to absolute white (just touch 100 IRE on the waveform monitor)

3. Using scopes, set the white and black balance

4. Set the look of the film by adjusting the luma curve and pushing the highlights and shadows on the color wheels

5. Add special effects, such as noise removal

Still from J. Van Auken's *Revelator*. ©2017 Revelator Films.

CHAPTER 14

Mari Cleven: Filming Documentaries on the Canon's C100 Mark II

Willem de Kooning's Woman-Ochre
https://uanews.arizona.edu/story/after-31-years-stolen-womanochre-returns
Film by Mari Cleven

The return of a stolen $160 million dollar painting, missing for over thirty years
(from *Willem de Kooning's Woman-Ochre*)
Courtesy of Mari Cleven ©2017 University of Arizona.

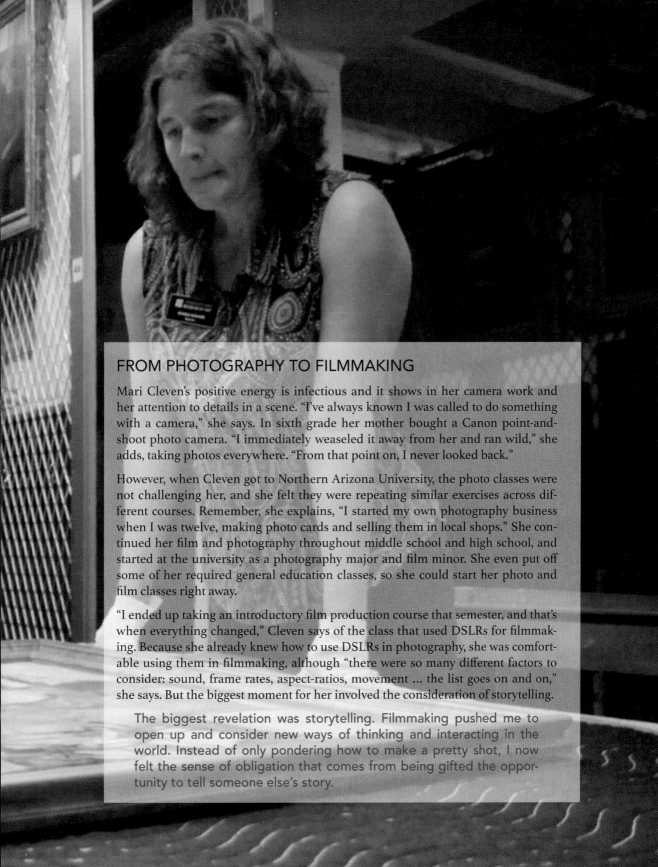

FROM PHOTOGRAPHY TO FILMMAKING

Mari Cleven's positive energy is infectious and it shows in her camera work and her attention to details in a scene. "I've always known I was called to do something with a camera," she says. In sixth grade her mother bought a Canon point-and-shoot photo camera. "I immediately weaseled it away from her and ran wild," she adds, taking photos everywhere. "From that point on, I never looked back."

However, when Cleven got to Northern Arizona University, the photo classes were not challenging her, and she felt they were repeating similar exercises across different courses. Remember, she explains, "I started my own photography business when I was twelve, making photo cards and selling them in local shops." She continued her film and photography throughout middle school and high school, and started at the university as a photography major and film minor. She even put off some of her required general education classes, so she could start her photo and film classes right away.

"I ended up taking an introductory film production course that semester, and that's when everything changed," Cleven says of the class that used DSLRs for filmmaking. Because she already knew how to use DSLRs in photography, she was comfortable using them in filmmaking, although "there were so many different factors to consider: sound, frame rates, aspect-ratios, movement ... the list goes on and on," she says. But the biggest moment for her involved the consideration of storytelling.

The biggest revelation was storytelling. Filmmaking pushed me to open up and consider new ways of thinking and interacting in the world. Instead of only pondering how to make a pretty shot, I now felt the sense of obligation that comes from being gifted the opportunity to tell someone else's story.

In the end, she created a story about a man from a local homeless shelter. But rather than just showing up and shooting footage, she took the time to "forge a strong relationship" with him. "He opened up to me about traumas in his past that moved me," Cleven adds. "Being able to share in his experiences, and finding ways to visually communicate that story, inspired me to pursue film full-time." She switched her major to film, because, as she puts it, "I flourish on being able to have experiences that help me feel more connected and integrated in the world." And, for her, she discovered how film is the "best medium" for her to "impact change and be actively engaged in shaping how others connect to experiences around them." However, it's not easy, and she notes how "it takes a lot of work—and a lot of effort," but she "finds the process and end product exceptionally rewarding."

Cleven grew up challenged with health issues, "dramatically impacting my daily life," she says, "and it's something I still struggle with." Filmmaking gives her an outlet away from those challenges, allowing her to "channel" her energy "into crafting a shot and let everything else fall away," she explains.

> Being able to craft images behind a lens gives me some semblance of control. It allows me to capture my unique way of viewing the world, and takes me outside myself. Even now, when I'm actively shooting, I get lost in the bliss of flow. I'm all consumed with the task at hand, and in those moments, I'm content.

The all-consuming aspect of filmmaking would reach a climactic point in her job at the University of Arizona.

WILLEM DE KOONING'S WOMAN-OCHRE

https://uanews.arizona.edu/story/after-31-years-stolen-womanochre-returns

Over thirty years ago, Willem de Kooning's *Woman-Ochre* was stolen from the university's art museum in a brazen fifteen-minute heist that involved a woman distracting a security guard and a man cutting the painting out of its frame. Recently, the owner of a furniture and antiques store in New Mexico, David Van Auker received the painting in an estate sale. Several customers said it looked like an original and, after doing some research, Van Auker researched the heist and returned it to the university's museum after discovering that it was the original painting. Professor Mancy Odegaard of the Arizona State Museum authenticated the painting, and Cleven was there to capture *Woman-Ochre*'s return.

Cleven was responsible for covering the story for the university on the painting's return. Although she doesn't typically do news stories, her images would soon be broadcast around the world as news outlets got wind of the story and used some of her footage. It was different from her normal job. "Shooting the de Kooning story was a whirlwind of adrenaline, anticipation, and in the end, elation," Cleven exclaims. "With so many negative stories in the news right now, it was refreshing to cover a story with a happy ending," she explains. And in the end, her footage would be the "only record ever of *Woman-Ochre*'s return to the museum. No pressure, right?" No, not when the painting's worth $160 million.

The story became a shooting challenge. "Because the piece hadn't been authenticated," Cleven says, "we had to proceed with caution. The theft is still an open FBI investigation, so not only did we have to deal with lawyers, NDAs, and the police, but we had to be sensitive to the fact we potentially had a 160-million-dollar painting in our care!"

It was a bit of an adrenaline rush, Cleven exclaims, and as a filmmaker she "knew this was a once-in-a-lifetime opportunity." Ultimately Cleven felt that the story was what "Hollywood films are made of—a priceless piece of artwork is stolen and then recovered over thirty years later. A world-renowned conservator had to come in and meticulously inspect the artwork in order to authenticate the piece. We all joked about who would be cast in the starring roles of the film," Cleven laughs.

With that pressure over her head, Cleven juggled three elements when shooting:

Sound

I knew it would be important to identify the key players in the room and get a mic on them before the action took off. A lot of the best soundbites occur organically in the heat of the moment, and I didn't want to miss anyone's reactions to seeing the painting for the first time. Particularly the moment the conservator finally declared, yes, the de Kooning is real! You can't recreate those moments, so always push to mic someone up.

(See Figure 14.1.)

FIGURE 14.1

Mari Cleven captures the moment when the authenticity of the de Kooning painting was revealed.

(Film by Mari Cleven. ©2017 University of Arizona.)

Let It Roll

I tried to do long takes and let the camera roll. Not only does this keep the natural sound rolling (it was feeding directly into the camera), but I wanted to make sure I had steady shots that let the action unfold.

Coverage

To the above point, I also knew a news package would need to be short and sweet. Getting proper coverage with cutaways was essential. Close-ups, such as the paint strokes between the canvas and frame, were integral to the story. Proper coverage of a scene gives you way more options in post, and helped me craft a tighter story by being able to rearrange natural sound-bites with specific shots.

(See Figure 14.2.)

FIGURE 14.2

Cleven's detail shot shows the brush strokes of the original frame *Woman-Ochre* was cut from, with the edge of the canvas matching the paint stroke of the returned art.

(Film by Mari Cleven. ©2017 University of Arizona.)

The following nine-shot sequence (Figures 14.3–11) reveals Cleven's eye for details and it is a master-class example of how to shoot coverage in a scene and reveal emotion. In an attempt to capture the unveiling of the painting, Cleven sets up a sequence that includes one cutaway to a head-shot sequence, but all of the other cuts in this sequence reveal a variety of shot sizes and camera angles.

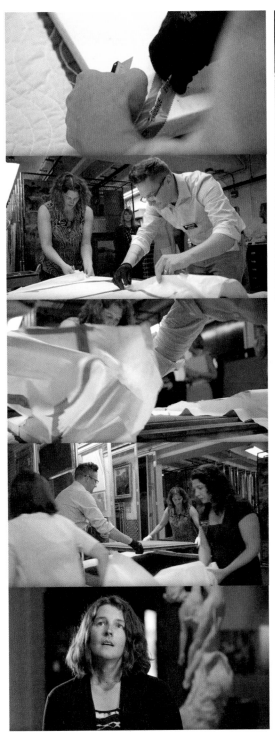

FIGURES 14.3–14.11

In this sequence, we can see how Cleven shot a variety of shot sizes and camera angles to visually tell the story of the unveiling of *Woman-Ochre* and the emotions captured. The flow of shots go down on the first column, then back up to the second column. One head-shot interview tells the story.

(Film by Mari Cleven. ©2017 University of Arizona.)

NOT ALL GLITZ AND GLAM

Cleven loves the production process—especially if she can shoot outdoors. "I love getting to interact with different individuals, all with varying ideals, goals, and knowledge," she says. "Getting to share in their perspectives and gain insight into their world gives me another nugget of knowledge or experience to take with me throughout the rest of my life." As a documentary filmmaker, she loves learning about other people. "I've been blessed to have opportunities and learn about topics I never otherwise would have been exposed to. Filmmaking allows me to continuously learn and be a student of life!" In addition, she loves being behind the lens, allowing her to "actively capture events as they unfold." Cleven is a kinesthetic learner, and she uses the camera as an extension of her body, her sensibilities. "By shooting," she explains, "I enter that flow state where nothing else matters and I can see the vision come together in my head. Pure magic."

But it's not all fun. "I always dread prepping an edit," she says. "Having to transcribe or re-listen to interviews is tedious," she adds. And watching and logging footage takes hours of work. She also feels that pulling select shots "can be wearisome," she admits. Because she loves the outdoors so much, she really "struggles being plugged into [her] computer for hours on end." But, despite the labor, she realizes that some of those tedious moments "are necessary for a well-produced product," she explains. Cleven realizes that she can't just jump in and start editing. The preparation allows her to gain a "firm grasp of everything I've recorded," she says. "It's like running a marathon. No one enjoys the long hours of training, but without putting in the initial leg-work, you can't be successful." Making movies can be hard, but the payoff is an exciting film.

A creative field like filmmaking "isn't all glitz and glam," Cleven says. "It's showing up every day and putting in the hours," she explains. The key part to this? You have to do it "even when you don't want to. It can be painful. It's not as sexy as people try to make it out to be," she adds. "But, like anything, nothing great is ever easy. Only by putting in the hours do you learn, grow, and come away with an edit you can be really proud of," she explains.

Cleven distinguishes the differences from really enjoying a shot and loving a final project. "I'm particularly partial to any project that gets me outdoors, in the natural environment," she says. "But sometimes my favorite shoots aren't my favorite films, and vice versa." A shoot can be "stressful and crazy," she says, "but I love the final product." That type of unpredictability is "half the fun!" she exclaims. "Or so I tell myself," she adds.

RADIOCARBON DATING GETS A POSTMODERN MAKEOVER

https://research.arizona.edu/stories/radiocarbon-dating-gets-postmodern-makeover

Before taking on the de Kooning story, and after graduating from Northern Arizona University with a degree in filmmaking, Cleven applied for a job at the University of Arizona's Research, Discovery, & Innovation (RDI) division. Her responsibility? "'Making science cool; it's what we do,'" Cleven jokingly says about her job. "The University of Arizona is teeming with groundbreaking research endeavors," she adds, and her job is to translate difficult concepts into short films.

"I don't know if you've ever tried talking to scientists about mass spectrometers and other do-dads, but, suffice it to say, trying to distill these massive feats of inquiry often proves to be a challenge," she laughs. "I see my job as taking these academically daunting ideas and translating them into digestible stories any lay person could understand and relate to. I want to remind viewers the human connection behind these scientific undertakings—the deeper 'Why?' that connects to their life."

In her shot film called, *Radiocarbon Dating Gets a Postmodern Makeover*, Cleven had to tell the story of how researchers at the University of Arizona "plan to use the annual precision of tree rings, in combination with carbon-14, to underpin big questions related to the rise and fall of civilizations." It's a big topic. Her intent was to focus on "the topic of radioactive isotopes and hit upon a universal truth, thus providing a human connection to this scientific endeavor."

So she used a bit of dialogue from one of her interview subjects to set up the story. "The first line you hear is," Cleven says, "'A part of how we feel about ourselves as people comes from our identity and knowing about our past.' Boom. Right away I'm hooking the viewer by appealing to the human pursuit of identity." Rather than focus on the scientific concepts of "carbon-14 or calibration curves," she explains, which are "merely the tools being utilized to explore the deeper 'why,'" she examined a "universal truth," a process that she explains in this way: "Every person who clicks 'play' will, in some shape or form, relate to this shared human experience." Her research subject, Dr. Charlotte Pearson, then says, "'The study of archaeology, people, time, and environment is a way to understand ourselves better and our future, to learn something about humanity.'" By opening with these words, Cleven was able to meet her goal from the "get-go to set up this conflict, the human pursuit of meaning, and use the rest of the film to illustrate one way researchers are looking to solve that problem."

But as a filmmaker, Cleven realized that the words are not the most important aspect of a film. It's the visuals that really draw an audience in and the dialogue adds context. The opening of *Radiocarbon Dating*, shows a variety of poetic shots of trees. She also set up the shot with motion. "Trees provide great lines and depth in terms of composition" and, since the story involved the use of tree rings, the poetry of the shot fits the theme of the film. So the camera movement allowed her to "capitalize on their full potential," she explains. In addition, she adds, "I wanted the viewer to feel physically drawn into the piece. Instead of passive still shots, I actively looked to pull the eye in with flares and flow." (See Figure 14.12.) In this way, she fulfilled one of the key rules of storytelling in filmmaking: "Every choice you make as a filmmaker should creatively serve the story you're tasked with telling," including camera movement.

FIGURE 14.12

Cleven wanted lens flares and camera movement to help draw the audience into the flow of her story in *Radiocarbon Dating Gets a Postmodern Makeover*.

(Film by Mari Cleven. ©2017 University of Arizona.)

Camera movement adds a "feeling of flow and movement" to shots, but the movement should be "motivated," she says. "Always think about why you're moving the camera, and what you want to convey, or have the audience focus on, in relation to that motion," she explains.

If the "goal of this piece was to demonstrate the power of tree rings," Cleven explains, then there's going to be a "lot of technical concepts that go into this research," but that's not the way to draw a general audience into your film. So the tree shots reflected her desire for the "viewer to initially connect to the natural world," she adds. It helped structure the theme of the short film:

> You don't need a PhD to appreciate trees. That's something most people see every day. It's an easy concept to translate both in the natural world and in the laboratory. My goal by opening the piece in nature, spending the middle portion in the laboratory, and coming full circle back out on the landscape, is to remind viewers that the work being done in the laboratory connects back to the outside world.

Cleven is conscious of how shots should be composed. There are "fundamental tricks," she says, which include "depth of field, framing, leading lines, and the rule of thirds." In addition, she "visually stacks different foreground elements by using a telephoto lens to compress the image. This adds a sense of depth to a 2D image." Furthermore, she's consciously always trying to use "framing in my wide shots," because it "gives a feeling of intimacy and makes an otherwise bland shot dynamic," she adds. "I really enjoy playing with the balance of a frame and considering how to direct the viewer's eye. All of these tools, coupled with match frame cuts and camera movement, make for a fun time."

But when faced with the challenge of shooting inside a laboratory, Cleven feels that she "constantly battles with visual ways to illustrate scientific topics." She can face a "lack of visually engaging material" or even being forced to shoot in "spaces not conducive to filming." In these situations, she says, "I always try to get subjects to interact with something— equipment or other people." In this way, even "if the task isn't the most stimulating, I can cover the action in an interesting way." She is always conscious of filming a "variety of shot types, angles, and compositional

FIGURE 14.13
Cleven reveals a close-up inside the frame of a monitor that reveals how her subject, Dr. Charlotte Pearson, interacts with a photo to help illustrate her point, visually.
(Film by Mari Cleven. ©2017 University of Arizona.)

FIGURE 14.14

The shot is a bit wider, but provides more context. We see, now, that Dr. Pearson points to a monitor.
(Film by Mari Cleven. ©2017 University of Arizona.)

tools" so she can "cut together a sequence that is more or less engaging." (See Figures 14.13 and 14.14.)

By starting it as a detailed close-up followed by a wider shot providing more visual context, Cleven helps to draw the viewer into the world of her subject. Cleven loves the details. "There's beauty in the details," she says, but those kinds of shots, she adds, "give me a lot of leverage in post. They are cutaways, which means I can cut into a detail, and then cut out to a reframed scene without visually jarring the viewer with a jump-cut or unnatural transition."

As to the use of light and lenses, Cleven likes to shoot with zoom lenses. Typically she'll shoot with the budget zoom lens, the 17–55mm/f2.8 and 70–200mm/f2.8 zooms. Cleven loves the flexibility of the zoom lens.

> Shooting in a documentary style, often with little control over my surroundings, leaves me in need of flexibility. Having variation in focal length is critical for me to get complete coverage of a scene. Especially when I don't have access to locations beforehand, I need to be able to roll with my surroundings and make anything work.

Lighting in documentary work can be a challenge, but lighting is "what gives shape and depth to an otherwise two-dimensional image. It brings a subject to life," she says. "Lighting also plays a big role in the way a viewer feels, whether they're conscious of it or not. A high-key scene that's bright, soft, and lower in contrast provides a completely different aesthetic than a dark, low-key, contrasty image. Think about the mood you want to convey and use lighting to deliver that experience."

DREAM DELIVERY SERVICE

https://vimeo.com/197961512

In a side project, Cleven profiled Mathias Svalina, a poet traveling the country on his bicycle delivering personalized "dreams" to subscribers. Her short film earned a professional regional Emmy Award. It's a film she jumped on quickly. "By the time I found out and connected with Mathias, he was getting ready to leave town," Cleven laughs. "I believe I filmed his last delivery before he hit the road."

Cleven chose a slight slow motion look to this film in order to "convey a dream-like aesthetic," matching the theme of the subject—a person who delivers written dreams. Structurally, she chose to include two major scenes, a sequence showing Svalina's writing and a sequence showing his delivery.

Even though she shot his writing at a local coffee shop, "a crowded, uncontrolled environment," Cleven explains, it became the perfect place to "convey Mathias' sense of isolation, even in a room full of people." So when she edited the piece, she decided to show the first shot when we "see Mathias alone," she says. "I composed

FIGURE 14.15

Svalina sits alone in a coffee shop as he writes. Cleven composed him small in the frame, with all this empty space around him, and an empty chair in front of him.

(Film by Mari Cleven. ©2017 Mari Cleven. Used with permission.)

him small in the frame, with all this empty space around him. An empty chair in front of him." (See Figure 14.15.)

Then she built a "sound bed comprised of clinking plates, friends talking, and laughter," she explains. The sequence includes a "cut to a shot of a woman laughing, and then a tilt up to Mathias, where his narration begins: 'I feel like a creature who's in a world where I don't know how the rules work, and I don't know how to make sense of things," she says. By framing him "by the laughing women," Cleven adds, it "visually communicates his inner thoughts of isolation." At the same time,

FIGURE 14.16
Cleven composes Svalina between people who are enjoying themselves in order to show the social isolation as he writes.
(Film by Mari Cleven. ©2017 Mari Cleven.)

we hear Svalina speak, revealing a larger theme of the film: "But in the kind of contained space of writing, inside the containment of writing, is when I feel the most like the closest to being human." (See Figure 14.16.)

But Cleven doesn't just have Svalina talk about how he finds a moment of being human. She captures his writing, obviously, but her intent was to visualize his humanity by recording "his subtle mannerisms," she explains. This included shots of him chuckling to himself, "clearly wrapped up in his own imagination,"

FIGURE 14.17
As Svalina writes, he chuckles to himself, a moment that Cleven feels reveals "his singularity" in being human..
(Film by Mari Cleven. ©2017 Mari Cleven.)

she adds. "I keep Mathias in context as an outsider by showing him in relationship to those in the café, always cutting back in to express his singularity." (See Figure 14.17.)

Then the second half of the film shows him delivering the stories, showing his morning delivery route, "getting an introspective glimpse into his inner thoughts," Cleven says. "As he's packing up envelopes in his book bag," she explains, "I transition to an early morning shot of him grabbing his bicycle. Then I cut to a wide of him riding, similar in idea to the opening wide, but this time doing the thing he would describe as, 'the thing my body was made for.'" Unlike many films that include subjects talking in an interview, Cleven decided never to show the interview, because, as she says, "I want the audience to stay wrapped up in Mathias' head, hearing his inner dialog."

The end is in contrast to the "isolation created in the beginning of the film," Cleven says. "By the end you see Mathias laughing, enjoying himself." This provides a "full circle," she feels, because through writing, "Mathias found the one thing that makes him feel like a complete, functioning being in the world." She shot this project with Canon's 17–55mm and 70–200mm/f2.8 zoom lenses on the C100 Mark II.

CAMERA CHOICES AND THE POSTPRODUCTION PROCESS

Although Cleven is a gear head and likes trying out new equipment like other filmmakers, she states, "I've always been of the opinion that gear is only one component of a production. While it plays an essential role, knowing how to craft a shot and tell a story are more important." The story is number one. But when it comes to specific gear, she factors in the "budget, crew size, delivery, and the overall needs of the project." But at the small operation she's in at the university—with limited money and resources—and shooting as a one-woman band, she "wanted a camera that hits all my technical and aesthetic requirements in an affordable price range."

Furthermore, "Having to direct, shoot, and produce everything on my own meant I needed a stable system in the field," Cleven adds. She chose the Canon C100 Mark II, because of its ability to shoot cinematically, as well as two XLR inputs "to feed and monitor audio through." It also shoots 60 fps, contains six stops of ND filters built in, and is relatively low-priced storage, since it records on two SD cards. "I shoot primarily documentary work," Cleven says, "so for me this camera provides a lot of important touch points at a very affordable price."

She feels that one of the disadvantages of the C100 is its lower resolution (full HD), as well as a lack of high frame rates for slow motion work, and its limited recording codecs (AVCHD and MP4 recording). "There's no option to record in ProRes or 4K," she complains, but the 4K "isn't always an advantage if you're shooting a big doc and have to consider hard drive space or if you need to turn a news story quickly," she adds. "I think the key advantages of this camera is its ability to perform in the field, ease of use for solo operators, battery life, media storage, built-in ND and XLR inputs, and affordability. You get a lot for the price and don't need to spend a lot of extra money outfitting the camera."

Cleven loves using the C100's Canon log setting, but it does require that every shot be graded. "While I like having latitude in post," the Canon log "only works if you have time built into your postproduction schedule," she notes. For example, "I shot C-log for the de Kooning piece," she says. "However, because I had to cut that video so quickly, and package a press kit for media, I wish I had shot it in a different format. It took me longer to grade the final product."

When grading, Cleven uses the Lumetri Color panel in Premiere. She feels it's "awesome." Since Premiere provides grading "tools in the editing software, there's no round-tripping the work," she notes. However, when faced with "bigger proj-

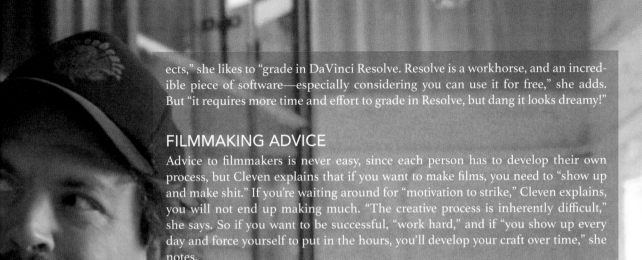

ects," she likes to "grade in DaVinci Resolve. Resolve is a workhorse, and an incredible piece of software—especially considering you can use it for free," she adds. But "it requires more time and effort to grade in Resolve, but dang it looks dreamy!"

FILMMAKING ADVICE

Advice to filmmakers is never easy, since each person has to develop their own process, but Cleven explains that if you want to make films, you need to "show up and make shit." If you're waiting around for "motivation to strike," Cleven explains, you will not end up making much. "The creative process is inherently difficult," she says. So if you want to be successful, "work hard," and if "you show up every day and force yourself to put in the hours, you'll develop your craft over time," she notes.

In a reversal of expectations that you need to push your ego in order to be successful at filmmaking, Cleven advises, "be humble." She explains what she means by this: "We all have different strengths, weaknesses, and journeys to follow on our filmmaking path. Know that you have value, and with the right attitude and work ethic, people will take notice." She adds, "Leave your ego at the door." But an important aspect in learning how to make films, involves seeking out mentors and other individuals who will "help push you," Cleven advises. "Everyone you meet provides unique value; treat them with kindness and respect. You never know how the people you encounter today may turn into a key connection down the line."

As for learning about how to make better films using online resources, Cleven feels that Stillmotion or Muse Storytelling is a great resource in learning how to tell better stories. "I love their story-centric approach to filmmaking," she says (see https://musestorytelling.org/). She also recommends http://nofilmschool.com. "I read articles on that site regularly." Cleven also is "a big podcast fan" and she likes listening to Chase Jarvis Live—"it's fantastic and provides insights from a vast array of creatives," she adds. She also recommends checking out Jarvis's "The Daily Creative" YouTube series (https://www.youtube.com/user/achaser123). Creative Live is another "fantastic resource for any kind of artistic or entrepreneurial endeavor," Cleven says (see https://www.youtube.com/user/creativelive). "You can watch free webinars every day on tons of topics from software, lighting, filmmaking, photography, marketing, design, business, and so much more."

A still from Bibbi Abruzzini's *Children in captivity: Freeing Nepal's Prison Babies.*
(Courtesy of Bibbi Abruzzini. ©2017 Zoomin.TV)

CHAPTER 15

Bibbi Abruzzini: Filming Documentaries on Canon's 5D Mark IV

STORYTELLING

Bibbi Abruzzini knew that she wanted to be a storyteller ever since she was seven or eight years old. Storytelling has always been a tradition in her family, she says, "be it around the dinner table or under a tent with a torch in hand in the middle of Italy." Her grandfather was an architect and filmed a series of documentaries about architecture in Rome, and he "transmitted to me his passion for art and images," she adds. "As a kid I used to cut and paste pictures from *National Geographic* and make up stories about faraway lands and people."

Storytelling was ingrained within her since she was a child, but Abruzzini didn't know she wanted to make films until she worked as a multimedia journalist in Asia, working for a Chinese news agency in Kathmandu. She felt a certain amount of empowerment, when she discovered that that editors could change her words but not her images.

Abruzzini began to focus on how photography and cinematography felt new to her as a storytelling tool. "When I started, I knew very little about visual art," she explains, but she "felt like discovering something new and the process was introspective" to her.

One of Abruzzini's biggest inspirations for her documentary work includes Jean Rouch, who practiced a participatory and ethnographic approach to his films. "Participatory is a word we hear with increasing frequency in filmmaking," Abruzzini says. "It encourages an active participation from the film's subjects," she explains. From her filmmaking she wants a collaborative approach that creates a "rich sense of place and a strong focus on humanity," she adds.

This participatory approach becomes Abruzzini's favorite aspect of filmmaking, an approach that allows for the process of finding the story more important than forcing a result from the story. She looks forward to waking up on a Saturday and seeing the world through a lens and interacting with people. Filmmaking for her is about creating "meaningful connections with my subjects," she says. "It's about questioning my way of telling stories. Ultimately, by enabling people to present themselves, I hope to encourage a more honest and inclusive building of knowledge." In addition, she likes the moment in postproduction when the footage begins to look like a film and how the "images acquire different meanings depending on their placement in the edit."

But filmmaking doesn't come easy to Abruzzini. She says it involves a "gigantic physical and mental effort," and often includes some "doubt to my approach" and often involves not fully planning properly. It also becomes all-absorbing when she commits to a project, which "sometimes includes negative repercussions on my personal life," she says. As an example, she recently traveled to Lebanon to shoot two short documentaries: one in a Palestinian refugee camp in Beirut, and another one in Southern Lebanon about a grandmother who has turned her village into an example of sustainability. "Both projects were badly planned," she laughs, looking back at it. "For almost two weeks I could barely rest," she says, which ended up impacting her "performance in the field." She's still learning how to find a "healthy balance between filming and planning." In the end, she resorts to a maxim by Magnum photographer Alex Webb, who, she explains, says that "photography and visual storytelling is a kind of work that is 99.9% failure, but then 'something utterly unexpected happens, something utterly serendipitous.'"

Abruzzini feels that documentary filmmaking can be "easily integrated into other art forms." As such, she reads "as much as possible about modern art history and cinema. I also spend a lot of time reading anthropological research and essays," she adds, in order to "deepen my understanding of society and cultures." She likes to read I read Bigthink (http://bigthink.com) and she watches at least two or three documentaries a week. At the same time, she is "deeply influenced by photography" and spends time on the websites of LensCulture, Magnum, *The New York Times* lens blog, as well as watching their Op-docs sections, and *Huck* magazine. She was inspired by the work of some of her university professors such as Bill Carter (Miss Sarajevo), as well as by visual storytellers and photographers such as Alex Webb and Eugene Richards. She follows the work of Paula Bronstein and documentary filmmakers such as Joshua Oppenheimer, Sharmeen Obaid-Chinoy, Ari Folman, and Sarah Polley, among others.

BLENDING CINEMA AND ANTHROPOLOGY

The first step in finding a story, she says, involves getting to know yourself and developing yourself. The best stories "arrive only when we are ready to tell them," she says philosophically. This doesn't happen until you have a sense of the kinds of stories you want to tell, which includes connecting to people. Don't let the camera become a filter or a wall to this connection, detaching yourself from your subjects' stories, she says. "Use your camera to get closer rather than further away." To help with this connection, "live in the present and make the best of the opportunity you have to interact with your subjects," she explains. For example, she doesn't want the camera to be a distraction, especially during interviews. "A technique I use particularly with kids is to show them how the camera works and let them film with me for a couple of minutes," she explains. "As a result the camera is not seen as the enemy or something to be afraid of anymore." She also develops a style of interviewing that is conversational, allowing for "meaningful and relaxed" discussions, "so that the camera just becomes part of the scenery, like a lamp, or an object."

Abruzzini advises that you will encounter some stories that "have never been told, while others will be the same rationalized version of their problems. Learn how to tell the difference." With that difference in mind, she also feels that interacting with the community you're in provides a foundation for strong storytelling. "I try to understand the community I am going to film and find ways of representing their issues creatively by blending cinema and anthropology." By this she means that she values connections with people with respect. "I spend days and sometimes months in close contact with my subjects," she explains. "I try to understand their routine and find beauty in their gestures." In her short film about young women skateboarders in Nepal, Abruzzini says she filmed a young skateboarder, Rezina, as she was getting ready to leave the house. "Silence reigned in the room," Abruzzini notes. "It wasn't that sort of awkward silence, it was comfortable. Rezina was putting her socks and shoes on, doing her hair, and looking out of the window. I found that whole routine beautiful in its simplicity and normality." (See Figures 15.1 and 15.2.) This leads to visual intimacy, but that takes trust and it takes time to build trust. "I spend a lot of time trying to establish mutual trust and emotional connections with the people I'll film," she states.

At the same time, Abruzzini feels visual storytelling is an intuitive process. This process leads to deeper storytelling. "Yes," she explains, "I film what I see. As a result, what I shoot is simply a reflection of the people that I meet and my interaction with them." This involves practicing what she calls "social listening" in order to "constantly evolve my approach to a story." As she was researching her project on homelessness, *Brian*, in Phoenix, Arizona, she engaged in social listening as a constant. "Social listening" allowed "me to go beyond appearances and understand how to best tell the story by giving members of the community power to decide how they were going to be portrayed," she explains. "I didn't want the word 'homeless' to be a defining and static characteristic for the subjects of the documentary. Through social listening I could relate to and be curious about their unique stories, scrap labels, and have an exchange as equals." (See Figure 15.3.) One of the most important aspects in her approach to filmmaking is her philosophy is about "receiving and giving." She adds, "If someone is opening up to me, I feel compelled to trust them and do the same."

FIGURES 15.1 AND 15.2

Bibbi Abruzzini films Rezina as she gets ready to go outdoors to skate in Nepal. Her filmmaking techniques captures gestures and looks that reveal an intimacy of emotion not often found in new pieces.

(Film by Bibbi Abruzzini. ©2017 CafeBabel.)

FIGURE 15.3
Brian locates a place to sleep in the streets of Phoenix, Arizona.
(Film by Bibbi Abruzzini. ©2017 Bibbi Abruzzini.)

Through this process, she helps the viewer "get a glimpse into a place through the stories and expressions of its people. I try to make certain that my work is immersive, emotive, authentic, and fearless," she adds. Through a process of self-discovery and living that honestly, Abruzzini quotes photographer Sarker Protick to explain the types of stories she chooses to do: "I believe our own individual philosophies towards life reflect in our work and images."

Whenever Abruzzini takes on a new project, she tries to be the "best person possible," opening herself up to an authentic life. This process of creating deep connections to people in an authentic way builds a trust that allows her to become a "clever shadow, using the camera as a tool of personal development and interrogation of others," she explains. By this she means to "make sure that subjects know that they are being seen with mindfulness without judgment." She feels that there is no objective stance, no way to become invisible to your own sensibilities. "I think it's unrealistic to believe the filmmaker's perspective will not affect the story." But unlike news stories that rely on heavy narration, what she calls "voice-over clues," she wants her images to shape the ways views "make meaning," giving them the "ability to interpret actions and words independently" of a reporter's narration.

CHILDREN IN CAPTIVITY: FREEING NEPAL'S PRISON BABIES
(See http://www.msn.com/en-us/video/pop/children-in-captivity-freeing-nepals-prison-babies /vp-BByhvWQ)

One of Abruzzini's favorite news stories includes a project about Indira Ranamagar, who has spent over twenty-five years helping children of prisoners in Nepal, who often grow up with their parents behind bars, Abruzzini explains. "When no guardian is available, arrested parents from low-income backgrounds must choose between bringing their children to jail with them or letting them live on the streets," she adds. When Ranamagar was forced by her husband to choose between him or helping the children, she chose the children.

"There are over eighty children still living in prisons across Nepal," Abruzzini says, but "thanks to Indira's efforts, some have a chance at a life not peering through bars." In filming the story, she traveled with Indira across Southern Nepal when some political protests were occurring in the region. She was "overwhelmed" when filming in women's prisons, but there was one moment in particular, she said, that she will never forget. "It's a moment I didn't even have the strength to film," she notes. "A little boy—he might have been eight or nine years old—who lives with his mom in prison, started crying as he wanted to come out to play with us. All you could see was his face behind the bars and those tears flowing down his eyes. Eventually we asked the security guard whether he could hang out with us for thirty minutes and she agreed. It was upsetting, but it made me realize how important it was to cover that story and be there in that moment." She did film him playing outside with "some of the rescued kids," she adds. "I think that he was crying not necessarily because he was sad about his mother, but more because he was tired of not having the freedom to play and be with all the other children. There was no possibility for him to be spontaneous in prison."

Abruzzin's participatory filmmaking approach occurred in the making of *Children in Captivity*. With a shared collaboration with Indira, she would have never been able to film in Nepal's prisons, as they made connections with both the women and the guards. "On one occasion in particular," Abruzzini says, "Indira encouraged me to travel with her to Illam, in far Eastern Nepal, to visit a farm in the hills where she was teaching some of the rescued children how to work in the field of perma-culture. I knew that it was going to take at least six hours' driving around the region, but as a filmmaker I decided to trust her." By convincing her to go, Indira became a collaborator in the film (as well as a participant). And it was worth it. "When we got there it was absolutely beautiful and it added another layer to the story that I wouldn't have been able to give without sharing ownership of the project." (See Figure 15.4.)

This participatory and collaborative approach, Abruzzini practices makes for better storytelling. "They are the better people to tell their own stories," she says, "if they are given enough space and freedom to express themselves and give a direction to the project." Therefore, she "always tries to be flexible and open to sugges-

FIGURE 15.4
In Nepal, children of mothers sent to prison, but go with them to prison.
(Film by Bibbi Abruzzini. ©2017 Zoomin.TV)

tions, not letting myself become confined by scripts, plans, and storyboards," she explains. "As the collaboration between subjects and filmmakers deepens, a lot more scenarios open up," she adds, "and we need to be ready for them."

S.K.A.T.E. NEPAL

(See http://www.cafebabel.co.uk/society/article/skate-nepal-rolling-over-gender-inequality.html)

Abruzzini feels a connection to women's issues. She says that in Nepal, 40% of women are married by the age of 18. "Girls and young women are often confined to certain roles according to society's expectation," she says. So she wanted to tell a story that defied this expectation. "I decided to film a group of young skateboarders pushing the boundaries for women in Nepal," she says. There is a female collective from New Zealand, she explains, who make "the sport more accessible and less intimidating." In her documentary, she explores issues of identity, gender equality, and "what it means to be a woman skateboarder in South Asia."

As with her other projects, she prefers a collaborative approach to filmmaking. "I wanted this collaborative documentary to address conflicting views of reality in Nepal" in order to create a "social intervention." She intended and hoped the documentary would become a "vehicle for social change involving collaborative practices with participants to bring about some form of new awareness," she adds. She collaborated with Rezina, who is an amateur skateboarder, and members of the female collective Refurb Skate, "in order to reverse intercultural dynamics and challenge traditional power relations," she explains. (See Figure 15.5.)

FIGURE 15.5
A girl practices her skate moves in Nepal.
(Film by Bibbi Abruzzini. ©2017 CafeBabel.)

Ultimately, Rezina gave Abruzzini access to the skateboarding subculture in Nepal. Without her help she wouldn't have been able to do the film. "She put me in contact with her family and found possible girls and women that we could film," Abruzzini says. "She also acted as a mediator, convincing people to be interviewed and appear on camera. As a result, the participatory and collaborative approach to the story made Rezina much more than a 'subject,' but an ally, a friend, an assistant, a filmmaker," she adds.

Initially, she wanted to focus on one character, but she realized that "it wouldn't work." She decided to "expand the scope of the documentary" and spend several months on it, filming at least three days a week at the skate park in Kathmandu and around Nepal in order to find her stories of women.

In the end, she says, "I tried to put myself at the disposal of the subjects and invent part of the film with them." But not everyone is going to be interested in skate culture and she didn't want to turn this into a skate video. In order to widen the potential audience interest, "I tried to find a different angle to the story so that it had an emotional impact on viewers."

BRIAN

(See https://bea2016.secure-platform.com/a/gallery/rounds/1289/details/24149)

Emotions flow from Abruzzini's shots, and the participatory aspect of her filmmaking opens up a sense of trust that allows her to record such emotions on camera. One of her significant experiences involved collaborating on a documentary with Brian Noel, a homeless person she met in Phoenix, Arizona while working on her Master's documentary project at Northern Arizona University. Noel, who is a "videographer" recording his experiences on the street, has posted hundreds of videos on YouTube. "What distinguished Brian from other passionate, aspiring filmmakers, was his raw technique and provocative videos on social '(in)justice'," she explains.

"If in the virtual world this 58-year-old man could be a 'star,'" Abruzzini says, then in the real world, Brian is an "invisible member of the hidden homeless population in the United States." His YouTube channel becomes a platform so he can be heard, allowing him to be treated as an "equal" in contrast with his "bum persona" in the analog world.

As with her other films, she collaborated with Brian. "We joined creative forces to produce a documentary film exploring the dreams and realities of homelessness in Arizona through observational and collaborative filmmaking." This form of participation "allowed Brian to gain greater control over the identity and image of people struggling with homelessness," she explains. At the same time it Abruzzini to gain a deeper understanding of what it is like to be homeless.

When it came to filming the project, Abruzzini would spend at least two days a week hanging out with Brian. "And most of the time we wouldn't even be filming," she says. "We would just get to know each other and find better ways to tell the story on camera." In addition to exploring what it is like to be homeless, she says that "Brian witnessed a lot of important moments in my life, from trying to live in the US as an Italian, to living in a hostel. He became a confidant for me as well. Reciprocity is what defined our relationship," which relates to the collaborative nature of the film, she explains. But it wasn't easy. "Brian was really skilled in rationalizing his issues so it took me months to get an emotional answer from him," she says. "This collaborative process was challenging at times because the line between being a filmmaker and a friend, or in Brian's case, also part of his survival strategy, got blurred." However, this approach allowed them to be "completely honest about the documentary; what was going to be included and what wasn't," she says. "In particular in Brian's case, it was important to craft, film, and edit the story together. There were parts of his personality and his history that he didn't want to unveil to viewers." The film became a living, but filtered document, showing what it is like to live on the streets of Phoenix.

COMPOSITION, CAMERA MOVEMENT, AND DETAIL SHOTS

Abruzzini developed her skills as a photographer before shifting to filmmaking. "I seek with my eyes the beauty of imperfection," she says. She feels that this approach leads to genuine authenticity, rather than a polished view of the self. "With Brian, for instance," she says, "I remember a sequence in which I filmed his rugged, blistered hands, his nicotine-stained fingers, and his vanishing tattoos. I knew that objectively they might not have been very flattering but if helped viewers to feel to feel that Brian was not just a projection on a screen—he was real." (See Figure 15.6.)

FIGURE 15.6
Such details as nicotine-stained fingers helps the viewer realize the reality of Brian's situation. (Film by Bibbi Abruzzini. ©2017 Bibbi Abruzzini.)

As for composition, it comes to her spontaneously as an "intuitive and lonely process." She explains that when she is shooting action footage (or b-roll), she needs to "distance" herself "from reality and the present." She admits that this is a "difficult feeling to explain, but it is as if for an instant you are invisible, holding your breath in another dimension in which time and space have a different meaning. In this surreal space I am on my own, and it's not something that I could share with anyone else."

She loves to capture images and feels that the camera creates a unique language. "Visual storytellers are often accused of being intrusive," she says, "but for me we are taking ourselves out of the picture—seeking anonymity to record the rest of society. In particular when it comes to composition I need my Zen space and commit to a degree of self-erasure." This process allows her to get into an intuitive flow when shooting, part of which includes recording detail shots, which "allows you to show viewers things in a different way, in an intimate way" she adds. "As filmmakers we might notice those small details, weird juxtapositions, and nuances." This might be as simple as "someone holding a cigarette, a mother caressing their child, or a woman looking in the distance," she notes, but it is such details that "take us closer to reality, to those everyday gestures that we take for granted." Technically, when she is focusing on details, she uses "layers to give image depth and boost interest of viewers. For me showing details is not about the micro, but about the macro of our existence."

When she engages in camera movement, she like to make them "poetic" in order to "allow people to enter a certain mood. I usually start slow like if two people were first introducing each other. You start with a handshake, not with an intimate question about your family. I use poetic movement so that a degree of communion can be found between the story and viewers." In her most recent project about refugee camps in Lebanon, she begins by showing details of a "chaotic neighborhood in the middle of Beirut." But she saw several sheets hanging from the buildings and took inspiration from that. "They are disorganized, but move slowly as if dancing in the air," she adds. "I tried to use these slow camera movements while shooting as well."

> I use poetic movement so that a degree of communion can be found between the story and viewers.

As for lenses, she keeps a fixed prime 50mm handy, and for flexibility she carries a Canon 17–40mm and 24–105mm zooms. "The 50mm is definitely my favorite lens. It's a portrait lens and creates an intimate feeling through its image, allowing me to get close and capture faces and expressions. Although it's not extremely flexible, its f/1.4 aperture allows me to create significant shallow depth of field and easily shoot night scenes."

When it comes to lighting, Abruzzini "almost exclusively uses natural light," unless she's interviewing someone. "I use light as both part of my composition—to exclude and include through selective exposure—and to convey a specific mood," she explains. When using natural light, she prefers magic hour, shooting early in the morning and before sunset in order to avoid "harsh light." At the same time, she likes to use urban street lights at night. "I have always been fascinated by the cinematographic nature of urban night lights," she says. In *S.K.A.T.E. Nepal*, lighting played a crucial role in making the documentary more cinematic and emotional, she adds. "The documentary starts at sunset and night as one of the protagonists talks about the challenges of being a woman skateboarder in Nepal, where the sport is heavily associated with masculinity. I decided to film at night for the opening scene to create a sense of loneliness and intimacy." (See Figure 15.7.)

FIGURE 15.7

Street lamps and cars light the face of Rezina as she discusses what's it's like to be a girl in Nepal who wants to skate.

(Film by Bibbi Abruzzini. ©2017 CafeBabel.)

POSTPRODUCTION PROCESS

I start by selecting some key clips and organizing them according to themes. Once I have some structure I start looking at how they work better. I usually have the beginning and the end of my documentaries in mind before starting editing. All the rest changes through out the postproduction. Feedback is extremely important to me. I usually do a first screening with fellow videographers and friends to get their honest feedback. I try to integrate as much of their ideas into my project. For *S.K.A.T.E. Nepal* I asked for help from some of the people I filmed and even got some additional skateboarding footage that made the documentary much better. For me the postproduction process is deeply collaborative. I meet with musicians, animators, storytellers, and subjects to make the documentary as much as a collaborative effort as possible. I like to give everyone involved ownership of the project and post-production plays a vital role in allowing this.

CAMERA

Abruzzini loves shooting with the Canon 5D Mark IV. "It's one of my favorite cameras when working alone in the field." She does not often work with a crew due to a limited budgets on her projects, but working alone also allows her to "establish personal connections with my subjects," she says. Because of her solo shooting style, it's "extremely important for my equipment to be relatively light and easy to carry," she explains. "In this sense the Canon 5D Mark IV was the best option for me to shoot projects such as *S.K.A.T.E Nepal* or the documentary in refugee camps across Lebanon," she adds.

The 5D Mark IV became a useful documentary tool in the Shatila refugee camp in Lebanon. "I was not allowed to film, as they were controlled by political organizations who didn't want to appear on camera," Abruzzini explains. The small form factor of the 5D "allowed me to move fast and be fairly discreet. It was also a great camera to have, as it managed to capture the colors and details of Lebanon. From filming faces to landscapes, I found it a very flexible camera." She also liked the touch screen and the ability to use auto-focus, which "made it easy for me to use rack focus," she adds. She also liked the ability to shoot some scenes in slow motion and in 4K. In addition to shooting video, she also shoots photos, so the camera is ideal with working in both worlds. However, shooting just video allows her to get into smaller spaces and allow for the intimacy of a small camera.

She feels that the 5D Mark IV expresses a "distinct look compared to other cameras. It heavily influences the aesthetics of my documentaries, their saturation and tones," she explains. "I prefer to keep its natural look for the final version of my documentaries." The advantage with the camera is its small size and flexibility, but without a rig the lack of image stabilization makes it difficult to follow her subjects around so she tends to keep the camera more static than she wants. The Canon C100, on the other hand, is easier to handle when following her subjects, she says.

Behind the scenes photo from *Tangerine*, a feature made on an iPhone. Sean Maker operates a Steadicam Smoothee, an iPhone 5S, and a Moondog Labs anamorphic lens adapter for the shot.
(Photo by Shih-Ching Tsou. Courtesy of Magnolia Pictures. ©2015 Magnolia Pictures)

Conclusion

From Film to Low-Budget Cinema Cameras

My first short movies were shot on the Canon L2 Hi8 mm video camera. When I was doing doctoral work at NYU's Tisch School of the Arts in the mid- to late 1990s, I enrolled in NYU's filmmaking boot camp one summer, and we shot on 16 mm black and white film with no sync sound—Arriflexes that had three prime lenses that you could rotate into position. After that, I purchased the first generation Panasonic DVX100 24p miniDV camera and shot two fiction shorts and several documentary projects. Before shifting to DSLRs, I shot a short festival-accepted documentary on a Sony A1U HDV miniDV camera, a $2,200 camera (nearly the price of a Canon 5D Mark II body).

I know digital video.

And my footage from these cameras never looked as good as the two-minute rolls of film I shot on that Arriflex at NYU. Not even close. The smooth, creamy shots were unlike anything I've ever seen on video. The sharpness of the glass was incomparable, but it wasn't the digital sharpness found in video cameras. However, I lived with shooting on video because it was affordable, and artistic sensibility— that cinematic feel I had previously seen in 16 mm film—was compromised due to budget.

Until now.

In the fall of 2009, I started watching videos on Vimeo by DSLR shooters. The stuff looked good. I wanted one. I did more research and convinced my colleagues at Northern Arizona University's film department (really more of a broadcast focus back then) to get one—the Panasonic GH1 (the only other serious contender at the time for around ~$1300). One of my students, Shannon Sassone, shot her short fiction project with it in my intro video production class. She was amazed at the quality of the image. And I became convinced that DSLRs could be used in the classroom. None of the prosumer video cameras we had matched the image quality of the Panasonic GH1 and later Canon's low-end Rebel T2i.

I bought a Canon 5D Mark II, there was no going back. The footage coming out of the camera—if not the same as those shorts I shot with an Arriflex—was the best thing I've seen since then. The image was "thin" compared to the "thickness" of film emulsion, but the image was cinematic.

Later, I decided to write a book proposal that would address the cinematic needs of these student shooters, as well as for independent filmmakers, video production houses doing client work, and video journalists who saw the potential of these cameras but didn't know where all the resources were to make effective use of DSLRs as low-budget cinema cameras. I wanted to bring together some of the best thinkers and practitioners practicing this form of cinema—from Philip Bloom, who pioneered the sharing of information about DSLRs on his blog, to Shane Hurlbut, ASC, who had access to nearly any camera in the world but shot some projects with the Canon 5D Mark II just to see what it could do.

It's one thing to ignore shooters who get excited about putting up test shots online. It's another thing to look at Philip Bloom's *San Francisco People* and *Skywalker Ranch*, or Hurlbut's cinematography in Po Chan's *The Last 3 Minutes* and not realize that there's something going on here—something different from the kinds of video we've seen over the past twenty years.

Then Philip Bloom announced ten million views on his website as of June 1, 2010, and we're not talking about a celebrity site, but a working man's view of DSLR cinema and how he did it (see http://philipbloom.net). Other blogs sprouted up that were focused on DSLRs, but have now shifted to creating cinematic projects using a variety of cameras: Shane Hurlbut: http://hurlbutvisuals.com; PlanetMitch: http://blog.planet5d.com; Vincent Laforet: http://blog.vincentlaforet.com; and Dan Chung: http://newsshooter.com. All of these sites reveal a democratization of the cinema look, an inside peak at how to do good work.

And when Lucasfilm jumped on board, the tremor became an earthquake (at least for those of us joining the DSLR cinema revolution). As Hurlbut is fond of saying, Canon knocked over the applecart, burned it up, and decided to make applesauce.

At first, it looked like Hollywood was going to eat the applesauce Hurlbut helped try to envision. The season finale of *House MD* (2010) was shot on a Canon 5D Mark II. "We started testing on episode 19, which I was directing," Greg Yaitanes says in an interview with Philip Bloom.[1] "We would run the 5D next to our film cameras just to see how the 5D was reacting to our lighting, what our sets looked like, how actors looked, anything we needed to be aware of. And we were very happy with these tests." Everyone was surprised by how good the image looked. Everyone on the production and postproduction team agreed—including those handling

---

[1] Bloom, Philip. "Greg Yaitanes *House* Interview transcription." Transcription by Oli Lewington. http://philipbloom. net/other-stuff/case-studies/greg-yaitanes-house-interview-transcription/.

special effects; even the studio executives said it was good enough for broadcast, Yaitanes explains. In the end, he said it looked "gorgeous … It allowed us to tell a story that we never told before." The DSLR camera changed how the story was told. There was no examination of test charts. There was what they saw on-screen, and there was the emotion of the story.

Indeed, Yaitanes embraced the aesthetics of the camera. And despite banding issues—which does tend to occur when the camera overheats—he and his team didn't let that bother them. "We struggled a bit with banding. That was every once in a while and frankly it's part of a look," Yaitanes said to Bloom. "You can try and fight these things away and wish they weren't there, but then you're just comparing that aesthetic to something else. I'm not trying to create a film aesthetic. I'm trying to create its own aesthetic. I want it to be its own look, its own style. If there's some banding … some motion blur, then for me, who cares? I feel like the story trumps all. These are, again, tools. These are, again, things that give you a look."[2]

> I'm not trying to create a film aesthetic. I'm trying to create its own aesthetic. I want it to be its own look, its own style.
> -Greg Yaitanes

Those of us living in the DSLR world felt that between Lucasfilm, Hurlbut, and Yaitanes, among others, that more Hollywood films and dramatic television shows would be shooting with DSLRs. But, as noted in the Introduction, Hollywood never fully embraced the DSLR as a cinema camera. Perhaps it was the 8-bit banding issues, the lack of professional audio inputs, lack of professional monitoring (such as waveforms), and ND filters, among other weaknesses not found in prosumer and professional video cameras. But camera companies did take note. And so low budget cinema cameras were released over the past few years and former DSLR shooters embrace them. Those who who shot their films on DSLRs were always eager for low budget cinema cameras, thinking, perhaps, they'll now become "filmmakers." But the camera doesn't make a film look good. The filmmaker does that. The DSLR cinema revolution proved that. So this book was revised with that in mind. Students and other low budget filmmakers can still shoot outstanding images with a DSLR, or a mirrorless camera, or a cinema camera. What doesn't change is the techniques of visual storytelling, sound design, and lighting to help make stories strong.

If anything, I hope this book shows how you can develop that cinematic look—if not the look of film, then something else that looks as good. When Yaitanes went to film school, there was only film. But he wished that it "was not the only medium in which people would look at [motion pictures]. Back then no

---

[2] Bloom, P. "In-depth Interview with Greg Yaitanes, Executive Producer and Director of *House* Season Finale shot on Canon 5DmkII." 19 April 2010. http://philipbloom.net/2010/04/19/ in-depth-interview-with-executive-producer-and-director-of-house-season-finale-shot-on-canon-5dmkii/.

one would take something you shot on video seriously in terms of a narrative." Conventional video never really delivered an alternative look that felt cinematically strong.

But now all that has changed. The DSLR cinema movement forced manufacturers to create high-quality but inexpensive cinema cameras—and the DSLR digital video aesthetic, a cinema aesthetic made possible by an HD codec combined with a large sensor, small form factor, and interchangeable lenses—is now found in new kinds of cameras that many independent filmmakers can afford. If people can shoot a feature with an iPhone (when paired with proper apps and lenses), then there's really not much more that can be said to convince people of what this revolution created. What began as a 30 fps video on a stills camera (Canon 5D Mark II), designed for print journalists needing the convenience of shooting "a little bit of video" to supplement their in-the-field assignments for newspaper websites, become a common tool for independent cinema projects and shaped the future aesthetic for shooters who now use higher-end cinema cameras.

Some people still shoot strong projects with DSLRs and small mirrorless cameras, as seen from the case studies described in this book, while others are using cinema cameras that contain S35 mm, S16mm, or micro four-thirds sensors—all with interchangeable lenses. Some of these cameras still shoot full HD, while others shoot in 4K.

The biggest change that occured since the second editon of this book (2012) involved the release of low-end RAW cinema cameras. The promise of RAW includes a wide latitude of exposure and a strong color bit-depth that gives filmmakers the ability to shoot images as "thick" as film, allowing for strong postproduction possibilities. Joe Rubinstein and Elle Schneider created the Digital Bolex D16 camera, announced at the SXSW film festival in Austin, Texas in March 2012—the Kickstarter campaign hoped to raise $100,000 to get the first 100 production models built. Within a day or two of the announcement—with a nudge from Philip Bloom—they received over $260,000. The camera was released and it still provides some of the best images in any low-budget cinema camera on the market, today. Filmmakers have shot images comparable with high-end cinema cameras (such as Arri and RED). Despite this, the company ceased production of the cameras in summer 2016. Perhaps it came out too soon to grab a large enough market.

Just a month or so after the Digital Bolex South by Southwest (SXSW) Film Festival announcement, Blackmagic Design—the maker of quality production and postproduction hardware and software (such as DaVinci Resolve)—announced their own cinema camera that shoots 2.5 K RAW for under $3,000. And they later released their Pocket Cinema Camera that can also shoot a compressed form of RAW for $1000. To compare this camera to the Digital Bolex, however, involves understanding the power of the sensor. The D16 used a high-end CCD designed by Kodak that cost as much as the Blackmagic Pocket Cinema Camera.

In either case, the future of low-budget cinema cameras will be about shaping the film look, rather than being limited by the amount of exposure needed. More and more cameras will release RAW capabilities to meet the market and desire of filmmakers to control more of the production in post. Blackmagic URSA Mini and their Pro version allows for RAW shooting in a camera designed for professional cinema use. The Canon C200 was their response to Blackmagic. Panasonic announced their EVA-1 that shoots 10-bit cinematic images using Canon's lens mount. They will update their firmware to allow the camera to shoot RAW by the time this book is published. The gloves are being thrown down and new technologies are coming out that make filmmaking cheaper and cheaper.

Because of the cheaper costs, quality digital filmmaking—image-making for cinema—is no longer just for the Hollywood elite, but for you and me, the independent filmmakers, as well as event video shooters, students, video journalists, documentary filmmakers—the do-it-yourselfers who have been desiring cinematic quality on an affordable camera for the past twenty years but had to simply make do with miniDV and prosumer HD cameras that just didn't cut it due to their compressed images, fixed lenses, and small sensors.

We can now gear up for a cinema-type project for the price of an iPhone (and some additional money for software, lenses, and a gimbal) and not worry that our vision will be compromised. There is no excuse to shoot crappy-looking movies. You can still shoot bad images with these cameras, but that'll be due to a lack of skill, and not the camera.

I hope this book helps you make the best-looking films on the lowest possible budget. It can be done. And you can do it.

In short, this book is designed to give you a strong foundation for cinematic storytelling. My new book, *Basic Cinematography: A Practical Guide to Visual Storytelling*, slated to come out in 2019, will take you to the next level.

INDEX

A

Abruzzini, Bibbi 254–267
Act of Valor xv, xvi, xxii
Adobe Premiere Pro 125, 128
Ajmani, Asha 84–87, 91
ambient sound 61
anamorphic 230–233
angle of view for a lens 5
Anselmi, David 66, 121
anthropology 189–191, 256–259
Apple Final Cut Pro 77, 78, 90,
    125, 128
*A Ride for Liberty: The Fugitive
    Slaves* 92, 93
Art of the People 188–203
Atomos Ninja Flame 4K and
    Shogun Flame 4K 144
Audio-Technica 141
audio mixers and preamps
    142–143
  Azden field mixer 143
  Sound Devices MixPre-D
      field mixer 69, 143
  Tascam 143
  Zoom H6 69, 70, 143
audio quality 58–62
automatic gain control (AGC)
    60–68
Avid Media Composer 128
Azden field mixer 143

B

Baker, Sean xxv–xxvii
Bandit 22–25, 56
BeachTek adapter 68
Benro monopod 145
Bingham, George Caleb 178,
    179
bit depth 88
Blackmagic Design 128, 129,
    130, 132, 135, 142, 144
  Pocket Cinema Camera 137,
      153
  Production Camera 4K 137
  URSA Mini 4.6K 137
  Video Assist 144
blocking 11–15
Bloom, Philip xx–xxii, xxx, 44,
    103, 176–187

boom poles 68
Brian 257, 263–265

C

CAME-ARGO gimbal 147
Cameron, James 50–51
Canon 5D Mark II xiii, xv–xx,
    29, 45, 73, 103, 119, 124,
    204, 209, 210, 220, 224
Canon 5D Mark III 189, 198,
    202
Canon 5D Mark IV 22–25, 56,
    136, 255, 266, 267
Canon 7D 45, 177, 180, 182, 184,
    186
Canon 80D 136
Canon C100 Mark II 20, 21,
    136, 163–165, 169, 173, 174,
    238, 252
Canon C200 136
Chan, Po 11–13, 204, 207, 209,
    210, 212, 216–220, 222, 224
characters in film 101–106
Charters, Rodney xviii–xix,
    xxii
*Children in Captivity: Freeing
    Nepal's Prison Babies* 254,
    255, 260, 261
chrominance compression
    132–134
Chungking Express 154, 155
"cinematic" look 19, 160, 173
cinematographer, role of 5,
    31, 61
cinematographers, role of
    118–119
Cine Meter II App 47
Cinevate Inc. Duzi Camera
    Slider 146
Civil War 92, 93
Cleven, Mari 238–253
codecs 82–84
color balance 27
color correction 78, 79, 83–85
  definition of 96
color grading 78, 83
  definition of 96
color temperature 26–29

composition 1–5, 153, 156, 158,
    198, 199, 229, 230, 264, 265
Convergent Design Odyssey
    7Q+ video recorder 144
Cooke lenses 178, 180, 186
The Courage Closet xxvii–xxix,
    149, 150

D

Darg, David xii–xiii, xxviii–
    xxxi
A Day at the Races 176–187
Dear Tom 18, 29–32, 39, 152–161
depth of field 40–45
dialogue 94
Digital Bolex camera 84, 88,
    128–130, 135
DJI Osmo gimbal 150
DJI Ronin-M gimbal 147
dollies 16
    See sliders and jibs
Doyle, Christopher 154, 155
dramatic needs 103, 117–119
Dream Delivery Service 249–253
DSLR cameras 8, 10, 16
dynamic microphones 62

E

Edelkrone SliderPlus 146
Edwards, Derek 207, 222
"emotional equivalency" to
    human vision 5
environment 94
exposure and exposure meters
    40–49
external audio recorders 60, 61,
    66, 69, 135, 142, 143
external hard drives 148
external onboard microphone
    67, 68

F

f-stops 36, 40–45
false color 46, 47
FiLMiC Pro app 150
filmmaking advice 253
filters 48, 49

focal length of a lens 5–8
Foley 94
The Foley Artist 94, 95
Fragments 2–4, 20, 21, 162–175
frame rates 50, 51, 90, 131
Freefly Movi Gimbal Stabilizer 150

G

Garn, Jake 1, 2
gimbals
  CAME-ARGO 147
  DJI Ronin-M Gimbal 147
  ikan ECi Beholder 147
"golden hour" for shooting 29, 33
"golden mean" ratio 1–5
Gordon, Harwood 11–13
Grand Canyon National Park 189, 190

H

handheld cameras 15–17, 145
"hard" lighting 20, 21, 23, 32
headphones 70
histograms 39
Holms, Oliver 94, 95
Holterman, Tim 207, 223
"hooks" in film stories 117, 119
Horseshoe Bend 195
Hurlbut, Shane xv–xvii, 13, 15, 16, 27, 29, 124, 131, 204–225

I

ikan ECi Beholder 147
Induro carbon fiber tripod 145

infrared filters 45, 49
In the Mood for Love 154
ISO settings 35–39, 57

J

Jane, Eli 205, 210–213
Johnson, Eastman 92, 93
JuicedLink Preamp 68

K

Kar-wai, Wong 154, 155
Kessler Crane Pocket Jib Traveler 146
Kirkov, Kiril 188–203
KJ, Sam 226, 228, 229, 231, 235
Kodiak 2.0 Power Bank
Koji Color 96–98
Kolar, Rachel 220, 222
Kowa Prominar lenses 233

L

Laforet, Vincent xiii–xvi, xviii, xxxiv, 9, 16, 103, 119, 120, 124
Lancaster, Kurt (author) 6–7, 11, 40–47, 73, 76, 77, 84, 85, 86, 87, 91, 94, 97, 98, 122–125, 129, 132, 136, 254, 255, 258–260
The Last 3 Minutes 11–15, 29, 204, 205, 207–209, 211–217, 220, 223, 225
L-cuts and J-cuts 90, 91
lavalieres (lavs) 140, 141
  Sennheiser G3 wireless
lenses 5–10, 40, 48, 139, 180
lighting 19–33, 153, 154, 158–160, 165–167, 169, 174, 233, 234
  placement of 21–24
  setups 29–32
  source direction 21–24
Livio, Mario 1
log curve 52–54
log footage 237
Lucasfilm xx, 178
Lucas, George 102
luminance compression 132–134

M

Magic Lantern 60, 70
Manfrotto tripod 145
Mathers, Jim 48
microphones 140, 141
  lavalieres (lavs) 140, 141
    Sennheiser G3 wireless
  Rode VideoMic Pro 141

shotgun mics 140
    Audio-Technica 141
    Rode Shotgun 141
microphone types 62–67
monopods
  Benro 145
  Manfrotto 145
Moondog Labs 149
Mooser, Bryn xii–xiii, xxviii–xxxi
Multimedia iKlip 150

N

neutral density (ND) filters 45, 48, 49, 57

O

Occupy Wall Street 58, 73
olloclip lens adapter 149

P

The Painter of Jalouzi xii–xiii, xxviii–xxxi, xxxvi–xxxvii
Panasonic AU-EVA1 138
Panasonic GH5 226–230, 233
Panasonic Lumix DC-GH5 138
panning 15–17
Pearson, Charlotte 245–248
photos and movement 92, 93
pistol grips 68, 140
pixel sizes 129, 132, 133
postproduction 252–253, 266
  workflow 234
Primary xxxvi
prime lenses 10, 139
Pythagoras 1

R

Rabiger, Michael 106, 107
Radiocarbon Dating Gets a Postmodern Makeover 244–249
Ramsey, Brent (Canon) 162, 164, 165, 169, 173
The Rat Pack 207
Reichmann, Michael 39
Renaud, Brent and Craig 14, 103, 104

resolution 78–82
Revelator 236, 237
Reverie xiv–xvi, xxxiv, 8, 9, 16, 36, 37, 103, 105, 119, 120
rhythm and pacing 98, 99
Rode NTG-2 shotgun microphone 64–65, 141
Rode VideoMic Pro 141
room tone 94
Rubinstein, Joe 129
rule of thirds 1, 4, 247

S

sampling 83–88
scopes 234, 237
screen text 93
sensors 129, 130
shadows 21–25
shotgun microphones 62–66
Shutterfreaks 1–4
shutter speed 8, 50, 131, 132
shotgun mics 140
Simon, Joe 162–175
S.K.A.T.E. Nepal 261–263, 265–267
sliders and jibs 146
  Cinevate Inc. Duzi Camera Slider 146
  Edelkrone SliderPlus 146
  Kessler Crane Pocket Jib Traveler 146
smartphone cinema gear
  DJI Osmo 150
  FiLMiC Pro app 150
  Freefly Movi Gimbal Stabilizer 150
  Kodiak 2.0 Power Bank 150
  Moondog Labs 149
  Multimedia iKlip 150
  olloclip 149
  Steadicam Volt 150
Smith, Neil xviii–xx, 180–182, 186
"soft" lighting 20, 21, 23, 24, 29
software comparison chart 77
Sony Alpha7R II Mirrorless 138
Sony PXW-FS5 XDCAM 137

sound design 93, 94, 98, 99, 199–201
Sound Devices MixPre-D 69, 143
sound effects 94
sound mixing and mastering 96
sound quality 61, 62
speed of the lens 139
Spielberg, Stephen 202, 208
spot meter 70, 72
stabilization devices 15
Steadicam Merlin 17
Steadicam Volt 150
story 192, 193
story structure 117–120
storytelling 255
Svalina, Mathias 249–253

T

Tangerine xxiii, xxv–xxvii
Tascam 143
Tembleque, David 152–161
Terminator xv, xvi
The Delivery Men 162, 164, 174
The Kitchen 105
Thomas, Jeremy Ian 181–183, 185, 186
timeline 90, 91
Tracking Alewives for the Passamaquoddy 76, 84–87, 96
tripods
  Induro carbon fiber 145
  Manfrotto 145

U

Uncle Jack 101–103, 105, 106, 117, 118
underexposure 46–48

V

Van Auken, J. 226–237
video field recorders
  Atomos Ninja Flame 4K and Shogun Flame 4K 144
  Blackmagic Video Assist 144
  Blackmagic Video Assist 4K 144

Convergent Design Odyssey 7Q+ 144
video journalism 10, 65, 120
"video" look 50
visual anthropology 190, 191
visual storytelling 227–229, 256, 257

W

Walker, Lindsay xxvii–xxix, 149, 150
Weber, Alex 215–217
Wexler, Haskell 101, 102
What If 1, 34, 156, 157
white balance 26–29
Whitethorn Jr., Bahe 192, 193, 196
Whitethorn Sr., Bahe 191, 192, 197
wide-angle lenses 5–10
Willem de Kooning's Woman-Ochre 238–243
Willis, Gordon 118
Wilson, Randall 192, 198, 199, 201, 202
Winans, Jamin 100–103, 105, 120
Wonderful People 29, 32
workflow pipeline 89, 90
writing exercises 106–110
Wupatki National Monument 192, 196, 198

X

XLR inputs 135
XLR inputs and adapters 58–60, 67, 68

Y

Yedlin, Steve 79–82

Z

Zacuto 169
Zahney, Keno 194, 195
Zeiss lenses 6, 7, 10, 40–44, 73, 186, 223
zone system and zone scale 35–39, 44
Zoom H6 69, 70, 143
zoom lenses 8, 10, 139
Zsigmond, Vilmos 19